THE TWO KINGDOMS

The
Two Kingdoms

ECCLESIOLOGY IN
CAROLINGIAN POLITICAL
THOUGHT

✠

BY KARL FREDERICK MORRISON

PRINCETON, NEW JERSEY
PRINCETON UNIVERSITY PRESS
1964

❖

This book, in manuscript, received a McKnight Foundation Award in 1963.

❖

Publication of this book has been aided by the
Ford Foundation program to support publication, through
university presses, of works in the humanities
and social sciences

❖

1. Church and state — History
2. Political science — History.

To My Parents

PREFACE

"Destruction cometh, and they shall seek peace, and there shall be
none. . . . The law shall perish from the priest, and counsel from
the ancients. The king shall mourn, and the prince shall be clothed
with desolation, and the hands of the people of the land shall be
troubled." EZEKIAL 7:25-27.

DESTRUCTION and the decay of law are the background of this study. In the last years of Charlemagne, the political order which he had
established fell into decline, and internecine wars in the
time of Louis the Pious and for thirty years after his death
first divided the Frankish Empire into several kingdoms
nominally subject to the emperor, then brought about the
effectual secession of those kingdoms from imperial control, and finally even dissipated the powers of central
government in the splinter kingdoms. But the study of
secular and ecclesiastical law, the framing of sometimes
sophisticated legal pronouncements, and the formulation
of thoughts concerning the rightful structure and powers
of government continued throughout this period. Between
the imperial coronation of Charlemagne on Christmas
Day, A.D. 800, and the death of the great lawyer Hincmar of Rheims eighty-two years later, almost to the
day, the study of law and patristic writings led to a refined ecclesiology among the Franks which, in turn, significantly modified conventional elements of political
thought to the benefit of the Frankish clergy. Our theme
is this modification, the fruit of devotion to law in a time
of increasing lawlessness.

Hincmar and his brethren did not violently reject the

political thought of Charlemagne and his circle. Rather, they took advantage of the progressive weakening of independent imperial and royal authority and the increasing reliance of their kings on clerical support, and they insisted that the privileges of the clergy and the limits upon the temporal authority implicit in earlier thought be made explicit in laws and covenants between king and clergy. Their great fear was that the law would perish from the priest, and that the loss of clerical privileges and the collapse of all legal order in civil and ecclesiastical matters would ensue. Frankish thinkers reformulated the doctrine, present in the Gospels and affirmed by the Church Fathers, that the Church and the temporal government were two kingdoms, that they were distinct institutions each under its own laws and administrative offices, and that they were coordinate, though still separate, in a predominantly Christian society. Since priests could perform sacramental functions beyond the power of laymen, a functional dualism always mitigated the claims of temporal rulers to dominance over the Church such as those which Charlemagne asserted; and consequently no fundamental change occurred in royal ideology when in the course of the ninth century the adversities which enfeebled the Frankish kings brought them to terms with their dualistic clergy. Their powers greatly impaired by economic disorder and by constant military requisitions within and on their frontiers, the Frankish rulers bargained for clerical support by accepting the dualistic position, and their acceptance was formalized in the coronation ceremony, a covenant between the king and his clergy, between the kingdom of this world and the kingdom of the Church.

On another level, the conciliarist ecclesiology which complemented and even inspired dualism was a counter-doctrine affirmed by Frankish clergy who questioned the monarchical construction of Church order which contemporary popes maintained. But neither ideological premises nor urgent necessity led to compromise between the dualists and the papal monarchists; their opposition remained unresolved.

The first duty of a person writing about Carolingian history and political thought is to acknowledge his obligation to the previous editors and analysts whose care and industry have supplied the beginning of any fruitful enquiry in this field. I hope that my own very great debt to earlier studies will be appropriately clear in the critical apparatus. And yet, I must observe that many scholars have in large measure neglected the ecclesiological and legal approach to Carolingian political thought, which some have construed in terms of theology or of the revival of classical Antiquity, and to which a very few have come by an occult path through the mists of Teutonic folklore. This book is an attempt to put the political thought of the ninth century into the context of the legal thought from which it chiefly derived. It may also be said at the outset that, in opposition to one dangerously condescending school of interpretation, the present study maintains that even Carolingians, however barbaric their mode of life, were capable of logical thought, that they were fighting out some exceedingly difficult questions of political theory, and that their answers command respect.

Research for this study was begun at Cornell University under the terms of the George Lincoln Burr Fellowship, and it was continued with assistance from the American Numismatic Society and the Graduate Faculty Research Fund of the University of Minnesota. I am also under a heavy obligation to the learned institutions where research was done: Cornell University, The Catholic University of America (Institute for Study and Research in Mediaeval Canon Law, Inc.), the Library of Congress, Das Institut für die Erforschung des Mittelalters (Monumenta Germaniae Historica), Die Bayerische Staatsbibliothek, Stanford University, the University of California (Berkeley), and the University of Minnesota.

Wise and long-suffering scholars have most kindly advised me throughout the period of research and writing. Professors Josef L. Altholz, H. Grundmann, Robert S. Hoyt, Stephan Kuttner, Liutpold Wallach, Helene Wieruszowski, and Shafer Williams, and the Research Assistants of the Monumenta Germaniae Historica—Drs Lietzmann, Mayer, Reindel, Schaller, and Weigle—gave great assistance and encouragement. I am particularly indebted to Professor Brian Tierney for his always judicious advice, and to Professor Ralph E. Giesey for his patience, and for help given freely at a critical moment. Three persons who gave me gentle but sure direction when this study began have not lived to receive or reject the final work, and I can only record both my obligation to them and the profound regret that we can no longer see light in their light: Ernst H. Kantorowicz, M. L. W. Laistner, and, finally,

Theodor E. Mommsen, whose life, though full of sorrow, was likewise full of grace.

KFM

To Aghion Oros
19. September, 1963.

ADDENDUM

J. Devisse's study, *Hincmar et la Loi* (Dakar, 1962. Faculté des lettres et des sciences humaines. Publications de la Section d'histoire, no. 5) came to hand only after I had corrected the page proofs of this book. It consists of two parts: the first and by far the larger is a compendium of Hincmar of Rheims' citations of Frankish (pp. 9ff, 64ff) and Roman law (pp. 14ff, 41ff) and an enquiry into their sources; the second is a rather brief critique of Hincmar's thought concerning the nature of law. It may be pointed out that, despite the meticulous care of his research and the usefulness of his results, M. Devisse does not offer a complete inventory of citations in the first portion of his study (e.g., he omits the citation below, p. 88 n. 34). As for the second part, our two analyses of Hincmar's legal thought are, on the whole, complementary; wishing to devote a second study to Hincmar's use of ecclesiastical law (p. 88), M. Devisse does not discuss that subject with which we have been most concerned. There are, however, some points in common and some points of difference. For example, M. Devisse has attributed to Hincmar the thesis that the validity of secular law depended upon the conformity of that law to principles of Christian morality (p. 75f), and he also maintains that Hincmar considered the king to be bound by those principles and by the laws they inspired. Of the king, he writes: "Transgresse-t-il les lois humaines, il tombe automatique sous leur autorité et cesse, par ailleurs, de mériter le nom de chrétien. Et il perd sa fonction de roi" (p. 79). This interpretation discounts the independence of secular from ecclesiastical law which was a critical element in Hincmar's thought (see below, pp. 94ff, 229). The interested reader may wish to consult the review by M. Garaud (*Cahiers de Civilisation Médiévale, X^e-XIIe Siècles,* vi [1963], p. 192f), who suggests further modifications of M. Devisse's interpretive section.

ABBREVIATIONS

Bouquet—M. Bouquet, *Recueil des historiens des Gaules et de la France.* 24 vols. Paris, 1738-1904.

Br. Th.—Breviarium Alarici Codicis Theodosiani in T. Mommsen et al. edd., *Codex Theodosianus.* 2 vols. Berlin, 1905.

Cod. Th.—Codex Theodosianus, as above after Br. Th.

CSEL—Corpus Scriptorum Ecclesiasticorum Latinorum.

DC II—G. Tessier ed., *Recueil des Actes de Charles II le Chauve, Roi de France.* 2 vols. Paris, 1943, 1952.

Hist. JB.—*Historisches Jahrbuch.*

Hist. Zt.—*Historische Zeitschrift.*

Jaffé—P. Jaffé—S. Loewenfeld, *Regesta Pontificum Romanorum,* vol. I. Leipzig, 1881.

Mabillon, Acta SS. O. S. B.—J. Mabillon, *Acta Sanctorum Ordinis Sancti Benedicti.* 9 vols. Paris, 1668-1701.

Mabillon, *Analecta*—J. Mabillon, *Vetera Analecta.* Paris, 1723.

Mansi—J. D. Mansi, *Sanctorum Conciliorum Nova et Amplissima Collectio.* 53 vols. 1759-1778 (reprinted 1901-1927).

MGH—Monumenta Germaniae Historica

Series:

Cap.—Capitularia Regum Francorum

Conc.—Concilia Aevi Karolini

Conc. Suppl.—Concilia, Supplementum

Dip. Kar.—Diplomata Karolinorum

DK III—Diplomata Karoli III

DL II—Diplomata Ludovici Germanici

Epp.—Epistolae

Formulae

In usum schol.—Scriptores in Usum Scholarum

Ldl—Libelli de lite

Poet. Lat.—Poetae Latini Aevi Karolini

Regestrum Gregorii—Gregorii I Papae Registrum Epistolarum

SS.—Scriptores

SS. Rer. Mer.—Scriptores Rerum Merovingicarum

Migne—J. Migne, Patrologiae Cursus Completus.
  Series: *PL*—Series Latina. 221 vols. Paris, 1844-1864.
  PG—Series Graeca. 161 vols. Paris, 1857-1866.
Zt. für Schweiz. Gesch.—*Zeitschrift für Schweizerische Geschichte.*
ZfKG—*Zeitschrift für Kirchengeschichte.*
ZfRG—*Zeitschrift der Savigny-Stiftung für Rechtsgeschichte.*
  Series: GA—Germanistische Abteilung
       KA—Kanonistische Abteilung
       RA—Romanistische Abteilung

CONTENTS

CONTENTS

xvi

THE TWO KINGDOMS

CHAPTER I · INTRODUCTION

ROM the establishment of the Christian Empire in the fourth century until the present, the proper relationship of the ecclesiastical to the temporal power has been a question of debate. It was a new issue in the Middle Ages, an issue for which antiquity offered neither immediate answers nor great precedents which could have led toward a final resolution. Complex definitions of law, offices, institutions, and patterns of relationships had to be worked out before any systematic approach to the problem was feasible; and the legists and canonists in the twelfth century were the first to attempt such thorough formulations. Political thought in the early Middle Ages, therefore, was not fully jurisprudential, for jurisprudence as a science did not then exist. But it was legal, and it centered upon one problem: the legal status of the Church in the world. The unsystematized political thought from the fourth to the twelfth century was juristic ecclesiology.

This orientation was powerful among ecclesiastical writers as soon as Church-State relations became an actual problem; it was largely produced by juristic uncertainty in the age of Constantine the Great and his successors. The place of the Church in the Empire was anomalous then, for it was not clear whether Christianity, accepted as the Roman state religion, should be governed by Roman precedents: that is, whether Christianity, the successor of State paganism, should be governed by the civil power under the *ius publicum* as its predecessor was. Two conflicting answers emerged. The imperial court maintained that the Church was under civil authority wholly in its temporal quality and partially in its inner discipline. In response, the Church Fathers declared that, since the very essence of the Church was the Faith and the sacramental union of Christ and the believer which the Faith insured, the Church could not be governed by persons who had not been consecrated to teach the Faith and administer the sacraments, much less by the non-Christians in the imperial bureaucracy. Consequently, they argued, ecclesiastical order should not be subjected to administration by temporal law, which was entirely foreign to the Church, and the government of the Church must retain its independence and its integrity. In other words, imperial theorists construed human society in terms of unitary government headed by the civil authority, while the Fathers advocated the duality of ecclesiastical and temporal government.

The same conflict between the monism of temporal theorists and the dualism of ecclesiastical thinkers—the same opposition of organic to symbiotic union—occurred in the ninth century. And yet, this was more than a simple recurrence. The evolution of the Papacy as a dominant juridical power in the West, and the simultaneous development of the doctrine that Christendom was governed in a monistic fashion by the bishop of Rome, added a third dimension to the problem. Further, the appearance of the familiar jurisprudential question in the unfamiliar institutional context of Frankish Gaul led to the formulation of the dualistic response in new terms, terms which corresponded to the Germanic political structure. In the

4

Carolingian period, consequently, the history of the problem of Church-State relations—the difficulty of reconciling the demands of ecclesiology with concrete legal forms—began an entirely new course: for the first time in the West the problems arose of correlating the institutional freedom of the Church with the temporal responsibilities which churchmen owed their secular rulers; for the first time, also, the doctrines of royal monism, papal monism, and dualism came into conflict. Therefore, even if the ninth century had not given significant or original answers to the perennial question of institutional correlation, it would still have distinguished itself by posing the question in new and challenging ways. But the answers which it gave were of the greatest originality; and, in the development of European political thought, its formulations opened a period which lasted until the Conciliar Movement of the fifteenth century.

+

Despite the importance of Carolingian political thought, there is no agreement among modern scholars concerning even the broad principles of Frankish ecclesiology, which lay behind that thought. Some authors have taken the theological unity of Christian society as the dominant theme of Frankish political thought and have concluded, as Imbart did for the eighth century, "Il y a dualisme dans le pouvoir, non dans la société. L'Etat n'est autre chose que l'Église chrétienne, politiquement organisée."[1]

[1] Imbart de la Tour, *Les élections épiscopales dans l'Église de France du IXe au XIIe siècle* (Paris, 1891), p. 102. There can be no question of the theological unity of the Church; even church buildings were designed to express the oneness of Christ and His Church. See A. Weckwerth,

In his fundamental study, Faulhaber affirmed that there was no separation of Church and State in theory or in practice;[2] Eva Müller and, with more reserve, Louis Halphen have maintained that the two institutions were fully united in the one institution, the Ecclesia.[3] Arquillière went even further, asserting that the civil power was positively subordinated to the ecclesiastical within the unity of the Church.[4] And, most recently, Walter Ullmann has argued that the Franks were divided into two schools, those who supported the political monism of the Germanic kings ("theocratic kingship"), in which the Church was considered part of the State, and those who advocated the theological monism of the popes, in which temporal power was subordinated to papal.[5]

The argument *ad unitatem*, however, meets some diffi-

"Das altchristliche und das frühmittelalterliche Kirchengebäude—ein Bild des 'Gottesreiches,'" *ZfKG*, 59 (1958), pp. 37, 41f, and the interesting argument for representation of the two powers in ecclesiastical architecture, pp. 55ff.

[2] R. Faulhaber, *Der Reichseinheitsgedanke in der Literatur der Karolingerzeit bis zum Vertrag von Verdun* (Berlin, 1931), p. 93. See the related book by M. Hoechstetter, *Karl der Grosse, König, Patrizius und Kaiser als Rector Ecclesiae.* (Diss. Munich, 1931. Augsburg, 1934).

[3] E. Müller, "Die Anfänge der Königssalbung im Mittelalter," *Hist. JB.* 58 (1938), p. 317. L. Halphen, *Charlemagne et l'Empire carolingien* (Paris, 1947), p. 374 and *passim.*

[4] H. X. Arquillière, *L'Augustinisme politique*, 2d ed. (Paris, 1955), pp. 170ff.

[5] Walter Ullmann, *The Growth of Papal Government in the Middle Ages* (London, 1955), pp. 104ff, 155f, 167ff, and, more recently, *Principles of Government and Politics in the Middle Ages* (London, 1961), pp. 32ff, 117ff. For a penetrating critique of Ullmann's earlier book, see F. Kempf, "Die päpstliche Gewalt in der mittelalterlichen Welt," *Saggi storici intorno al papato* (*Miscellanea historica pontificie*, XXI. 1959), p. 117ff.

culties which even Imbart's acknowledgment of the duality of temporal and ecclesiastical power suggests. Translated to the area of law and governmental administration, this duality is of paramount significance. Since the functions of the royal and the episcopal offices were juridical, and the jurisdiction of the first was limited by civil law while that of the second was prescribed by the canons, a rather sharp institutional dualism obtained. The two offices derived from different sources; they were administered under different laws; they could not be joined in the hands of one man; and their obligations were completely distinct, as were the juridical units over which they ruled.[6]

Despite its lucidity, Tellenbach's argument for the essential unity of Church and State illustrates the strain upon the theological interpretation. The two institutions, he maintained, were not divided, but were rather one within the context of Christian society.[7] Moreover, in that union, the temporal power was regarded as being inferior to the spiritual.[8] On the other hand, Tellenbach writes, the spiritual power did not aspire to rule the earth[9] and, even in crucial political actions, the Frankish clergy did not assert its dominance over earthly princes. The clergy could neither bestow nor withdraw royal power through its sacramental actions: episcopal unction did not raise Louis the Pious to the throne, nor did excommunication depose him

[6] On the character of the royal office, see F. Kern, *Gottesgnadentum und Widerstandsrecht*, 2d ed. by R. Buchner (Münster, 1954), p. 55 n. 110: "Herrschaft ist Amt und Pflicht, nicht Besitzrecht."

[7] G. Tellenbach, R. F. Bennet trans., *Church, State, and Christian Society at the time of the Investiture Contest* (Oxford, 1948), p. 64.

[8] *Ibid.*, pp. 66f.

[9] *Ibid.*, p. 68.

7

from it.[10] From these inconsistencies with the evidence has forced upon Tellenbach's argument and upon the judgments of other scholars, one must conclude quite the reverse of Tellenbach's thesis: clearly, the union of Church and State in practice was not total, organic, or institutional.

Other authors, seeing the legistic distinction between the ecclesiastical and the civil powers, have emphasized the political dualism in Frankish thought. Among these, Lilienfein and Voigt were the first, maintaining that dualistic thought derived from the clergy's disillusionment with temporal rulers following upon the disorders of Louis the Pious's reign and equally from the clergy's attempt to find their own legal and administrative stability. David has drawn the lines still more clearly between temporal and spiritual administrative powers and, at the same time, has indicated the juristic difficulty with which we shall be particularly concerned later. He wrote: "Traditionnellement la doctrine chrétienne reconnaît l'existence autonome de deux sociétés. Elle ne cherche pas à équiper l'*auctoritas pontificalis* d'un appareil juridique, susceptible d'exprimer concrètement son poids plus lourd que celui de la *potestas regalis*."[11] Most recently, Pacaut has joined

[10] *Ibid.*, p. 65.

[11] H. Lilienfein, *Die Anschauungen von Staat und Kirche im Reich der Karolinger* (Heidelberg, 1902), pp. 46ff. K. Voigt, *Staat und Kirche von Konstantin dem Grossen bis zum Ende der Karolingerzeit* (Stuttgart, 1936), pp. 316ff. On the historical problems of Charlemagne's last years and the early reign of Louis the Pious, see F. L. Ganshof, "La fin du règne de Charlemagne, une décomposition," *Zt. für Schweiz. Gesch.*, 28 (1948), pp. 433-452, and "Louis the Pious Reconsidered," *History*, 42 (1957), esp. p. 173, a commentary on the essay by T. Schieffer, "Die Krise des karolingischen Imperiums," *Aus Mittelalter und Neuzeit, Festschrift Gerhard Kallen* (Bonn, 1957), pp. 1-15. M. David, *La Souveraineté et les limites juridiques du pouvoir monarchique du*

these scholars by affirming an absolute duality between temporal and spiritual authority in late ninth-century thought; and Fichtenau, questioning the reality of a political monism under Charlemagne, has clearly proved that Louis the Pious accepted the principles of juristic dualism.[12] Finally, though he declined to make any definitive statement, the judicious Carlyle observed that Church and State were discrete institutions in ninth-century thought, which he described as preceding "those mediaeval thinkers who thought of society as organized under the terms of complete unity."[13]

Neither the interpretation which sets Carolingian political thought in the light of theological monism nor that which casts it wholly in the form of institutional dualism is quite adequate. The first discounts the repeated and emphatic dualistic statements of ninth-century authors, and it consequently obscures the nuances of the nascent doctrine of corporations which was the focal point of dualism. The second does not allow for the interaction of theory and practice; it does not assess Carolingian thought as more than an academic abstraction or regard it as an

---

IXe au XVe siècle (Paris, 1954), pp. 107f. For another branch of Christian tradition, secular dominance over the Church, see W. Ensslin, "Auctoritas und Postestas," *Hist. JB* 74 (1954), esp. p. 668, and W. Ensslin, "Das Gottesgnadentum," *Studi bisantini e neoellenici,* 5 (1939), pp. 154-166.

[12] M. Pacaut, *La Théocratie: l'Église et le pouvoir au moyen âge* (Paris, 1957), pp. 55ff. H. Fichtenau, *Das karolingische Imperium* (Zürich, 1949), pp. 58ff, 230ff. Dualistic thought in the writings of Alcuin is discussed by L. Wallach, *Alcuin and Charlemagne* (Cornell, 1959), pp. 10ff.

[13] A. J. Carlyle, *A History of Mediaeval Political Theory in the West,* 1, 4th impression (London, 1950), pp. 184f, 253.

element in the real world to be judged according to the success it enjoyed in the face of internal tensions and rival doctrines. Abstract statements of legal principles by mediaeval thinkers were framed to serve concrete projects, and they stood or fell on the effect they had in contemporary institutional developments.

The first of these interpretations can be corrected by reference to the sources; but the nature of the sources themselves makes the aridity of the second interpretation virtually inevitable. Political writings in the Carolingian epoch were almost always occasional works, whose limited scope and lack of searching analysis constantly remind their modern reader that he is dealing with political thought, and not political theory. Timely repetition of conventional platitudes apparently served favored projects better than the composition of broad and analytical treatises; of the latter, none are known to have been written in the ninth century, and none survive.[14]

[14] Exception could be taken in favor of the nine formal essays on kingship (*Fürstenspiegel*) extant from the eighth and ninth centuries. The earliest of these is a letter written by a certain Kathvulf to Charlemagne (ca. 775), and the latest which we can date with certainty is Hincmar of Rheims's *De Ordine Palatii* (879). Between them were written Alcuin's *De Rhetorica* (801-804), Smaragdus's *Via Regia* (813/4-816), Jonas of Orléans's *De Institutione Regia* (ca. 834), Sedulius Scottus's *Liber de Rectoribus Christianis* (855-859), and Hincmar of Rheims's *De Regis Persona et Regio Ministerio* (873?) and *Instructio ad Ludovicum Balbum* (877). (See the discussion of the *De Rhetorica* as a *Fürstenspiegel* in Wallach, *Alcuin and Charlemagne*, pp. 6off.) The remaining treatise, a letter to a Carolingian king named Charles, is a simple reworking of a Merovingian letter; the revision probably belongs to the late ninth or early tenth centuries. E. Dümmler, "Ermahnungsschreiben an einen Karolinger," *Neues Archiv*, 13 (1887), pp. 191-196.

The essays are, therefore, relatively numerous. But two of them, the

One cannot censure the ninth-century Franks for failing to produce systematic seventeenth-century treatises on kingship. However helpful it might be to have such a treatise from the ninth century, the absence of one is perhaps as instructive as its presence could be. As their theological tracts show, the Carolingians were perfectly capable of producing coherent and highly technical essays on theoretical matters. Their failure to produce one on kingship indicates a general ignorance of the great questions of political thought, an indifference to government in the abstract, or the general acceptance of certain principles, which called for no debate.

Any study of Frankish ecclesiology and political thought, therefore, is a work of reconstruction and hypothesis. The modern scholar must play the synthesizer, deducing gen-

---

Kathvulf letter and the redaction of a Merovingian original, contain so little exposition as to prevent a clear understanding of their elliptical affirmations; and the others avoid principal issues of political theory, such as the character and limits of royal power, and accept theological maxims as sufficient substitutes for clear definitions of terms. Although it casts very considerable light upon Alcuin's political thought, *De Rhetorica* is primarily an essay on rhetoric, and its doctrines concerning government hold a secondary place. Likewise, Smaragdus's essay treats essentially of theological and moral virtues becoming to a king, rather than of the actual constitution and government of a state. Finally, Hincmar's treatises fall rather short of being genuine statements of political doctrine. His *De Regis Persona* is a catena of patristic and Scriptural quotations encrusting his revision of a synodal decree from the reign of Louis the Pious, and it is by no means a cohesive or an original exposition of theory. The very pragmatic *Instructio ad Ludovicum* and *De Ordine Palatii* contrast sharply in tenor and in content with the *De Regis Persona*, and they contain much of importance concerning the actual government of the Frankish realm; but their structure is topical and disconnected, and the information they offer about political institutions is incomplete.

eral theses from often unrelated statements addressed to quite specific issues. For this work, the letters and official acts of rulers provide much information. It would be impossible to establish currents in ninth-century papal thought without the large segments which survive from the correspondence of Popes Nicholas I, Hadrian II, and John VIII; and the excessively rare letters of the Frankish kings and their diplomata provide a fundamental schema of official doctrine by which information from other sources may be assessed. The correspondence of great churchmen like Hincmar of Rheims, and the synodal acts, doctrinal works, and juristic compendia such as those compiled by Benedictus Levita and Pseudo-Isidore also contain illuminating *obiter dicta* in the higher registers of political thought which must be gathered and placed in the context of contemporary intellectual tendencies.

This method invariably produces the sort of analytical study to which we have objected, an intellectual mosaic. Particular historical incidents which provided at specific times clear and full definitions of the political doctrines under discussion are needed to give the study cohesion. Ninth-century definitions of this sort occur in the trial of Bishop Hincmar of Laon. The documents surviving from the process are remarkably full and diverse, and, more important for our purposes, they illustrate clearly the three major political doctrines in which we are interested. The letters of Pope Hadrian II and Hincmar of Laon define papal monism. The letters of Charles the Bald, the charges he presented against the Bishop at the Synod of Touzy (recorded in the *procès-verbal* of the synod), and the position which Hincmar of Rheims attributes to

Charles in the three tracts known collectively as *Pro Libertatum Ecclesiae Defensione*, all set forth the monism of the Frankish kings. And the correspondence of Hincmar of Rheims, together with his controversial tracts, amply describes the position of the dualists and conciliarists. The conflict of these three doctrines and its ultimate outcome can still be discerned in the complete *procès-verbal* of the Synod of Touzy.

The dispute forms an intricate tapestry of treachery and betrayal. Hincmar of Laon, educated at the court of Charles the Bald, a vassal of his King, and one of the consecrators of Charles as King of Lorraine (869), was accused of having betrayed Charles by neglecting his sworn duties, by having entered into secret negotiations with Lothaire II and Pope Hadrian II against Charles, and by binding him with the anathema. In the later stages of the process, Hincmar's uncle, Hincmar of Rheims, entered equally severe accusations against him deriving from his position as nephew, student, and suffragan: that he had violated the normal bonds of kinship, that he had perverted the doctrine he had learned from his uncle, and that he had ridden roughshod over the obedience which he owed and had formally promised to his metropolitan.

For ten years after his accession to the see of Laon (858), the younger Hincmar had enjoyed the confidence of his uncle, the Archbishop of Rheims, and of his King; and he was honored by them both. In 868, however, he was charged with denying royal vassals the rightful inheritance of their benefices, deprived of some properties, and summoned before a secular court by Charles the Bald. His uncle came vigorously to his defense, denying the right-

fulness of Charles's procedure, and effected a brief reconciliation between the King and his nephew. Almost
immediately, however, Hincmar of Laon resumed by force
the villa Pauliacus which he had earlier ceded to Charles;
and the angry King summoned him to give account at the
Synod of Verberie early in 869. After a brief imprisonment
at the hands of the King, Hincmar was produced again
at the Synod of Gondreville (November 869) and at that
of Attigny (870). Having alienated the King by his maladministration of the temporal power of his episcopacy and
his uncle by his excesses in the spiritual office, he was
forced to defend himself again at the Synod of Touzy
(871), where he received his final condemnation. Although this synodal decision was contested by Pope
Hadrian II, Hadrian's death in 872 removed the most
powerful dissenting voice, and, in 876, with the permission
of Pope John VIII, Archbishop Hincmar ordained the
cleric Hedenulf to the see of Laon. At the Synod of Troyes
(878), after the death of Charles the Bald, John restored
the deposed bishop to the performance of priestly offices
and allowed him part of the revenues of his former see. In
these circumstances, the younger Hincmar died three years
later.[15]

In the formal arguments and counterarguments of this
process, the impact of law and ecclesiology upon political
thought is apparent. The dispute hinged upon two related
problems: upon the nature and competence of laws and
upon the delegation of authority. Since two systems of

[15] See H. Schrörs, *Hinkmar, Erzbischof von Reims* (Freiburg i. B.,
1884), pp. 315ff, and E. Lesne, *La hiérarchie épiscopale en Gaule et
Germanie (742-882)* (Paris, 1905), *passim*.

law and two corresponding governments, the temporal and
the ecclesiastical, were involved, the great questions of
mediaeval ecclesiology all arose in this trial. The critical
issues were classic: the degree to which the temporal ruler
was subject to ecclesiastical direction in his quality as a
member of the Church, the degree to which churchmen
were subject to their temporal rulers in their quality as
citizens of the temporal realm, the powers of temporal government in the administration of Church property, and
the proper structure of authority within the hierarchy of
the Church. The answers which the principals in the trial
gave to these questions convey the major formulations of
Carolingian political thought.

The absence of any authoritative codification of temporal or ecclesiastical law, of a commonly accepted system
of appellate jurisdiction in the Church, and of a fully developed doctrine of clerical immunities prevented the
formulation of any definitive and generally acknowledged
judgments on these matters. Such solutions as were offered
by the participants in Hincmar's trial came largely out of
the *loci communes* of mediaeval political theory. Together with the Fathers before and the scholastics after
them, all the principals in the case held the views that the
government of human society was bipartite—temporal and
spiritual—and that these two powers were divinely ordained, the temporal to serve the moral welfare of man-
kind in this world through the repression of evil, and the
spiritual to lead man to immortality through the teaching
of true doctrine. Like most other mediaeval theorists, they
also maintained that law was supreme in either order of
government, as the expression of true justice, that the Scrip-

tures, as the law of God, were above all other laws, and that no law contrary to Holy Writ was valid. Beyond this, the major parties in the dispute expressed themselves in clear and concrete terms on the nature of law and authority in civil and ecclesiastical government. They did not, it is true, compose any elaborate and consistent philosophical statements of their views. But the conceptual patterns of remarks made throughout the course of the trial, when artificially assembled, are coherent and indicate the doctrines and opinions upon which Charles the Bald, Hincmar of Laon and his papal supporters, and Hincmar of Rheims acted.

Charles's statements, written for the most part by Hincmar of Rheims but certainly representing the King's own convictions, do not touch upon the hierarchical relations between suffragan bishops, metropolitans, and popes, to which the two Hincmars principally devoted their efforts. Charles was concerned to vindicate the position of the king as legislator and as executor of temporal laws. He appealed to Roman law and to pertinent canons of Church synods, asserting that he was fully warranted in his proceedings against Hincmar of Laon, who, according to those authorities, had deprived himself of office and incurred punishment by the temporal power. Kings and emperors had by their edicts established ecclesiastical privileges and had assumed the responsibility of assuring their proper exercise, an obligation sanctioned by the Fathers of the Church. As a Frankish king, and as a successor of the Roman emperors, Charles affirmed that he must maintain the establishments of his predecessors in these functions.

Having defined his office in legal terms, Charles proceeded to the critical question of delegation of authority.
He acknowledged in strong terms the functional dualism
of kingship and episcopacy; but he further argued that
bishops, as persons who have received lands and temporal
powers from their kings in return for their oaths of fidelity
and support, were subject to the temporal ruler in all matters touching the royal interests, including the administration of the lands which they received in fief. Bishops, in his
view, received temporal authority from the king and
spiritual authority from their electors and consecrators,
and their exercise of the two kinds of power fell respectively under the surveillance of the offices which had
granted them. By perjury, calumny, and sedition, Hincmar
had betrayed his King and brought upon himself punishment by the civil power, in the royal courts.

The actions of Hincmar of Laon and his recorded
opinions on the nature of law and political authority are
so divergent as to indicate either an extremely flexible and
opportunistic mind or great fear which drove him to
abandon in practice the doctrines he had committed to
writing. Hincmar did not concern himself in his extant
writings with temporal law, and his considerations of ecclesiastical law focus upon the legislative power of the
papacy. For him, *auctoritas Petri* validated the judgments
of synods and councils; the *consuetudo* of the Roman
Church was the legally applicable custom of the universal
Church; and the decretals of popes were the authentic and
unchanging law of Christendom.

His comments upon authority likewise relate almost
entirely to the ecclesiastical side of his trial, and it is in

this connection that the inconsistency between his words
and his actions is most marked. He affirmed that the
bishop of Rome was the supreme judge in the Church;
papal jurisdiction was not merely appellate but even initial
in internal affairs of all metropolitan provinces. This assertion, as Hincmar elaborated it, amounted to a declaration that the metropolitan had no effective jurisdictional
powers over his suffragans in the administration of their
dioceses, since a bishop charged to defend himself before
his provincial synod could evade judgment at that level
by appealing directly to Rome. Hadrian II warmly supported Hincmar in this position, but the Bishop did not
hold to it steadfastly. Rather, he consented to trial by his
Metropolitan and comprovincials, and on several occasions
promised his obedience to Hincmar of Rheims in such a
way as to suggest that he accepted the position of his uncle
that metropolitans held full directive powers over their
suffragans, including the inviolable right of initial jurisdiction. He fell into similar inconsistency in his attitude
toward temporal jurisdiction; for while he stringently denied in his letters the power of royal courts to judge
bishops, he did himself voluntarily submit to judgment of
his case by the civil power, without the knowledge and
against the stated counsel of his Metropolitan.

Yet, Hincmar's theory is explicit, however greatly his
practice diverged from it. It is clear that he agreed with
Charles that the temporal authority which he held as
bishop derived from the king; but, against Charles's position, he maintained that bishops could be tried only by
other bishops even in cases involving the abuse of their
secular powers. In respect of ecclesiastical authority, he ex-

pressed the doctrine of the papal monarchy, that full legislative and jurisdictional powers in the Church were held by the bishop of Rome, from whom other bishops derived their spiritual powers and to whom they were directly subject.

These views and the doctrine of royal supremacy ran directly counter to the conciliarist-dualist doctrine affirmed by Hincmar of Rheims. At first his nephew's defender and later one of his chief accusers, the elder Hincmar drew upon an extraordinary knowledge of Roman law, of decretals, and of the canons in preparing his briefs—the most sophisticated commentaries on law and authority extant from the ninth century.

His remarks upon the nature of law deal largely with ecclesiastical law, although he did lay down as axioms that secular law in a Christian kingdom must conform to Christian principles, and that an imperial edict on an ecclesiastical matter must be considered void if the established authorities in the Church rejected it. The burden of Hincmar's thought was devoted to defining the components of ecclesiastical law and their interrelationships. His nephew had ascribed full legislative powers only to the bishop of Rome, but the Archbishop himself held that such powers resided only in the *assensus ecclesiae* as expressed in synods and councils. The canons of synods were the purest expressions of the *assensus*, and they were the peculiar law of the priesthood, the only fundamental and unchanging element of the Church's law. The other elements—papal decretals, imperial edicts, and custom— were binding on the Church only because the *assensus*, as expressed by synodal judgment, had approved them as needed complements of the canons; without this approval, they had no proper legal powers in ecclesiastical cases.

Hincmar's thought on the nature of authority corresponds to this general position. Supreme authority in the Church resided in the corps of the episcopacy, rather than in any one see; and all bishops alike were subject to the rule of the canons. Rome, he agreed, was the premier see; but her jurisdiction over internal affairs of other metropolitan provinces was strictly appellate, and its exercise was severely limited by the canons. Suffragans were subject directly to the supervision of their metropolitans, to whom they owed their consecration, even in the internal administration of their dioceses. In other words, Hincmar postulated that the episcopal powers descended from Christ to the Apostles, and from the Apostles to all bishops, among whom metropolitans acted as electors, consecrators, and superior judges. The Archbishop's views on the delegation of temporal authority turn upon the premise that it was of a quality completely different from that of spiritual offices. To his mind, there was a functional distinction between the clergy and the laity, reflected in two corresponding legal structures. The essence of the Church lay in the priesthood, and especially in the episcopacy; ecclesiastical property must be governed by churchmen, though it ought rightly to be defended by the royal power. Hincmar approved the Carolingian system by which high ecclesiastics became ministers of state, sharing in the honors and burdens of temporal government; but, at the same time, he denied the authority of the king, who bestowed those honors, to punish their wrongful use by higher clergy.

In his effort to defend these principles from violation by Charles the Bald, Hincmar invoked a new element in Frankish law: the coronation oath. The Archbishop reminded Charles that he had on several occasions—and, most important, at his coronation in 869—promised to preserve due law for every person and thus, in Hincmar's construction, to refrain from intervening in matters of discipline and doctrine among the clergy while, at the same time, guaranteeing the smooth operation of canonical procedure. Hincmar maintained that Charles had violated this oath by his measures against Hincmar of Laon, and threatened him with the loss of his office for this transgression. The royal oath, therefore, confirmed the state of affairs wherein temporal authority could be delegated to a bishop without his being responsible to the grantor for its exercise.

These three specific arguments and the three general doctrines they represent contain much that is important concerning the legal distinctions between the ecclesiastical and the temporal powers, the conciliar and the monarchical views of Church government, the nature of ecclesiastical law, the punitive and legislative qualities of the royal office, and the constitutional check upon the royal power which the Frankish clergy introduced in the form of coronation oaths. We shall return to these points in the subsequent discussion.

✝

If we consider as a unit Western political thought between late antiquity and the early modern period, the ninth-century segment is relatively unformed. The same problems which occurred in the trial of Hincmar of Laon would have been cast quite differently had the case been tried in the thirteenth or fourteenth centuries. But the same general questions of the nature of law and the delegation of authority would have arisen; the same moral and theological principles would have been invoked; and the major formulations concerning the conciliar or monarchical structure of authority within the Church and the relations between the two powers would have been repeated.

Three centuries of development of feudal institutions, including representative bodies and doctrines of contract and obligation, and the introduction of a wide knowledge of Roman and canon law in codified form, led to new formulations of basic terms. The scholastics, canonists, and legists devoted much thought to concepts of the "State" as a well-defined administrative order and of "public law," as the ultimate authority in civil matters, neither of which appears in ninth-century writings. Phrases such as "*honor*," "*status reipublicae*," and "*status ecclesiae*," to which the later authors attached precise meaning according to the abstractions of Roman law, held only the most indefinite sense for Carolingian thinkers;[16] and the paramount doctrine of sovereignty, which taught that the king was the

[16] For quite general treatments of the later meaning of the word "State," see especially F. Crosara, "Respublica e respublicae," *Atti del Congresso Internationale di Diritto Romano e di Storia del Diritto*, 4 (1953), pp. 227-261, esp. pp. 241ff; and A. O. Meyer, "Zur Geschichte des Wortes Staat," *Die Welt als Geschichte*, 10 (1950), pp. 229-237. On the canonistic usage of the terms *status ecclesiae, status regni, plena auctoritas, plenitudo potestatis* and the like, see B. Tierney, *Foundations of the Conciliar Theory* (Cambridge, 1955), pp. 50ff, 143ff.

source of law and that, as such, he was in himself an undying corporation, was totally foreign to them.[17] In ninth-century judgment, only God was sovereign, and only His kingdom was a true state. As the painstaking researches of Conrat and Krüger have shown, such knowledge of Roman law as did exist in the ninth century (and the knowledge of Hincmar of Rheims was extensive) was both fragmentary and unsystematized; for the Franks knew Roman law only from excerpts in intermediary sources, such as ecclesiastical canons and barbarian law codes, especially the Lex Visigothorum.

The great contributions of Roman and canon law lay in the future. The tripartite division of law into natural law, the law of nations, and civil law, distinctions between private and public law, doctrines concerning the legal relevance of custom, principles such as that of equity, the construct of the *plena potestas* of pope and emperor, and the fully defined role of the pope or king as establisher and interpreter of law—all these critical doctrines were largely or wholly unknown to the early Middle Ages.

By comparison with later mediaeval thought, ninth-century doctrines were tentative and very partial. But in the later period, men were still grappling with the problems of definition which had tantalized the early theorists. We have, for example, used the word "monism" to define the political doctrines implemented by ninth-century popes and kings. By this is meant the doctrine that one of the

[17] On the development of this critical doctrine, see R. E. Giesey, *The Royal Funeral Ceremony in Renaissance France* (Geneva, 1960), pp. 177ff, and E. H. Kantorowicz, *The King's Two Bodies* (Princeton, 1957), pp. 314ff.

two powers, civil or ecclesiastical, holds directive and punitive authority over the other. We have also used the word "dualism" to indicate the doctrine that the two powers were discrete and of equal dignity in this world, each existing under its own discipline and law. "Monism" and "dualism" are words often used by historians to specify the stated doctrines. They do not occur in mediaeval sources, and with good reason. As the subsequent discussion suggests, there were always elements of monism in dualism, whether theorists postulated the subjection of Christian kings to the clergy in religious matters or of clergy to kings in temporal matters; and there were always elements of dualism in monism, whenever so-called monists admitted that each of the powers had some functions into which the other might not intrude. Thus, even when doctrines are, on balance, monistic or dualistic, one will always find exceptions to the rigid application of these definitions. Neither Hincmar of Rheims in his age nor Innocent III in his succeeded in removing this conceptual ambiguity.

The ninth-century, therefore, shared some logical difficulties and some political doctrines with the later and more highly cultivated ages. The positions stated in the trial of Hincmar of Laon are sufficiently sophisticated to show the fallacy of saying that ninth-century men, however simple their doctrines by comparison with those of subsequent authors, had no idea of what the Church or the temporal office was, or of what the relationship of the two powers should be. Carolingian thinkers dealt with concrete problems for which they advanced concrete solutions. That these solutions were not so elaborate in their legal refinements as were the later ones does not obscure the fact that they were full and satisfactory answers for the men who framed them, and worthy precedents for later formulations.

In the following study, we shall discuss those aspects of political thought to which the Carolingians made direct and important contributions, particularly in ecclesiology, in the definition of law, and of the proper limits of ecclesiastical and temporal authority. We shall first outline the two principal political doctrines of Carolingian thinkers, royal monism and clerical dualism, and then, in three subsequent sections, we shall consider the ecclesiology which underlay dualistic thought, the challenge of royal supremacy to that ecclesiology, and the reconciliation between the claims of ecclesiastical liberty and those of royal supremacy which the Carolingian clergy attempted to establish by covenant.

CHAPTER II · THEORY AND COUNTERTHEORY

1. Charlemagne and Royal Monism

FRANKISH political thought in the time of Charlemagne was roughly analogous to incipient papal monism. But it contained certain tensions which prevented Carolingian "monism" from being complete, and which ultimately gave rise to genuinely dualistic thought. Under Charlemagne, social dualism existed within a political monism that centered upon two major premises: that the temporal ruler was the leader and the guarantor of the appropriate laws—though not necessarily the ideological or administrative head—of all social orders, and that the clergy, as a distinct social order, was secured in its peculiar legal constitution by his functions. Comparable in some respects to the theological monism of the later ninth-century popes, the royal monism of Charlemagne preserved more distinctly than the other doctrine the principle of functional and institutional dualism: "Just as kings are over all offices, so are bishops over those things which pertain to God."[1]

---

[1] MGH Epp. IV, no. 3 c. 11, pp. 23f. Scholarly writings on political thought at the court of Charlemagne have focused upon the Imperial Coronation in A.D. 800. F. L. Ganshof, *The Imperial Coronation of Charlemagne: Theories and Facts* (Glasgow, 1949), and P. E. Schramm, "Die Anerkennung Karls des Grossen als Kaiser: Ein Kapitel aus der Geschichte der mittelalterlichen 'Staatssymbolik,'" *Hist. Zt.* 172 (1951), pp. 449-515, provide excellent summaries of relevant secondary literature. The paucity of original sources makes it difficult to determine whether the initiative for the coronation came from Leo III or his court, from Charlemagne, or from Alcuin and his

Much in contemporary writings and in the actions of
Charlemagne himself suggests a political structure whose
civil head was also the chief of the clerical order and the

---

circle; one can only conclude with Schramm that "die geschichtliche
Zeugnisse, die es betreffen, sind so gründlich hin und her gewendet
worden, dass von ihnen kein neuer Aufschluss mehr zu erwarten ist."
Ibid., p. 39f. Ganshof and Schramm both maintain that the Frankish
court, particularly Alcuin and his closest associates, prompted the
coronation. But this does not exclude the influence of local Roman
conditions emphasized by K. Heldmann, *Das Kaisertum Karls des
Grossen* (Weimar, 1928), and E. Caspar, "Das Papsttum unter
fränkischer Herrschaft," *ZfKG*, 54 (1935), pp. 132-36, or the
Byzantine relations stressed by E. Pfeil, *Die fränkische und
deutsche Romidee des frühen Mittelalters* (Münich, 1929), and
M. Lintzel, "Das abendländische Kaisertum im 9. und 10. Jahrhundert," *Die Welt als Geschichte*, 4 (1938), pp. 421-447. Those
circumstances may very well have led Leo III and his advisors to
favor the imperial accession of Charlemagne, if not to propose it. The
coronation, however, cannot have been simply a papal plot (cf. W.
Ohnsorge, *Das Zweikaiserproblem im früheren Mittelalter* [Hildesheim,
1947], p. 23), and the opinions of other authors that the initiative
came from the Franks or from the Alcuinian circle surely contain
some truth. See L. Halphen, *Charlemagne et l'empire carolingien*
(Paris, 1947); A. Kleinclausz, *Charlemagne* (Paris, 1934), and *Alcuin*
(Paris, 1948); L. Levillain, "Le couronnement impérial de Charlemagne," *Revue d'histoire de l'Eglise de France*, 18 (1932), pp. 5ff; H.
Löwe, *Die karolingische Reichsgrundung und der Südosten* (Stuttgart,
1937); E. E. Stengel, "Kaisertitel und Souveränitätsidee," *Deutsches
Archv*, 3 (1939), pp. 1-56. The political doctrines of the papal and
Frankish courts, the civil condition of Rome, and Byzantine relations
probably all prompted the coronation of Charlemagne; but it would
be mere pedantry to attempt to single out one of these causes as predominant. For the historical background of the Frankish coronation,
see W. Levison, *England and the Continent in the Eighth Century*
(Oxford, 1946), pp. 116ff.

Students of Frankish political thought at the court of Charlemagne
have, on the whole, defined that thought as centering upon the figure
of the "priest-king." For them, the extreme measures Charlemagne
took in ecclesiastical affairs, the parallels contemporaries drew between

arbiter of spiritual matters. Popes Hadrian I and Leo III allowed Charlemagne a large part in the administration of ecclesiastical discipline and in problems of hierarchical

---

Charlemagne and David, the prophet-king, and the heavily theological character of court ceremonial and political thought, all point to a theoretical construct in which the king was vested with quasi-priestly, or quasi-episcopal, attributes and powers as well as with characteristics of the royal office. German scholars are accustomed to write descriptively of a "Priesterkönigtum." J. Hashagen, "Spätkarolingische Staats- und Soziallehren," *Deutsche Vierteljahrsschrift für Literaturwissenschaft und Geistesgeschichte*, 17 (1939), pp. 301-311, F. Kampers, "Rex et Sacerdos," *Hist. JB*, 45 (1925), pp. 495-515, and W. Ullmann, *The Growth of Papal Government in the Middle Ages* (London, 1955) are extreme statements of this grotesquely exaggerated interpretation. See also E. Eichmann, *Die Kaiserkrönung im Abendland*, 1 (Würzburg 1942), p. 325. The work of M. Bloch, *Les rois thaumaturges* (Strasbourg and Paris, 1924), pp. 69f, and E. H. Kantorowicz, *Laudes Regiae: A Study in Liturgical Acclamations and Mediaeval Ruler Worship* (Berkeley, 1946), pp. 47f, 56f, 63, and *passim*, has done much to set the sacral kingship of the Carolingian epoch in its proper perspective. But it remained for H. Fichtenau, *Das karolingische Imperium*, to point out that David was a prophet, not a priest, that parallels drawn between him and Charlemagne did not ascribe priestly or episcopal qualities to the Frankish King, that the actions of Charlemagne in ecclesiastical affairs were natural expressions of secular, Germanic political convention, and that court ceremonial did indeed acknowledge Charlemagne as an earthly counterpart of Christ, but of Christ as King, not of Christ as King and Priest. For supporting information, see R. Folz, *Le Souvenir et la légende de Charlemagne dans l'Empire germanique médiéval* (Paris, 1950), pp. 7, 39ff. In his recent study, W. Mohr (*Die karolingische Reichsidee*, Münster, 1962) cautions against the "Königpriestertum" interpretation (p. 15), but the "Davidic" concept of kingship which he attributes to Charlemagne is but a slight modification of the older interpretation. The present chapter attempts to show that Charlemagne's views were monistic, or nearly so, without including any sort of "pontifical kingship." On the hypothesis that the same principles which governed his thought before A.D. 800 continued to govern it afterwards, no particular attention has been drawn here to the Imperial coronation. The reader is, however, referred to the studies cited above.

order,[2] and the subjects of the King were likewise disposed
to enhance the royal character with trappings of sacerdotalism. Theodulf of Orléans praised Charlemagne by writing
that St. Peter, who held the keys of Heaven, had commanded Charlemagne to hold similar keys in governing
the Church, the clergy, and the people.[3] Alcuin summoned
his David to "defend, teach, and propagate the truth of
the apostolic Faith," to be a preacher of the law of God—
like a bishop, a rector and doctor—to preserve the purity
of the Faith and root out doctrinal error, and to exercise
the clerical functions "*praeesse et prodesse*."[4] Charlemagne,
he wrote, was the incorruptible and supreme ruler, "catholic in Faith, king in power, pontiff in preaching."[5] And
Paulinus of Aquileia solemnly acclaimed his Ruler as
"king and priest."[6]

Nor was this inclination to see in the earthly king an
image of the heavenly King and Priest confined to writings.
Court ceremonial and the architecture of Aachen, Charlemagne's "second Rome,"[7] seem a studied design to set the
Frankish ruler apart as the King of Glory.[8] More telling,
the King exercised great power in Church affairs. Charlemagne himself maintained that ecclesiastical lands were
committed to his governance[9] and that the granting of

[2] MGH Epp. III, no. 65, p. 593; no. 51, p. 573; no. 93, pp. 631f. See
also MGH Epp. v, no. 5, p. 61.

[3] Carm. 32, MGH Poet. Lat. I, pp. 523f.

[4] MGH Epp. IV, no. 202, p. 336; no. 41, p. 84; no. 171, p. 281; no.
257, p. 414. Cf. *Regula S. Benedicti*, c. 64, 8, CSEL 75, p. 149. The
phrase is also frequent in St. Augustine.

[5] Adversus Elipandum I, 16. Migne PL. 101, 251.

[6] MGH Conc. I, no. 19 D, p. 142.

[7] MGH Poet. Lat. I, p. 368, v. 94.

[8] See Fichtenau, *Das karolingische Imperium*, pp. 59ff.

[9] MGH Cap. I, no. 29, p. 79, "episcopia et monasteria nobis Christo

bishoprics was in the will of God and in the power of the king.[10] So too, the exercise of the pontifical office fell beneath his supervision.[11] Indeed his assertions of authority in the discipline and trial of prelates[12] were so decided that Pope Hadrian I defended himself against the threat of deposition by him,[13] and Alcuin felt it necessary to argue against the trial of Leo III under imperial auspices.[14] Syn-

---

propitio ad gubernandum commissa. . . ." See also the Gesta Episcoporum Cenomannensium, c. 17, Mabillon, *Analecta*, p. 289.

[10] Monk of St. Gall, Gesta Karoli I, 4, MGH SS. II, pp. 732f. See also Charlemagne to Hadrian I in E. Munding, ed. *Texte und Arbeiten herausgegeben durch die Erzabtei Beuron*, I Abt. Hft. 6 (Beuron, 1920), p. 4, "Cor enim regis in manu Dei consistere credimus nutuque illius huc illucque vertit. Ideoque non nostro arbitrio, sed Dei credimus esse pastorale illi culmen concessum." See also the similar passages in Charlemagne's letters to Gerebald of Liége (MGH Cap. I, no. 124, p. 245), Constantius of Chur (MGH Dip. Car. I, no. 78, p. 112), and Amalarius of Trier (MGH Epp. v, no. 3, p. 244).

[11] E.g., Charlemagne's letter to Gerebald of Liége, MGH Cap. I, no. 122, p. 241, and Gerebald's response, *ibid.*, no. 122, p. 242.

[12] See Paschasius Radbertus, Vita Adalhardi, c. 37, MGH SS. II, p. 528: Charged before Charlemagne, Adalhard of Corbie addressed his episcopal colleagues, "Nolite, quaeso, fratres mei, nolite attendere, quasi quod de nobis agitur, in hominis sit potestate. Fateor enim, etiam si idem aliud delegerit, quam quod a Deo semel prolatum est, non posse penitus retractari, nisi primum hoc opere compleatur, neque possunt compleri disposita, si non idem annuerit. . . . Interim vero, quaeso, parcite a Deo collato nobis principi, quod non sua quodammodo sed Domini nostri, cui peccavimus, interdum utitur voluntate." See also the Gesta Episcoporum Cenomannensium, c. 20, Mabillon, *Analecta*, p. 291; Monk of St. Gall, Gesta Caroli, I, 16, MGH SS. II, p. 737. Charlemagne himself asserted that he was the supreme appellate judge in some ecclesiastical matters. See MGH Conc. I, no. 19 G, c. 6, pp. 166f. MGH Cap. I, no. 130, p. 257; no. 97, pp. 203f; no. 33, c. 15, p. 94.

[13] MGH Epp. III, no. 92, pp. 629f, against the suggestion by Offa "ut per suam videlicet adhortationem atque suasionem nos a sede sancta dignitatis nostrae, quod absit, eicere deberemini et alium ibidem de gente vestra institueremini rectorem." Cf. MGH Epp. IV, no. 100, p. 146.

[14] MGH Epp. IV, no. 179, p. 297. Cf. L. Wallach, "The Roman

ods submitted their decrees to him for review and correction;[15] the reformation of liturgy and the purification of Scriptural texts fell under his direction;[16] and orthodox dogma found in him an earnest censor, defender, and propagator against Spanish and Byzantine error.[17]

Yet upon this extension of power into spiritual government, there was one principal limitation: Charlemagne was a layman, and even he acknowledged that he was subject to episcopal counsel in doctrinal matters.[18] He intervened in ecclesiastical affairs, not on any principle of dominion over the Church, therefore, but rather on the premise that God had granted the imperial power to him "not simply for the *governance* of the world, but most of all for the *defense* of the Church. . . ."[19] The same authors whose apparently extreme ascriptions of omnicompetence to Charlemagne we have quoted in fact set definite limits to his actions, by denying him the priestly character. In acclaiming Charlemagne as *"rex et sacerdos,"* at the Synod of Frankfurt (794), Paulinus attributed only temporal functions to his King: the subjugation of barbarian peoples, the defense of the Church, and, most important, the secur-

---

Synod of December 800 and the Alleged Trial of Leo III," *Harvard Theological Review*, 49 (1956), pp. 123-142, and the literature cited there.

[15] See MGH Conc. I, no. 37, p. 274; no. 38, p. 293; no. 19 D, pp. 130f; no. 29, p. 230. See especially the letter of Paulinus of Aquileia to Charlemagne, MGH Epp. IV, no. 15, pp. 517f.

[16] MGH Cap. I, no. 22, p. 61, no. 30, pp. 80f.

[17] See also the Admonitio of one of his missi, MGH Cap. I, no. 121, p. 239, an admonition to orthodoxy of faith.

[18] MGH Epp. IV, no. 304, pp. 462f.

[19] *Ibid.*, no. 308, p. 471, a citation of Leo I, Ep. 156, c. 3, Migne PL. 54, 1130.

ing of priests in their sacred ministry and in their enjoyment of the privileges of canon law. Charlemagne, he
wrote, was to fight with material arms against visible enemies; his bishops were to combat invisible enemies with
spiritual weapons.[20] Alcuin, too, held that the priestly
power was distinct from the royal, for the priestly bore the
key to the kingdom of heaven and the royal carried the
sword to punish malefactors.[21] "The duty of the priests,"
he wrote, "is to declare the words of God. Yours, o princes,
is to obey them humbly, to fulfill them diligently."[22] And
in matters of dogma and ecclesiastical discipline, Charlemagne himself acknowledged the Roman Church as the
supreme guardian and interpreter.[23]

While he construed Church-State relations politically,
Charlemagne did not, therefore, arrogate to himself priestly functions or prerogatives. Instead, he brought to bear
two premier theses of Germanic thought: that the king
was a military leader, the civil ruler of all members of the
human society subject to him, and that his first duty was
to guarantee to each man the benefits of his peculiar law.

The first thesis is manifest in Charlemagne's views of
the unity of society and of the Church as a warring institution under his direction.[24] He saw the general supervision

[20] MGH Conc. I, no. 19 D, p. 141f, and MGH Epp. IV, no. 18 a, p.
525.

[21] MGH Epp. IV, no. 255, p. 413. Cf. *ibid.*, no. 17, p. 45; Liber de
virtutibus et vitiis, c. 6, Migne PL. 101, 617.

[22] MGH Epp. IV, no. 18, p. 51.

[23] Libri Carolini, I, 6, MGH Conc., Suppl., p. 20. See also Charlemagne's prologue to the Codex Carolinus, MGH Epp. III, p. 476. Cf.
Astronomus, Vita Ludovici, c. 4, MGH SS. II, p. 608: Charlemagne
commended his sons, Louis and Charles, to Saints Peter and Paul,
"quibus coeli terraeque potestas attributa est. . . ."

[24] See MGH Cap. I, no. 22, c. 62, p. 58; no. 29, p. 79; and no. 33,

of ecclesiastical affairs, consequently, as a public matter within the competence of the royal power.[25] To this essentially Germanic concept, the writings of St. Augustine, which Charlemagne is reported to have enjoyed and respected, added a religious lustre. Charlemagne's thought followed closely Augustine's image of the earthly city as an *umbra* of the heavenly, in which Christ ruled as king, and of its unceasing warfare against the city of the devil.[26] Given historical reality by the King's military expeditions against the Saracens, the Saxons, and the Avars, this Augustinian figure received striking expression at the Synod of Frankfurt (794). As the "lord of the earth," Charlemagne summoned the synod to combat the Adoptionist heresy; he sat among the bishops in their sessions and issued them procedural directions; he confirmed and promulgated their decrees.[27] Still, the royal summons was issued under papal authority; Charlemagne did not participate in discussions of doctrinal matters; and he accepted the synodal decrees without imposing his own doctrinal interpretations upon

c. 2, p. 92: "Precepitque ut omni[s]homo in toto regno suo, sive ecclesiasticus sive laicus, unusquisque secundum votum et propositum suum, qui antea fidelitate sibi regis nomine promississent, nunc ipsum promissum nominis cesaris faciat. . . ."

[25] It was *negotium publicum*. See Rimbert, Vita S. Anskarii, c. 26, MGH SS. II, p. 712. "Sic quippe apud eos [the Northmen] moris est ut quodcumque negotium publicum magis in populi unanima voluntate quam in regia constet potestate," an obvious comparison with Frankish practice.

[26] De Civitate Dei, xv, 1, 2, Corp. Christ. Ser Lat., pp. 454f. One may recall Charlemagne's oath, as recorded by the Monk of St. Gall, Gesta Caroli I, 3, MGH SS. II, p. 732, "Per regem coelorum!" See also Augustine, *op.cit.*, I, Praef.; x, 21; xviii, 41; xx, 11; v. 47, pp. 1, 294f, v. 48, pp. 637, 720f.

[27] MGH Conc. I, no. 19 E, p. 143.

33

them.[28] Without entering into the peculiar functions of bishops, "the rulers of the city of Christ through their diverse sees," Charlemagne exercised his office as the head of society, patterning his actions upon those of "Jesus Christ, our Lord, [who] governs that city with the royal power through which He rules, defends, and exalts the whole structure of the city."[29] Since, as king, he was vicar of God, the conduct of doctrinal as well as military warfare fell under Charles's general direction;[30] but in spiritual matters, the problem of higher strategy was proper to his bishops.

The functional dualism implicit in this position received legal formalization. As we have seen, Paulinus urged Charlemagne to honor the peculiar law of the priesthood; and indeed, from the very beginning of his reign, Charlemagne exercised his duty as the guarantor of laws to ensure the juristic separation of the clergy from the laity according to the terms of canon law. His earliest extant edict (769) is almost entirely a repetition of the capitulary of Carloman (742), in which the clergy were reserved to the law of the canons.[31] From then onward throughout his life, Charle-

[28] *Ibid.*, 19 C, p. 122: "Regiam scilicet vel canonicam placuit ei consuetudinem renovare."

[29] *Ibid.*, 19 E, pp. 160f.

[30] Cf. Jonas of Orléans's remark on the Synod of Frankfurt: De Cultu Imaginum, 1, Migne PL. 106, 309, "quibus milites Christi, ut pote invictissimis armis muniti ejus vesanam doctrinam propulsaverunt. Ejusdem namque principis jussu in unum coacti, adhibita etiam sanctae Romanae Ecclesiae auctoritate, eumdem Felicem damnaverunt. . . ." See pp. 239ff.

[31] MGH Cap. 1, no. 19, pp. 44f. See the fragmentary letter from Sigwald of Aquileia to Charlemagne (774/6), MGH Epp. IV, no. 8, p. 505: "Vestra est . . . sacrorum canonum inviolabiles sanctiones salubriter promulgatas nullo quolibet usurpationis titulo . . . mutilare. . . ."

magne frequently confirmed this principle in his legislation
and continually fostered the study of the canons.[32] In fact,
he was so eager to secure canonical administration in clerical affairs that he was even prompted to instruct Leo III
upon his accession to the throne of St. Peter "to adhere in
all regards to canonical sanctions and always to follow
upon the statutes of the Fathers."[33] These efforts of Charles
added an institutional quality to the functional division
of the priesthood from the laity. For the applicability of
royal power in episcopal elections, in the trial of bishops,
and in the administration of Church lands was increasingly
restricted by the juristic apparatus prescribed in the canons.
The effects of this tendency in political practice, to which
we shall return, were evident even before the death of
Charlemagne: in his later assemblies, he separated the
members of the clergy from the laity and charged them
with considering their own law among themselves.[34] Many
years later, Hincmar of Rheims described the canons as
the tribal law of the priesthood,[35] and Charlemagne may

[32] MGH Cap. I, no. 25, c. 5, p. 67; no. 89, p. 189; no. 33, pp. 91f, and
passim. See the Gesta Episcoporum Cenomannensium, c. 17, Mabillon,
Analecta, p. 288: "Sed illo in tempore jam sapientia ordinante atque
instigante domno Carolo, pollere cœperet et canonica auctoritas, prae-
cipiente iam dicto Carolo gloriosissimo Francorum Rege, enucleatim
perscrutari." See Charlemagne's Admonitio Generalis (789), MGH
Cap. I, no. 22, c. 60, p. 57, and *ibid.*, no. 34, c. 2, p. 100; no. 35, c. 25,
p. 103.

[33] MGH Epp. IV, no. 93, p. 138, and the related instructions in *ibid.*,
no. 92, pp. 135f. See also Charlemagne's interest in canonical episcopal
elections, MGH Dip. Car. I, no. 174, p. 234, Böhmer-Mühlbacher,
Regesta Imperii I, pt. I, no. 690, p. 285, MGH Cap. I, no. 89, c. 10, p. 189.

[34] MGH Cap. I, no. 71, c. I, p. 161; Annales Laureshamensis (a. 802),
MGH SS. I, p. 39; MGH Conc., I, no. 36, p. 259. See H. v. Schubert,
Der Kampf des geistlichen und weltlichen Rechts (Heidelberg, 1927),
pp. 30f.

[35] *Infra*, pp. 90, 98.

well have been applying the principle of the personality of the law in an ethnic sense when he commanded these divisions. Still, the largely monistic character of his political actions toward the Church gave rise to a major intellectual reaction among the Frankish clergy: the formulation of dualistic political thought and conciliarist ecclesiology.

2. *The Clerical Reaction: Dualism and Conciliarism*

The thought of the Frankish clergy departed from the political monism of Charlemagne toward an institutional separation of *Ecclesia* and *Respublica*. Unlike papal monists, the Frankish clergy did not assert hegemony over temporal government; they did not claim the power to bestow the royal office or to depose kings. Instead, they proposed to erect their order as a second government beside the temporal, a government to which the Christian king would submit in spiritual matters just as clerics submitted to him in temporal.

As we have seen, the distinction between clergy and laity was basically functional and, by extension, juridical in the time of Charlemagne. Two related concepts, conventional in ecclesiological thought, which first assumed importance among Frankish theorists in his reign, sharpened and enhanced that distinction: namely, the concept of the Church as a community apart from temporal government, unified and ruled by priests and bishops, and that of the clergy as a legal body reserved to its own law and to its peculiar courts. The effect of these concepts was the formulation of a dualistic doctrine of Church-State relations and of a conciliarist doctrine of Church government.

✛

The ground of this new position was the same as that of papal monism: the concept of the Church as a mystical union of all believers which derived its cohesiveness from the sacramental functions of priests. "The whole Church," said Florus of Lyon, "is one sacrifice of God and one body of Christ. . . . In Christ, we are one bread; in Christ we are incorporate and united."[1] To this union, the priestly function was essential. As Haimo of Halberstadt wrote about the Eucharistic Host: "The fullness of Divinity which was in Him [Christ] also fills this bread, and that divinity of the Word which fills heaven and earth and all that are in them, fills also the body of Christ, which is sanctified by many priests throughout the whole world and makes one body of Christ. And just as this bread and blood [*sic*] change into the body of Christ, so all in the Church who worthily eat it are one body of Christ."[2] And Hincmar of

[1] MGH Conc. II, no. 57, pp. 771f.

[2] Expositio in 1 Cor. 10:17, Migne PL. 117, 564. See also Agobard, MGH Epp. v, no. 3, c. 3, p. 159, "quoniam unus panis, unum corpus Christi, immo unus Christus secundum apostolum sumus. . . ." and the remarks by A. Bressolles, *Saint Agobard, évêque de Lyon* (Paris, 1949), pp. 90ff. Cf. Expositio in Epheses 4:5, *ibid.*, col. 718: "Unum est baptisma, quia omnes aequaliter per universam orbem baptizantur, qui signaculum fidei percipiunt." See also Florus of Lyon, MGH Epp. v, no. 13, c. 9, p. 271: "Prorsus panis ille sacrosanctae oblationis corpus est Christi, non materie vel specie visibili, sed virtute et potentia spiritali." Cf. Agobard of Lyon to Louis the Pious, MGH Epp. v, no. 3, c. 3, p. 159. For a general biography of Agobard, see J. A. Cabaniss, *Agobard of Lyons, Churchman and Critic* (Syracuse, 1953). Professor Kantorowicz cautions, "Corpus mysticum, in the language of the Carolingian theologians, referred not at all to the body of the Church, nor to the oneness and unity of Chris-

Rheims commented: "Christ consecrated the mystery of the peace of our unity at His table. Who save He is daily consecrated at His table?" Hincmar made the source of that unity explicit when he wrote that, "the priestly ministry is the very altar of God,"[3] a metaphor which suggested to his contemporaries that the priesthood itself constituted the *"corpus Christi."*[4]

This metaphoric relationship was critical in political thought. For it divided the ministrants of the sacraments from those to whom they ministered. In terms of law, it removed the clergy as a separate corporation from civil jurisdiction, and it exalted the spiritual power over the temporal in the context of the Church. Commenting upon confirmation of clerical privileges by the Emperors Theodosius and Valentinian, Florus of Lyon praised their statement that "the Church abides among the priests (*Ecclesia in sacerdotibus consistit*) and expands [from them] into the temple of God," and he observed that it was "a wondrous and true statement that the Church consists not of

---

tian society, but to the consecrated host." E. H. Kantorowicz, *The King's Two Bodies* (Princeton, 1957), pp. 195f. The historical evolution of the phrase "corpus mysticum" as a designation of the Church is traced by H. de Lubac, *Corpus Mysticum: L'Eucharistie et l'Eglise au moyen âge* (Paris, 1948). On the Carolingian period, see de Lubac, pp. 32ff, 40ff, 116. H. Fichtenau, *Das karolingische Imperium* (Zurich, 1949), p. 227.

[3] De Cavendis Vitiis, c. 10, Migne PL. 125, 924. Cf. Haimo of Halberstadt, Expositio in 1 Cor. 11:23ff, Migne PL. 117, 570: "Uno enim pane universitas ecclesiae designatur." Hincmar, Ad Regem de coercendo raptu viduarum, c. 4, Migne PL. 125, 1019. Baptism was similarly regarded. See Rhabanus Maurus, De clericorum institutione, I, 1, Migne PL. 107, 297, and Ennarratio in 1 Cor. 12:12, Migne PL. 112, 113, and Ennarratio in Coloss. 1; 18, Migne PL. 112, 515.

[4] See Rhabanus Maurus, De sacris ordinibus, c. 19, Migne PL. 112, 1179 (and De clericorum institutione 1, 33, Migne PL. 107, 324).

stones so much as of priests"; for the same reverence shown
the altar should be shown the priest.[5] Governed by one
distinctive law throughout the world, and performing
identical offices,[6] priests were legally set apart from others
as the mediators between God and man, as men discharging a sacred ministry.[7]

In this intellectual framework, the spiritual office was
far superior to the temporal.[8] Laymen must accept the
decrees of synods "as though they were the words of God
Himself."[9] For "the spiritual commonwealth of the universal Church"[10] was, in fact, not a *respublica*, but a
regnum, whose priestly rulers bore in their tonsure the

[5] F. Maassen, "Ein Commentar des Florus von Lyon," *SB der Akad.
der Wiss. zu Wien*, phil.-hist. Kl. 92 (1878), p. 324. Cf. Migne PL.
119, 421. The same edict is cited by Pope Gregory IV, MGH Epp. IV, no.
14, p. 78, "sanctam ecclesiam, quae in sacerdotibus maxime constat," and
by Benedictus Levita, II, 99, Migne PL. 97, 761f (See E. Seckel, "Studien
zu Benedictus Levita, VII," *Neues Archiv*, 34 [1908/9], p. 356.), and
Pseudo-Isidore, Ps.-Pius I, Ep. II, c. 7f, Hinschius, *Decretales Pseudo-
Isidorianae*, pp. 118f. On the manuscript problem of this edict, see F.
Maassen, *Geschichte der Quellen und der Literatur des canonischen
Rechts im Abendlande bis zum Ausgange des Mittelalters,* v. I (Gratz,
1870), pp. 321, 569f.

[6] Concilium Moguntiacense (888), c. 23, Mansi XVIII A, 70.

[7] MGH Cap. I, no. 178, c. 4, p. 367. See also Jonas of Orléans, De
institutione laicali, II, 20, Migne PL. 106, 208, and the letter of the
bishops of the dioceses of Rouen and Rheims to Louis the German,
MGH Cap. II, no. 297, p. 429.

[8] Hincmar of Rheims, De Divortio, Responsio VII, Migne PL. 125,
c. 769f.

[9] Synodus ad Theodonis Villam (844), MGH Cap. II, no. 227, p. 113.

[10] Walafrid Strabo, De Exordiis, c. 32, MGH Cap. II, p. 514. Cf.
Florus of Lyon, Comment. in Coloss. 1:24, Migne PL. 119, 390, a
citation of Augustine, Ennarat. in Ps. LXI, c. 4, "Ad communem hanc
quasi rempublicam nostram quisque pro modulo nostro exsolvimus
quod debemus. . . ." See also Hincmar of Rheims, De Divortio, Migne
PL. 125, 699, "unum regnum una est ecclesia. . . ."

symbol of their royal and sacerdotal office.[11] Rhabanus Maurus described this exaltation of the priesthood very concisely when he wrote that there were three orders in the Church: the laity, or the *ordo popularis*, the monks, and the clergy. The clerical order, he wrote, was set above the others since it performed divine services and "dispensed sacraments to the peoples." Like the tribe of Levi, the priests of the "present Church" were particularly elected by God to offer sacrifices, "to judge between the just and the unjust, to decide between the sacred and the profane ... and to teach the people of God all His laws and the precepts He has sent them."[12] In the same tenor, Agobard of Lyon wrote to Bernard of Vienne (822/9) that laymen were bound to obey priests. "For although righteous laymen [*iusti populares*] are more worthy of eternal life than unrighteous priests, still unrighteous priests can perform sacramental functions [*sacramentaria*] in which the salvation of the people consists, and righteous laymen cannot."[13]

This sacramental construction accordingly limited the authority of the king in the Church. As a layman who was also king, he was obliged to guarantee the exercise of canon law over priests, but not to pronounce or to administer canons; and although his duty was to defend his clergy in the performance of sacramental offices, he might not discharge those offices himself. Whatever his majesty as *pater patriae*, the king must always acknowledge

[11] Concilium Aquisgranense (816), MGH Conc. 1, no. 39, p. 318, quoting St. Isidore of Seville. Repeated by Rhabanus Maurus, De clericorum institutione, 1, 2, Migne PL. 107, 298.

[12] *Ibid.*, 1, 2, Migne PL. 107, 297. (Repeated in his De sacris ordinibus, c. 2, Migne PL. 112, 1166f.)

[13] CC. 7, 9, Migne PL. 104, 134, 136f.

the spiritual supremacy of his bishops, "the propitiators and reconcilers of the people to eternal salvation."[14] Jonas of Orléans praised the Emperor Theodosius for humbling himself before St. Ambrose, since "he knew that the imperial power which set him apart derived from the power of Him whose servant and minister Ambrose was."[15] And in the same tenor, Lothaire II, "the vicar of God on earth," submitted himself to the judgment and censure of his episcopacy, acknowledging his bishops as mediators between God and men, guardians of his soul, and ministrants of spiritual healing and chastisement.[16]

As a consequence of this concept of sacramental unity, there are statements from the time of Charlemagne[17] onward which imply the complete subordination of the royal power to the jurisdictional apparatus of the clergy. The tendency they represent appears to have been particularly strong during the reign of Louis the Pious, whose own conviction that he was *"in Dei servitio"* gave it impetus.[18] His public penances, at Attigny (822) and St. Médard (833), as well as his submission of his personal and official actions to episcopal scrutiny on other occasions,[19] enhanced the hierarchical position that the fulfillment of the royal ministry consisted principally in supplying the needs of

[14] MGH Cap. II, no. 272, c. 4, p. 310.

[15] De institutione laicali, II, 20, Migne PL. 106, 211.

[16] Mansi xv, 614.

[17] E.g., the letter of Odilbert to Charlemagne, MGH Cap. I, no. 126, p. 247: ". . . divinitus inspirati quae Domini sacerdotes diffiniebant, illa tamen principalis auctoritas confirmabat."

[18] Rimbert, Vita S. Anskarii, c. 25, MGH SS. II, p. 710. Cf. Louis' Admonitio of 823 cc. 2, 5, MGH Cap. I, no. 150, pp. 303f.

[19] Praeceptum Synodale (829/30), MGH Conc. II, no. 52, p. 683.

the churches and the poor.[20] The Synod of Paris (829) construed the royal duties entirely within this ecclesiastical context. While maintaining that the prerogatives of the king in ecclesiastical affairs were limited "by divine authority," and that Louis had transgressed those limits on diverse occasions, the synod wished to enlist the royal power primarily in its own service. The basis and the main characteristic of that power, it acknowledged, was the power of the sword, granted to the king by God to be exercised "for the terror of many . . . for the sake of God's vengeance." The king, acknowledging the "priestly power, vigor, and dignity," was to realize that he had no jurisdictional authority over the priesthood, but rather, that God had given priests power to judge kings. The temporal ruler, therefore, was to honor the persons and the reputations of his bishops, and to yield them his power in securing the regular meetings of synods, in enforcing ecclesiastical discipline, and, finally, in guaranteeing the full enjoyment of the episcopal *libertas*.[21]

The concept of the royal power as an auxiliary of the episcopal survived in the reign of Charles the Bald. Archbishop Wenilo of Sens, for example, wrote that Christ had divided the governance of His Church between bishops and kings "so that the most devout kings might accomplish and cause to be accomplished what holy bishops taught."[22] His contemporary, Hincmar of Rheims, though a pro-

[20] Relatio Episcoporum (820?), c. 8, MGH Cap. I, no. 178, p. 367. Cf. the Relatio Episcoporum de Poenitentia (833), MGH Cap. II, no. 197, pp. 52ff.

[21] Synod of Paris (829), Relatio, cc. 8 (quoting Rufinus, Hist. eccles. x, 2), 17, 27, MGH Conc. II, no. 50, pp. 673, 676, 680.

[22] Wenilo of Sens to Amulo of Lyon (843/5), MGH Epp. VI, no. 81, p. 73.

nounced dualist, was also capable of extreme hierocratic views. In writing to Louis the German during Louis's invasion of the lands of Charles the Bald (858), Hincmar admonished the King to remember that he was a "son of the Church"[23] and that his first duties were to preserve ecclesiastical privileges. He must honor bishops "as fathers and vicars of Christ," obey their spiritual counsel, and enable them to perform their episcopal ministry in peace, lending them the coercive power of the civil arm in ecclesiastical cases when necessary, guaranteeing their right to hold provincial and diocesan synods, and defending ecclesiastical properties.[24] He expected similar services of the young Kings Louis III and Carloman, hoping that they would be taught to "humble [their] spirit before the priests and bend [their] head before the great" and to reserve to the Church and her rulers their due privileges.[25]

By far the most imperious statement of this position, however, issued from the Synod of Meaux-Paris (845/6). The bishops in that assembly applied to themselves the Scriptural sentence: "See, I have this day set thee over nations and over kingdoms to root out and to pull down, to scatter and cast down, to build and to plant" (Jeremiah 1:10). All "sons of the Church," including the King, "who, through God's action excels all other sons of the Church by virtue of the royal dignity," were subject to their correction; Charles the Bald himself was threatened

[23] Epistola Synodalis Carisiacensis (858), c. 15, MGH Cap. II, no. 297, p. 440.
[24] Ibid., c. 7, p. 431f. Cf. Hincmar's Instructio ad Ludovicum, Migne PL. 125, 987.
[25] Ad Carolum III Imperatorem, c. 3, Migne PL. 125, 991. The Scriptural citations are Eccli. 4, 7, and Ps. 18, 8.

with the anathema.[26] Whatever perversity earthly power, cupidity, ignorance, or weakness had introduced into the Church or human concourse was to be cut off by priestly action.[27] The bishops regarded the royal power as an instrument for eliminating evil practices and the decay of ecclesiastical discipline: the King must remove monasteries and other ecclesiastical properties from the hands of laymen and give them to those canonically qualified to rule them; he must restore ecclesiastical lands illicitly withdrawn from the control of the Church and respect their immunities; and, finally, he must leave the episcopal administration unimpeded by royal intervention except when a bishop should request it. The juridical integrity of the kingship has disappeared in these decrees; it has been absorbed into the concept of the king as personally subject to the Church, as the *filius ecclesiae*, whose duties as a king and as a man were "to fulfill and to cause to be fulfilled what holy bishops taught."

The historical settings of these statements, however, do not allow one to assume that they express prevalent concepts. In the same letter we have cited, Wenilo justified the nomination of bishops by kings and urged the consecration of two persons so advanced. Engaged in a harsh struggle with Louis III for free and canonical election in the see of Beauvais, Hincmar did not resist his King with spiritual censures or threats of temporal punishments, but rather he professed himself willing to suffer at the hands of his earthly lord.[28] Finally, the judgments of the Synod of

---

[26] MGH Cap. II, no. 293, c. 78, p. 419; prologue, pp. 395f.
[27] *Ibid.*, prologue.
[28] Ep. 20, c. 9, Migne PL. 126, 120.

Meaux-Paris were by no means commonly held. Of the eighty-three canons which the synod presented to Charles the Bald for promulgation, only nineteen were accepted: the hierocratic position had been most emphatically rejected.[29]

+

On the whole, the Frankish clergy argued on sacramental grounds, not to subject temporal to ecclesiastical government, but rather to erect ecclesiastical government irrefrangibly as an integral political entity apart from secular institutions. As the Synod of Paris (829) declared in an unwitting corruption of the Gelasian text, "There are two August Empresses by which this world is principally governed, the hallowed authority of pontiffs and the royal power."[30] The powers were separate in origin, administrative order, and purpose:[31] while he might participate to

[29] Annales Bertiniani (a. 846), MGH in usum schol., p. 33.

[30] MGH Conc. II, no. 5 D, p. 610, 1, 3. The same reading is preserved in the decrees of the Synod of Aachen (836), *ibid.*, no. 56 A, p. 705, in Benedictus Levita, I, 319, Migne PL. 97, 742, and in one variant of the Episcoporum ad Ludovicum Relatio (829), MGH Cap. II, no. 196, c. 3, p. 29.

[31] Cf. Rhabanus Maurus, MGH Epp. v, *fragmenta*, c. 23, p. 528: "Duae dignitates atque potestates inter homines constitutae reperiuntur. Una ex humana inventione reperta, hoc est imperialis atque regalis. Altera vero ex divina auctoritate instituta, hoc est sacerdotalis. Quarum una hominum corpora parat ad mortem, altera animas nutrit ad vitam." See also the decree of the Synod of Quierzy (857), MGH Cap. II, no. 297, c. 15, pp. 439f, the edict of Cologne (843), *ibid.*, no. 254, pp. 254f, and that of the Synod of Ver (844), *ibid.*, no. 291, c. 12, p. 387: "Saeculares honores saeculares possideant, ecclesiasticos ecclesiastici sortiantur." The distinction between excommunication, the ultimate penalty of the Church, and capital punishment, that of the temporal power, should also be noted. E.g., Hincmar, De Divortio, Responsio II, Migne PL. 125, 643, and MGH Cap. I, no. 26, c. 11, p. 69. Cf. Annales Bertiniani

some extent in ecclesiastical affairs,[32] the king remained
a layman, a son of the Church.[33] In temporal matters, the
temporal ruler sustained the Church,[33a] but bishops ruled
their king in spiritual matters: "Bishops," declared the

(a. 866), MGH in usum schol., p. 84: "Karolus Willelmum . . . quasi
contra rem publicam agentem secus Silvanectum civitatem decollari
fecit." See also the parallel but independent administrative structure
sketched by Walafrid Strabo, De Exordiis, c. 32, MGH Cap. II, p. 515.

[32] Cf. the Synod of Soissons, MGH Cap. II, no. 258, pp. 263f, of
Charles the Bald, "ubi posthabitis saecularibus curis ipse quoque rex
adesse dignatus est . . ." and the Synod of Worms (868), Mansi XV,
867, of Louis the German, "jussione . . . Ludovici regis, cujus tanta
erga Deum devotio extat, ut non solum in rebus humanis, verum etiam
in causis divinis maximam semper sollicitudinem gerat."

[33] See the comment of the eleventh-century chronicler Anselm of
Liége on the defense offered by Lothaire II to Nicholas I (MGH SS.
VII, p. 199): "Rex se esse laicum, canones ignorare confitetur, sed super
hoc in omnibus se episcopali paruisse iuditio." Contemporary accounts
place similar weight on episcopal counsel: MGH Epp. VI, no. 53, p. 347,
Liber Pontificalis, Vita Nicolai I, ed. Duchesne, v. II, p. 160. See also
Hincmar of Rheims, De Divortio Lotharii, Responsio I, Migne PL.
125, 640: "laici conjugati laici regis conjugem judicent." Cf. the comment of Louis the German and the Synod of Metz (859), MGH Cap. II,
no. 298 B, p. 446, and the words of the Synod of Meaux-Paris (845/6),
c. 78, ibid., no. 293, p. 419: "Indignum valde est ut qui in regia dignitate
ceteros ecclesiae filios auctore Deo praecellitis neglegentius quae Dei
sunt exsequi videamini." Cf. the early tenth-century letter of John XII
of Ravenna to Berengar (S. Löwenfeld, "Acht Briefe aus der Zeit
König Berengars," Neues Archiv, 9 [1884], p. 530): "Dupliciter enim
deo servire regi iubetur, fideliter serviendo, quia homo est, et leges
iuxta precipientes et contraria proibentes convenienti vigore servando,
quia rex est." The lay character of the king, of course, was central to
this limitation.

[33a] See the Visio Audradi, Bouquet VII, 289, the Synod of Thionville
(844), MGH Cap. II, no. 227 c. I, p. 113, and passim. Cf. the comment
of Charles the Bald to Ado of Vienne (MGH Epp. VI, no. 23, III, p.
177): "Vobis enim et omnibus episcopis suis omnem ecclesiam suam
Christus deus noster commisit. . . ."

Synod of Savonières (859), "govern and correct the kings of kingdoms, the nobles, and the people committed to them in the Lord."[34] By the later years of Louis the Pious, the realms of the "two Empresses" were so definitely divided that Archbishop Angilbert II of Milan refused obeisance to Lothaire I because the King was not "the Lord God."[35]

The character of the institutional division toward which the Frankish clergy was striving received formulaic clarity in the writings of Hincmar of Rheims. No one, he wrote, might be both king and bishop or govern both the temporal commonwealth and the ecclesiastical order.[36] For it was "Christian doctrine" that the offices of the pontiff and the king should be discrete, even though the members of both orders participated in the nature of Christ, the true King and Pontiff.[37] Two elements separated the two offices: first, the power of the bishop to confer sacra-

---

[34] MGH Cap. ii, no. 299, c. 2, p. 447.

[35] Andrew of Bergamo, Chronicon, c. 11, MGH SS. iii, p. 234: The occasion was Lothaire's return to Italy after his defeat in 833/4. "Volebat imperator dicere, quod ille (Angilbert) in ipso consilium fuisset, et venientes nobiles eum in gratia miserunt; sed dum ante imperatore ducerent, ille vero tantum caput inclinivit et verba salutatoria dixit; ad pedes vero noluit venire propter reverentiae honorem ecclesiarum. Tunc imperator dixit: 'Si contenis te, quasi sanctus Ambrosius sis!' Archiepiscopus respondit: 'Nec ego sanctus Ambrosius, nec tu Dominus Deus.'"

[36] Ep. 27, Migne PL. 126, 181. Cf. Ep. 44, *ibid.*, 126, 266, "sin autem cum ille [Lothaire I] inter principes et ego inter episcopos ante Regem regum et Episcopum episcoporum venerimus. . . ."

[37] Ad episcopos, c. 1, Migne PL. 125, 1007. Hincmar is paraphrasing the letter of Gelasius I to the Emperor Anastasius. A. Thiel, *Epistolae Romanorum Pontificum*, pp. 349ff. See also Hincmar's De Officiis Episcoporum, Migne PL. 125, 1087.

ments and, second, the difference between secular law, which the king was to execute, and canon law, which the bishop discharged.[38]

These limitations, which state in legal terms the functional separation of *Ecclesia* and *Respublica*, indicate the primary effect of canon law upon Frankish political thought: the reservation of the clergy as an institution distinct from the political commonwealth, an institution whose supreme authority resided in the priestly community as a whole.

The earliest explicit claim for the removal of the priestly commonwealth from the power of the temporal occurred about the middle of the reign of Louis the Pious. According to his biographer, Wala of Corbie addressed the imperial assembly at Aachen in 828/9, maintaining that episcopal elections and the administration of ecclesiastical property should be removed absolutely from the control of temporal men and administered canonically: "*Habeat igitur rex rempublicam libere in usibus militiae suae ad dispensandum; habeat et Christus res ecclesiarum, quasi alteram rempublicam, omnium indigentium et sibi servientium usibus, suis commissam ministris fidelibus.*"[39] Others, notably Agobard of Lyon, also advocated the division which Wala suggested, and the *respublica altera* was recognized by civil rulers in their laws.[40] Even the char-

[38] *Ibid.* See also De Ordine Palatii, cc. 7, 8, MGH Cap. ii, p. 520, and his Ep. 22, Migne PL. 126, 135: "In quibus nihil de civili judicio, cujus cognitores non debemus esse episcopi, ponere, sed quae ecclesiasticae definitioni noscuntur competere, quantum occurrit memoriae, breviter studui adnotare."

[39] Epitaphium Arsenii, ii, 2, MGH SS ii, p. 548.

[40] E.g., MGH Epp. v, no. 5, c. 19, p. 174; MGH Cap. i, no. 138, c. 2, p. 276. On the historical part of the royal immunity in producing

acteristic royal duties of administering justice and promulgating laws were somewhat restricted by the legal apparatus of the ecclesiastical commonwealth. For example, Haimo of Halberstadt limited the competence of temporal judges in ecclesiastical cases to the rather special instances of the murders of popes, bishops, priests, and deacons.[41] And the rôle of the king in regard to the canons themselves was simply corroborative: he could only confirm the rulings of the canons or, when necessary, supplement them according to the counsel of his clergy.[42]

The case for the institutional integrity of the clergy was most clearly stated by the three major jurists of the period, Benedictus Levita, Hincmar of Rheims, and Pseudo-Isidore. All three maintained that civil authorities were absolutely external to ecclesiastical jurisdiction.[43] In this view, the sacramental functions of the priesthood were fundamental, "for it is not rightful," wrote Benedictus, "that ministrants of the Divine Service be subject to the

---

the dualism under discussion, see F. L. Ganshof, "L'immunité dans la monarchie franque," *Recueil de la société Jean Bodin*, v. I₂ (Brussels, 1958), pp. 171-216, with a summary of relevant secondary literature.

[41] Expositio in Rom. 13:1-4, Migne PL. 117, 481: "Sunt nempe quaedam enormia flagitia, quae potius per mundi judices quam per antistites et rectores ecclesiarum judicantur, sicut cum quis interficit pontificem apostolicum, episcopum sive presbyterum sive diaconum. Huiusmodi reos reges et principes mundi damnant."

[42] Cf. the declaration of Carloman (884), MGH Cap. II, no. 287, p. 371: "illa quae contra malum rapinae et depraedationis a sanctis patribus sunt *promulgata* et a christianissimis regibus auctoritate regia *confirmata*." MGH Epp. VIII, fasc. I, no. 160 b, c. 9, p. 138.

[43] Cf. Conventus in Villa Colonia, MGH Cap. II, no. 254, c. I, p. 255: "eisdem [sacerdotibus] vero regalis potestas et inlustrium virorum strenuitas seu reipublicae administratores, ut suum ministerium competenter exequi valeant, in omnibus rationabiliter et iuste concurrant."

judgment of temporal powers."[44] The power of temporal government, wrote Hincmar, was divided among several kings; but the Church was unified by the exercise of identical priestly functions throughout the earth,[45] functions which both marked the clergy as the spiritual rulers of all believers and reserved them to their own juridical institutions.[46] Similarly, Pseudo-Isidore maintained that, through the unction they received at ordination, priests were set apart from laymen to teach and govern them in spiritual matters[47] and that they were at the same time removed from the censure and judgment of laymen.[48]

The jurists further agreed that, just as laymen were unable to administer sacraments, they were also denied authority over those who exercised sacramental powers. To be sure, Benedictus repeats the words of the Synod of Paris (829) that "the body of the entire Holy Church of God is divided into two chief persons, the priestly and the royal,"[49] but he allows the king only two ecclesiastical functions as a *"potestas extera"*:[50] to bear "the sword of God"[51] against those whom priests expelled from the Christian community and against external enemies of the

[44] II, 390, Migne PL. 97, 796.

[45] E.g., Ad Regem De Coercendo Raptu Viduarum, c. 8, Migne PL. 125, 1023: "unam Christi ecclesiam et unum Christi altare et unum sacrificium quod ubique uni Deo et una religione constituitur et offertur." See also *ibid.*, c. 1, col. 1017.

[46] See below, pp. 68ff.

[47] Ps.-Anacletus, Ep. I, c. 12, Hinschius, *Decretales Pseudo-Isidorianae*, p. 71; Ps.-Urbanus, Ep. I, c. 7, p. 145; Ps.-Telesphorus, Ep. I, c. 3, p. 111, and *passim*.

[48] Ps.-Pontianus, Ep. I, c. 2, p. 147; Ps.-Clement, Ep. III, c. 70, pp. 57f; Ps.-Marcellus, Ep. II, c. 9, pp. 227f; and *passim*.

[49] I, 319, Migne PL. 97, 742.

[50] III, 11, col. 804.

[51] II, 432, col. 802.

Church and to promulgate laws "for the utility of the Church."[52] Moreover, in his ecclesiastical legislation, the king must frame his laws according to the law of God[53] and with the counsel and assent of his clergy.[54] The administration of Church lands, episcopal election, and the trial of clerics, however, were all regulated according to the canons apart from any royal intervention.[55]

In the same tenor, Hincmar commended the Holy Church, the Christian people committed to the King by God, to Louis the Stammerer to be defended, but not to be ruled.[56] Hincmar's concept of the royal ministry was simple: he wished the king to direct himself and the good among his people in the way of righteousness and to chasten the wicked.[57] Under the ultimate guidance of Christ,[58] the king must administer justice according to the law of God,[59] and, when petitioned by his clergy, he must

[52] Praefatio, cols. 699f.   [53] Addit. III, 18, col. 874.

[54] III, 123, cols. 811f; Addit. IV, 32, col. 894; and *passim*.

[55] II, 403, col. 797, rubric, "Quod episcopi inter se corrigere, si quid ortum fuerit, debent"; Addit. IV, 3, cols. 887f; Addit. III, 2, col. 873; III, 468, col. 860; I, 261, col. 831; III, 375, col. 844, and *passim*.

[56] MGH Cap. II, no. 304, p. 461, at the moment the scepter was bestowed. Cf. De Officiis, Migne PL. 125, 1089, "res ecclesiasticae . . . in tuitione atque defensione Christi consistunt, qui eas terrae principibus atque primoribus ad defendendum et conservandum, non affligendum vel usurpandum sive praesumendum commisit."

[57] MGH Epp. VIII, fasc. I, no. 126, p. 65. Cf. Ad regem de coercendo raptu viduarum, c. 18, Migne PL. 125, 1031, "ut quicunque his fructibus tanquam brutae et perniciosae bestiae insidiantur, vestra custodia repellantur, vestra etiam severitate corrigantur."

[58] See his reference to Christ in LV Capitula, c. 11, Migne PL. 126, 325, "coelestem ac terrenum principatum, cunctam videlicet rempublicam regens, et universam militiam, tam coelestem et spiritalem quam terrenam et temporalem, distinctis in ordinibus disponens ac moderans, et supernae atque mundanae curiae praesidens. . . ."

[59] De Ordine palatii, c. 21, MGH Cap. II, p. 524.

strengthen and supplement the canons with his own edicts.[60] In ecclesiastical matters, however, he was always to "honor the bishops as fathers and as vicars of Christ" and to obey their spiritual counsel.[61] His laws did not supersede the canons, and he might not pronounce on matters of doctrine.[62] Moreover, the king had no power whatever over the persons of bishops. In his conflict with Louis III over the election to the see of Beauvais (881/2), Hincmar explicitly wrote that the part of the king in episcopal elections was merely to assent to the results of election by clergy and people.[63] And in an earlier dispute with Charles the Bald, he wrote "bishops ought not to be, and cannot regularly be judged in the consistory of kings or in the pretorium of judges, or in any way except by bishops in synod or in a private place, by the judgment of those deputed by metropolitans (*primates*) or of judges they themselves have chosen."[64]

The part Pseudo-Isidore assigned to temporal rulers in ecclesiastical matters is less well defined. All earthly princes, he wrote, must obey priests, stand ready to serve them, and act as *cooperatores* of the law of God.[65] They might not presume to act against divine commands or the

[60] MGH Epp. VIII, fasc. I, no. 160 b, c. 8, p. 138.

[61] Epistola Synodalis Carisiacensis, c. 7, MGH Cap. II, no. 297, p. 432: "Eorum spiritualia consilia obaudite. . . ."

[62] See Ep. 25, Migne PL. 126, 170, and the related passage in De Divortio, Responsio VI, Migne PL. 125, 671. MGH Epp. VIII, fasc. I, no. 131 b, pp. 70f.

[63] Ep. 19, c. 3, Migne PL. 126, 112. See G. Ehrenforth, "Hinkmar von Rheims und Ludwig III von Westfranken," *ZfKG*, 44 (1925), p. 76.

[64] Pro Ecclesiae Libertatum Defensione, Migne PL. 125, 1064.

[65] Ps.-Clement, Ep. I, c. 39, Hinschius, *Decretales Pseudo-Isidorianae*, p. 43.

apostolic canons;[66] their own laws merely served to corroborate the canons.[67] On three points, however, Pseudo-Isidore was so clear and so firmly resolved as to be repetitious: namely, that bishops should not be under temporal control, that the lands of their churches be free from confiscation by worldly princes,[68] and that their persons be immune from accusation and trial by secular judges.[69]

Unlike papal theorists, therefore, the Frankish clergy denied temporal intervention in clerical affairs without subordinating the royal power to the ecclesiastical authority. Toward secular authorities, the Church maintained a dualistic relationship. The clergy was not an order in temporal society as were the Burgundians, who were privileged to enjoy their own law but were wholly under the temporal authority, or as Jewish merchants, who received immunities from the king. The clergy was rather as a second society, a *respublica altera*, with a peculiar law and a juridical apparatus completely distinct from that of the royal government. Yet, while independent in origin, administration, and purpose, the clergy must submit to the civil authority in civil matters, just as the Christian king must submit to the clergy in spiritual. Institutionally separate, kingship and episcopacy were thus necessarily united in the context of human society; but that union did not impair the legal integrity of either.

[66] Ps.-Calixtus, Ep. I, c. 6, p. 137, Ps.-Marcellinus, Ep. II, c. 4, pp. 222f, and the sources cited.

[67] Ps.-Euticianus, Ep. II, c. 7, p. 211; Ps.-Eusebius, Ep. II, c. 12, pp. 237f; Ps.-Eusebius, Ep. I, c. 2, p. 230, and *passim*.

[68] E.g., Ps.-Pius I, Ep. II, c. 7f, pp. 118f.

[69] Ps.-Cornelius, Ep. II, c. 4, pp. 173f, Ps.-Anacletus, Ep. II, c. 19, p. 76, Ps.-Fabianus, Ep. II, c. 12, p. 161, and *passim*.

Frankish dualism was one of the two answers which ninth-century churchmen gave to the fundamental question: "Where does governmental supremacy reside in this world?" One, rendered by papal theorists, was a theological construction of world order. According to it, the Church embraced human society as a universal mystical union whose head, by virtue of Christ's commission to St. Peter, was the bishop of Rome. The other, advanced by the Frankish clergy, was a sacramental view in which the Church, as the community of all believers, was only one of two principal institutions in human society, an institution whose unity and government derived from the sacramental functions of priests. The other part of society was the temporal commonwealth. Although both papal and Frankish views developed historically from the functional distinction between laymen and priests, the relationships between ecclesiastical and temporal powers and the form of Church administration which these two doctrines ultimately advocated were vastly different.

To be sure, both positions held that kingship and episcopacy were discrete juridical offices over unrelated areas of competence. Both acknowledged that the warrant for separation of those offices and their jurisdictional spheres was the functional difference between the priesthood and the laity. Both accepted the necessary coexistence of the two offices in the framework of human society.

The theological standpoint of the Romanists, however, led them to formulate a monistic government of the world and a monarchical government of the Church. Through the commission and guarantees given by Christ to St. Peter, the Roman Church—and her head, the vicar of St. Peter—became the guardian of the Faith that gave the mystical union of the Church its cohesiveness, the ruler and the supreme judge of the priests who operated in its mysteries, the ultimate monitor of faith for all Christians, the arbiter of all that touched the spiritual life of the Christian community. Finally, according to this position, the powers of temporal government were also directed— and, according to some theorists, bestowed—by the bishop of Rome.

The Franks, on the other hand, came to affirm a dualistic world government and conciliar sovereignty in the Church. This position preserved some of the political concepts prevalent in the time of Charlemagne which made the clergy a distinct social order governed by its own members according to its own law. It agreed, for example, that in temporal affairs the clergy should be regarded as a component of the state, obliged to yield to the royal power in matters of common civil necessity. But it went much further than the earlier position in requiring the obedience of temporal rulers to their bishops in spiritual matters. Kingship and episcopacy were distinct; and each was supreme in the area of its prescribed competence.

The sacramental concepts which effected the division of temporal and spiritual authority had one further significant result, for they placed the ultimate government of the Church in the corps of the episcopacy, and not in the charge of one ruler. All bishops combined in their persons the several clerical orders; all governed the lesser orders according to the same canonical rules; all alike could transmit the gift of the Holy Spirit through unction and the imposition of hands. Because of this view of the episcopacy as a body whose members shared identical sacramental powers and responsibilities, the dualists concluded that true supremacy in the Church resided in the episcopal order as a whole and, by extension, in the synods and councils whose decisions were produced and ratified by the consensus of the priestly order. *Ecclesia* and *Respublica* were distinct institutions; the government of the first rested ultimately in the episcopal, but not in the papal, cathedra, and that of the second, in the royal throne.[70]

[70] All authors agreed that the authority exercised by king, by bishop, or by pope was the authority of his office, not personal authority. The throne was symbolic of the episcopal and of the royal office. See Alcuin, MGH Epp. IV, no. 177, p. 293, "regalis throni potestas"; Walafrid Strabo, Glossa Ordinaria (to Matthew 27:19), Migne PL. 114, 173, "Pro tribunali: Tribunal sedes iudicum ut solium regum, cathedra doctorum"; Nicholas I, MGH Epp. VI, no. 88, p. 469, "de solio imperiali descendentes cathedram praesularem, ut ita fateamur, ascendistis"; Liber Pontificalis, Vita Leonis IV, c. 95, ed. L. Duchesne, v. II (Paris, 1955), 130; Adventius of Metz to Nicholas I, MGH Epp. VI, no. 8, p. 220, "in reverentissima summi principis cathedra verus apostolus residetis" (cf. the manifesto of Gunthar of Cologne and Theutguad of Trier, Annales Bertiniani [a. 868], MGH SS. in usum Schol., p. 68: "Nicolaus, qui dicitur papa et qui se apostolum inter apostolos adnumerat") and the acclamation of Leo IV by his synod in 853, Migne PL. 115, 658: "Justa et vera, catholica et apostolica definivit cathedra." Naturally, the person who sat in the throne was absorbed into its dignity. Cf. the letter of Gregory IV to the Frankish bishops, MGH Epp. V, no. 17, p. 230: "In tantum autem honoranda est cathedra pontificalis, et propter cathedram sedens in illa." See also the letter of Leo IV to Charles the Bald, MGH Epp. V, no. 39, p. 606; the acclamation of Nicholas I in the trial of John of Ravenna, Liber Pontificalis, Vita Nicolai I, c. 35, ed. Duchesne, II, pp. 157f; the letter of Anastasius to Nicholas, MGH Epp. VII, no. 1, p. 397; and the letter of John VIII to Charles the Bald, MGH Epp. VII, no. 9, p. 9. On the distinction between an incumbent and his office, see Hincmar of Rheims's remarks at the Synod of Metz (859), MGH Cap. II, no. 298 B, p. 446 and LV

The contrast between the political monism and hierarchical monarchy of papal writers and the corresponding dualism and conciliarism of the Franks is clearly illustrated by their use of the phrase *"vicarius Dei."* After the term entered papal correspondence toward the middle of the ninth century, the Curia tended to apply it only to the bishop of Rome as expressive of his universal competence. Pope John VIII, for example, claimed that, as vicar of God, he had elected and anointed Charles the Bald as emperor.[71] As vicar of Christ, he asserted his absolute supremacy over the Frankish bishops,[72] and he shared the attitude stated by the forger of the Donation of Constantine, who

---

Capitula, c. 4, Migne PL. 126, 302. Louis the Pious acknowledged that he was by nature equal to other mortals and was exalted only "by the dignity of governance." (Prooemium to the Capitularies of 818/9, MGH Cap. ii, no. 137, p. 274.) Cf. *Jonas d'Orléans et son "De Institutione Regia,"* ed. J. Reviron (Paris, 1930), p. 150: "ut plebem Christi sibi natura equalem recognoscant," and the offer of Lothaire II to defend his case before Nicholas I, "nihil nostrae regiae dignitati faventes, sed, quasi unus ex vilioribus personis, sacerdotalibus monitis parentes." MGH Epp. vi, no. 7, p. 218 (repeated with variants in no. 14, p. 232, and no. 18, p. 240). Charles the Bald confessed that "the person of our governance" might err "through ignorance, youth, or necessity." MGH Cap. ii, no. 254, p. 254. For similar thought see Hincmar of Rheims, lv Capitula, c. 14, Migne PL. 126, 327, a somewhat altered citation of the Moralia in Job, xxi, xv, 22 (Migne PL. 75, 203), and Wulfhad of Bourges's pastoral letter, MGH Epp. vi, no. 27, p. 191.

[71] Bouquet vii, pp. 695f.

[72] MGH Epp. vii, no. 7, p. 322. For earlier instances of the usage of the words *"vicarius Dei"* in papal correspondence, see the letters of Adventius and Anastasius cited above, note 70. Much later, the equation *"vicarius Dei =* episcopus" does occur, though with great rarity, in papal correspondence: *e.g.,* Paschal II, Ep. 501, Migne PL. 163, 426, "Non judicare aut opprimere episcopos, sed tanquam Dei vicarios venerari." See also the work of Maccarrone cited in the next note.

wrote that the pope was the "vicar of the Son of God" from whom all other bishops derived their authority.[73] He was "the vicar of Christ *on earth*."[74]

This position, which knows no limits in the administration either of secular or of spiritual affairs, differed considerably from the pluralistic Carolingian standpoint. For acknowledging that Christ was both King and Priest, the Franks saw no logical difficulty in affirming that the king was the "vicar of God *on earth*" and that bishops were "vicars of God *in the Church*." Indeed, that affirmation was wholly in accord with the conventional Gelasian statement that Christ had divided the government of the world between the royal power and the spiritual authority of bishops, assigning proper functions to each.[75] Neither the

[73] Hinschius, *Decretales Pseudo-Isidorianae*, p. 252: "ut sicut in terris vicarius filii dei esse videtur [papa] constitutus, etiam et pontifices, qui ipsius principis apostolorum gerunt vices principatus, potestatem amplius quam terrenam imperialis nostrae serenitatis mansuetudo habere videtur. . . ." On the dating of the Donation of Constantine, see the study by W. Gericke, "Wann entstand die Konstantinische Schenkung?" *ZfRG*, K. A. 43 (1957), pp. 1-88, who concludes that it was written in four stages between 754 and 796. The proposal of Silva-Tarouca that the Donation was written in the middle of the ninth century is strongly disputed by H. Fuhrmann, "Pseudoisidor und die Abbreviatio Ansegisi et Benedicti Levitae," *ZfKG*, 69 (1958), pp. 309-311. Cf. M. Buchner, "Rom oder Reims die Heimat des Constitutum Constantini?" *Hist. JB.*, 53 (1933), 137-168. The best synthetic study of the vicar-figure in ecclesiastical literature is M. Maccarrone, *Il Papa "Vicarius Christi"* (Rome, 1948).

[74] Supra, pp. 27ff.

[75] See Ep. xii, c. 2, Tractatus I B, c. 5, in Thiel, *Epistolae Romanorum Pontificum*, pp. 351, 562. Professor Ullmann's interpretation of the Gelasian statement as a clear expression of papal monism (*Growth of Papal Government in the Middle Ages* [London, 1955], pp. 19ff) was not foreshadowed by any Frankish author in the ninth century. E.g., on Alcuin, see L. Wallach, *Alcuin and Charlemagne* (Cornell, 1959), pp. 10ff: *Jonas d'Orléans et son "De Institutione Regia,"* ed. J. Reviron

subjects of Charlemagne nor those of his successors, therefore, intended to propound monistic doctrines when they
referred to their rulers as vicars of God; for they recalled
that temporal rulers shared only one species of government
with Christ, the King and Priest, "the Emperor who is
over all emperors."[76] Rather, their tendency was to emphasize the duality of world government. Writing to
Charlemagne before that dualistic thought had been clearly
formulated, Kathvulf declared that his King was the vicar
of God "over all His members." The bishop, he wrote,
took second place to the king, for he was only vicar of
Christ. Although Kathvulf's theology was errant, his
meaning was clear. The duty of the king was to establish
"the law of God over the people of God" together with
his bishops, to take counsel with them, and to honor their
law, the canons. As if to make his intent perfectly explicit,
he further referred to Deuteronomy 17:18f, a Scriptural
passage repeatedly cited in the ninth century: "And it
shall be, when he [the king of Israel] sitteth upon the

c. 1, pp. 134f; Hincmar of Rheims, Synod of Fismes, c. 1, Migne PL.
125, 1071, De officiis episcoporum, *ibid.*, col. 1087, and *passim*; MGH
Cap. 11, no. 196, c. (3) 111, p. 29; no. 297, p. 440 and *passim*.

[76] Paulinus of Aquileia, Liber Exhortationis, c. 8, Migne PL. 99, 205,
and c. 20, col. 212f. Cf. Hincmar of Rheims, De Divortio Lotharii,
Responsio XII, Migne PL. 125, 700: "Et non dicant reges hoc de
episcopis et non est de regibus constitutum, sed attendentes quia si sub
uno rege ac sacerdote Christo, a cujus nominis derivatione christi
Domini appellantur, in populi regimine sublimati et honorati esse
desiderant, cujus honore et amore atque timore, participatione magni
nominis domini et reges vocantur, cum sint homines sicut et ceteri. . . ."
See also Hincmar's letter to Louis the German, MGH Cap. 11, no. 297,
p. 435: "a quo videlicet Rege regum et Domino dominorum nomen
regis et domini mutuatis." Cf. H. Beumann, "Nomen Imperatoris,"
Hist. Zt., 185 (1958), pp. 515ff.

throne of his kingdom, that he shall write him a copy of
this law in a book out of that which is before the priests the
Levites. And it shall be with him and he shall read therein
all the days of his life, that he may learn to fear the Lord
his God, to keep all the words of this law, and these statutes,
to do them."[77] As the vicar of God, the temporal ruler
enjoyed no extraordinary powers over the clergy. Instead,
he was bound to perform the specifically royal functions
of establishing and executing the law, guided by the
counsel of his bishops.

Later writers preserved the same meaning when they
described Charlemagne's successors as God's vicars. When,
for example, Smaragdus of St. Mihiel admonished Louis
the Pious to act as the vicar of Christ in rooting out whatever wickedness he might find in the Church, he also admonished him to perform "the *royal* ministry which you
bear,"[78] to recall that he was a son of the Church,[79] and
to submit to priestly counsel.[80] His powers were not seen
as extending to the sphere of episcopal discipline and
doctrinal pronouncement. When Sedulius Scottus wrote for
the edification of Lothaire II thirty years later, he, too,
attributed only secular offices to his king. To be sure, God
"wished [the king] to be in the governance of His Church
as though His vicar, and granted him power over every
order of the exalted and the subject."[81] But Sedulius also

[77] MGH Epp. iv, no. 7, p. 503: "Post fidem Dei et amorem et timorem,
ut sepius habeas enchyridion, quod est librum manualem, legem Dei
tui scriptum in manibus tuis ut legas illum omnibus diebus vite tue...."

[78] Via Regia, c. 18, Migne PL. 102, 958.

[79] Epistola nuncupatoria, *ibid.*, col. 933.

[80] C. 20, *ibid.*, cols. 959f.

[81] *Sedulii Scotti, Liber de Rectoribus Christianis*, c. 19, ed. S. Hellmann (Munich, 1906), p. 86.

explicitly wrote that all royal power "was divinely constituted for the utility of the commonwealth."[82] In the service
of that utility, the king was charged with guarding the
privileges of the clergy and above all with guaranteeing
the clergy the right to celebrate synods frequently; he
himself was to pronounce on no ecclesiastical matter until
it had been duly considered and decided by his assembled
clergy.[83] Similarly, neither Lupus of Ferrières, who repri-
manded Charles the Bald for his lasciviousness, nor the
Synod of Pîtres twenty years later, which was concerned
to limit the exercise of Charles' power, meant to attribute
any save royal qualities to Charles when they called him
the vicar of God. As the synod states, God, "the King of
kings and Lord of lords, . . . wished him to be and to be
called king and lord, king on earth in His honor and
stead."[84]

This usage is perhaps most clearly defined by the records
of the Synod of Aachen (862). Meeting in the same year
as the Synod of Pîtres, the Lotharingian bishops declared
in words much like those of their West Frankish brethren
that their own King, Lothaire II, was the vicar of God, the
King. The occasion for the synod, however, was Lothaire's
attempt to secure a divorce from his barren wife, contrary to the judgment of Pope Nicholas I; and the lofty
tone of its decree indicates the enhanced authority it
derived from the opposition of the wishes of their King to
the sentence of the Pope. They had met, the bishops wrote,

[82] *Ibid.*, c. 4, p. 30.

[83] *Ibid.*, c. 19, pp. 84f, 86f.

[84] Capitula Pistensia (862), MGH Cap. II, no. 272, p. 305. See above
note 76. See also Lupus of Ferrières to Charles the Bald, MGH Epp. VI,
no. 64, p. 64: "Vicem vos gerere Dei quis ignorat?"

to recall Lothaire to himself, "*ut non immemor vocationis suae, quod nomine censetur opere compleat, ut rex regum Christus, qui sui nominis vicem illi contulit in terris, dispensationis sibi creditae dignam remunerationem reddat in coelis.*" Furthermore, to attain that end, they had received irretractable promises from Lothaire that he would obey their counsels, and that he would be "the true adjutor and tireless succourer of our order and of the entire sacred religion."[85] Lothaire himself had given the warrant for this attitude in his address to the synod: the government of the Faithful, he had said, was entrusted to two orders, the royal and the episcopal, and the temporal must acknowledge the spiritual as the higher in moral affairs.[86] The use of the term "*vicarius Dei,*" therefore indicates a duality of power not present in later papal thought but evident in Frankish writings from the late eighth century on.

In a sense, the common intellectual background both of papal and of Frankish thought was the modified social dualism prevalent in the time of Charlemagne. According to that earlier position, human society was divided into two social orders—clergy and laity—according to the performance of sacred functions by priests and the inability of laymen to perform them. By extension, clergy and laity were distinguished still further as separate juristic orders. But in the course of the ninth century, the political thought and the ecclesiological concepts of Romanists and Franks departed increasingly from that relatively simple division. The theological grounds of papal thought, dominated by

[85] Mansi, xv, cols. 611f, cc. I-III.
[86] *Ibid.*, col. 614.

the doctrine of Petrine primacy, oriented Roman political constructions increasingly toward monism, toward papal headship of every organ of government, temporal and spiritual. On the other hand, the Franks held more closely to the early functional division and elaborated upon it, positing duality of episcopal and royal governments. An examination of the background and nature of the Frankish concepts of political and hierarchical relationships will define more satisfactorily the differences between these two doctrines, one of which maintained that God's vicariate was borne in all matters by one prelate, while the other affirmed that kings and all bishops in discharging their respective offices had equal claim to the title "vicar of God."[87]

Mediaeval thought concerning the relations of the Church to secular government moved simultaneously in two dimensions, the legal and the theological. Always jurisprudential in nature, it varied in formulation as different authors oriented their positions according either to law or to theology. In general, later Carolingian authors considered the problem of Church-State relations in a legal, or corporative, framework which radiated from two juristic

---

[87] On the episcopal usage, see Benedictus Levita, III, 390, Migne PL. 97, 847; Hincmar of Rheims, Ep. 19, c. 10, Migne PL. 126, 117, and Ep. 24, col. 155; Adventius of Metz, Privilegium pro Abbatia Gorziensi, Migne PL. 121, 1149, "Cum enim vices Dei regis aeterni suscipit (episcopus); . . ." The term is applied to bishops frequently by Pseudo-Isidore. See Ps.-Evaristus, Ep. II, c. 4, Hinschius, *Decretales Pseudo-Isidorianae*, p. 90; Ps.-Eusebius, Ep. III, c. 17, p. 239; Ps.-Alexander, c. 12, p. 102. See Jürgen Fischer, *Oriens—Occidens—Europa: Begriff und Gedanke 'Europa' in der Späten Antike und im frühen Mittelalter* (Wiesbaden, 1957), p. 142 n. 18.

premises: that government of human society was not unitary, and that governmental supremacy was of two species, temporal and spiritual. From these principles, the Frankish clergy deduced an institutional dualism in which the *Regnum Ecclesiae*, the kingdom of the Church, coexisted with the secular kingdom in the context of one society, and in which each government preserved its peculiar laws and headship.

This doctrine was the tentative beginning of the later mediaeval doctrine of corporations. Indeed, the principal tenet of Carolingian dualists—that the universal Church existed as a corporation without the concession of the civil State and independently of temporal government although under the protection of the secular arm—was critical to the subsequent development of political thought. Still, the jurisdictional rights which lay debatable between the Church and the State were too numerous and too important for dualism to prevail in actual institutional relationships. As Gierke wrote in another vein: "In century after century, an unchangeable decree of Divine Law seems to have commanded that, corresponding to the doubleness of man's nature and destiny, there must be two separate orders, one of which should fulfill man's temporal and worldly destiny, while the other should make preparation here on earth for the eternal hereafter. And each of these orders necessarily appears as an externally separate realm, dominated by its own particular law, especially represented by a single folk or people and governed by a single government. The conflict between this duality and the requisite unity becomes the starting-point for speculative discussions of the relation between Church and State. The

64

medieval spirit steadily refuses to accept dualism as final. In some higher unity, reconciliation must be found."[88]

We have said that ninth-century Franks did not, on the whole, construe governmental supremacy in terms of unitary government. To do so, they would have been forced to resolve one preliminary question. They would have had to determine initially whether human society was primarily a mystical union, and so to be ruled by the spiritual authority of the Church, or whether it was fundamentally political, or civil, and so to be governed by temporal power. In other words, to define one particular resting-place of governmental supremacy, it would have been necessary first to determine whether the "body politic" was the Church, a purely sacramental institution ruled by the ministrants of the sacraments, or whether it was, more broadly, Christian society, a body whose interests encompassed and extended beyond the spiritual limits of priestly authority. Consequently, it would have been necessary to establish whether the administrative powers of ecclesiastical and of civil government were subject one to the other, and, if so, in what order.

Frankish writers, however, cast this problem differently. On one hand, they acknowledged that the Church was the body of the Faithful, a corporation of clergy and laity held together by the performance of the sacraments. But on the other, they posited, not one government of that body, but two discrete and integral institutions, *Ecclesia* and *Respublica*. [89] They set the clergy apart as a juridical unit with

[88] Adapted from the translation by F. W. Maitland, *Political Theories of the Middle Age* (Cambridge, 1900), pp. 10f.

[89] On the concept of the State and its relation to ecclesiastical func-

its own laws and administrative organs, a state unto itself; and, though subjecting it to the clergy in spiritual matters, they reserved to the laity temporal laws and juristic apparatus. For them, government was of two kinds, spiritual and temporal, and each kind reposed in the governmental institution corresponding to it.

The dualistic position, however, existed under a threefold tension. One source of that tension was the theological monism of ninth-century popes, which postulated unitary government of Christendom centering in the see of St. Peter. Another source was the precedent of royal monism, which had prevailed in theory and in practice during the reign of Charlemagne and which gave the temporal sovereign very considerable powers in ecclesiastical administration. Even after it had been modified by the efforts of ecclesiastical jurists to vindicate the independence of Church government from secular intervention, this monistic doctrine retained sufficient vigor under Charlemagne's successors to endanger the legal apparatus and privileges of the clergy. The third strain upon the dualistic position came from within dualism itself: namely, the division of sovereignty between the kingship and the episcopacy left no

---

tions, see E. Ewig, "Zum christlichen Königsgedanken im Frühmittelalter," *Vorträge und Forschungen*, III (Lindau, 1954), pp. 7-73, H. Helbig, "Fideles Dei et Regis," *Archiv für Kulturgeschichte*, 33 (1951), pp. 287ff, T. Mayer, "Staatsauffassung in der Karolingerzeit," *Hist. Zt.*, 173 (1952), pp. 477ff, and C. E. Odegaard, "The Concept of Royal Power in the Carolingian Oaths," *Speculum*, 29 (1945), pp. 279ff. See also the enlightening comments of H. Löwe, "Von den Grenzen des Kaisergedankens in der Karolingerzeit," *Deutsches Archiv*, 14 (1958), pp. 345-374. The outlines of the problem were suggested by L. Halphen, "L'idée d'état sous les Carolingiens," *Revue historique*, 185 (1939), pp. 59-67.

intermediate office between them which could authoritatively define their respective jurisdictions. There were no grounds for coordinating the two powers, and, in determining the legal competence of royal and episcopal courts, there was no third party and no process by which it could be decided whether a case involving both temporal and spiritual jurisdiction were "civil" or "ecclesiastical." The elegant symmetry which dualism had in theory was confused or lost in practice.

CHAPTER III · JURISTIC
PRINCIPLES OF CAROLINGIAN
ECCLESIOLOGY

1. Conciliarism

A. GENERAL VIEWS

THE first principles of any ecclesiological doctrine are theological, but complex problems of law are implicit in them and explicit in their elaborations. It has been generally agreed that divine sanction alone legitimatizes the exercise of authority in the Church, and yet the relatively few Scriptural passages which bear on this critical point admitted of several quite different interpretations. For mediaeval writers, the words of Christ to St. Peter—"Thou art Peter, and upon this rock I will build my Church; and the gates of hell shall not prevail against it. And I will give unto thee the keys of the kingdom of heaven: and whatsoever thou shalt bind on earth shall be bound in heaven and whatsoever thou shalt loose on earth shall be loosed in heaven." Matthew 16:18, 19—were especially important to any thought concerning the delegation of authority within the Church. There was, however, no consensus on the meaning of this text. By the end of the Middle Ages, two major ecclesiological schools had developed, the conciliarists and the papal monists. The first maintained that Christ had spoken to St. Peter as to the representative of all the Apostles, and thus of all bishops, the successors of the Apostles.

According to this construction, Christ delegated governmental authority equally to the Apostles; this authority was transmitted to their followers in the apostolic succession. Further, although St. Peter and his successors enjoyed a certain ceremonial preeminence, their real powers were the same as those exercised by all other bishops. True doctrinal, legislative, and disciplinary supremacy could be exercised only by the corps of the episcopacy in a General Council. Papal monists, on the other hand, interpreted the verses of St. Matthew to mean that Christ had elected St. Peter to be superior to the other Apostles, granting to him alone and to his successors in the Roman see full power (*plena potestas*) in the Church.

Although these two doctrines were not yet fully elaborated in the ninth century, their outlines were strongly drawn and ready for the development they received in the later Middle Ages. On the whole, papal monism did not have many vigorous advocates among the Franks, although, as we shall see in the instance of Hincmar of Laon, it did win some militant supporters. The predominant tendency in Frankish thought was to vest in the episcopal order as a whole both the supremacy in ecclesiastical jurisdiction and the legislative supremacy that the popes claimed as the privilege of St. Peter. This thought is strong even in authors who might on balance be considered pro-papal, and, in the discussion which follows, we shall indicate its vigor in the minds of some writers of that school.

The sacramental concept of the Church was as basic to thought concerning hierarchical order as it was in the definition of relations with the temporal power. All priests had the power to "make the body of Christ" with their mouths;[1] all fell beneath the rule of the canons. All bishops exercised full sacramental powers, including that to transmit the Holy Spirit; as successors of the Apostles, all joined in their office every lesser priestly function and enjoyed the same powers and dignity. Ultimate authority in the Church, therefore, was seen to rest in the body of the priesthood and in its episcopal rulers: *"Ecclesia in sacerdotibus consistit."*

The government of the priestly state fell to the clerical assemblies from whose active deliberations laymen were excluded,[2] to the parochial assemblies in which matters of the particular diocese were settled, to metropolitan synods where affairs general to one province were determined, and to universal councils which established law for the whole of Christendom.[3] In Frankish thought, the pope was not a sovereign ruler, but rather a premier bishop. Jonas of Orléans, for example, affirmed that the pope was not St. Peter nor an Apostle and that Christ had given the same powers to the other Apostles and their successors,

[1] MGH Formulae, no. 1, p. 550; Charles the Bald to Hadrian II, Ep. 7, Migne PL. 124, 877.

[2] To be sure, laymen might be present, even at the trials of bishops (e.g., at the trial of Hincmar of Laon, Mansi xvi, Acta Synodi, c. 4, col. 662; "adstantibus diaconibus cum laicis fidelibus"), but they did not debate or return sentence. See De ordine palatii, MGH Cap. ii, c. 30, p. 527.

[3] On local synods, see C. de Clerq, "La législation religieuse franque depuis l'avènement de Louis le Pieux jusqu'aux Fausses Décrétales," *Revue de droit canonique*, 6, p. 160; Flodoard, Historia Remensis Ecclesiae, iii, 22, MGH SS. xiii, p. 519; Herardus of Tours, Capitula, Migne PL. 121, 763. On the legislative powers of general councils, see MGH Epp. v, no. 3, c. 12, p. 163, no. 5, cc. 4, 20, pp. 167, 174f.

the bishops, as He gave to St. Peter and his.[4] Frankish
bishops threatened to depose Pope Gregory IV in synod
when they thought his actions contrary to the universal
law of the canons.[5] And even so staunch a Romanist as
Ratramnus of Corbie placed supreme authority in "the
generality of the whole Church."[6]

The outlines of this view of ecclesiastical government, in
which pure authority resided neither in pope nor in king,
may be illustrated best by the works of two major Frankish
jurists, Benedictus Levita and Pseudo-Isidore. Certainly, the
legal writings of these two men vary widely in treatment
and in purpose. Benedictus Levita presents a disordered
compilation of *sententiae*; and Pseudo-Isidore affords a

[4] De Cultu Imaginum, III, Migne PL. 106, 376, 378, 385. De institutione
regia, c. 2, ed. J. Reviron (Paris, 1930), pp. 101ff, 136f. The same
statement occurs in the Relatio (829) of the Frankish bishops to Louis
the Pious, MGH Cap. II, no. 196, c. (21) I, p. 35.

[5] See the letter of Gregory to the Frankish bishops, MGH Epp. v, no.
17, p. 231, and the reference of Hincmar, Ep. 27, Migne PL. 126, 180,
"et quomodo Gregorius subreptus cum Lothario patro suo [Charles]
repugnante in Franciam venit, et pax nostra in Francia ut antea non
fuit, et ipse papa cum tali honore sicut decuerat et sui antecessores
fecerunt, Romam non rediit." See also the Epitaphium Arsenii, II, 16,
MGH SS. II, p. 562, ". . . firmantes (pro dolor!) quod eumdem apostolicum, quia non vocatus venerat, deponere deberent," and the words of
the anonymous biographer of Louis the Pious (MGH SS. II, p. 635, c.
48), ". . . sed si excommunicans adveniret, excommunicatus abiret,
cum aliter se habeat antiquorum auctoritas canonum."

[6] See his Contra Graecorum Opposita, IV, 8, Migne PL. 121, 335:
"Illuc namque ambo principes [Petrus et Paulus] sunt directi, ubi
principatus eminebat mundi: quatenus Romana civitas, sicut imperiali
potentia totum sibi subjecerat orbem, sic religionis culmine, et apostolatus dignitate, totius mundi regnis praesideret." Cf. *ibid.*, IV, 8, cols.
343f, "auctoritatem quam beato Petro tam Christus *quam omnis
ecclesia* totiusque mundi principatus contulit, . . ." and III, 1, col. 272,
"Absit autem ut ista vel dicant vel sentiant, suamque velint tantummodo
vel sententiam, vel consuetudinem totius ecclesiae generalitati praeferre."

71

chronological arrangement of canons and of forged and genuine papal decretals. Further, the goal of Benedictus was to provide a general defense of privilege for the Frankish clergy, and that of Pseudo-Isidore was to compose a book of discipline universally applicable to the priesthood. Still, these papalists agree with the conciliarist, Hincmar of Rheims, upon one fundamental point of ecclesiastical government: that supreme legislative and disciplinary authority in the Church lay in councils. To be sure, the papal claims to primacy were modified rather than rejected. The three jurists attributed to Rome final appellate jurisdiction in episcopal processes and the authority to declare rules of discipline for all priests. At the same time, they limited the papal competence with the principles that the powers of definitive legislation and jurisdiction lay in councils; that the pope was the guardian, not the maker, of the canons, the universal law of the priesthood; and that the successor of St. Peter must frame his own actions with the counsel of other bishops and in accordance with the canons.

Perhaps because his compilation purports to consist of royal, rather than of ecclesiastical, documents the position of Benedictus toward the hierarchical organization is not so fully defined as is that of the other two jurists. Yet, his tendencies are clear: "The Holy Church is in the priests."[7] All bishops and priests are vicars of Christ;[8] to all bishops, through St. Peter, Christ gave the power to bind and to loose, and to all the clergy, represented by the disciples, He granted the gift of the Holy Spirit. "They are the glory of the Church, in whom the Church shines. They are the

[7] II, 99, Migne PL. 97, 761f.
[8] *Ibid.*

mighty columns founded on Christ upon which the whole multitude of believers rests."[9] Among bishops, the bishop of Rome was certainly the greatest; councils might not be held without his summons;[10] he might receive appeals of episcopal trials from synods and decide them definitively;[11] and his decrees were mentioned as inviolable precepts together with the canons. But the authority of Rome was derived from the canons framed by general councils; its exercise was subject to them.[12] And finally, in provincial jurisdiction, the judgments of the bishop of Rome, his interpretations of the canons, were themselves declared through synodal procedure.[13]

Pseudo-Isidore was of a similar opinion: the bishop of Rome was the premier bishop of the Church, the most authoritative interpreter of the canons; but ecclesiastical supremacy resided in the priestly—or, more particularly, in the episcopal—order. The theme of Pseudo-Isidore is well expressed in the Scriptural verse which recurs in his decreta: *"ne transgrediaris terminos antiquos quos posuerunt patres tui."*[14] And his doctrinal position is indicated

[9] I, 315, col. 741. E. Seckel, "Studien zu Benedictus Levita: VI," *Neues Archiv*, 31 (1905), p. 107; MGH Cap. II, no. 196, cc. 21, 22, pp. 35f.

[10] II, 381, col. 793; II, 341, col. 785.

[11] E.g., Addit. IV, 29, 30, col. 893.

[12] E.g., III, 244, col. 828; II, 341, col. 785, "unanimes divinis apostolicis constitutionibus serviatis, ut in nullo patiamini pia canonum decreta violari."

[13] Addit. IV, 24, col. 892. On diocesan and provincial synods, see I, 328, col. 745; II, 325, col. 783; III, 219, col. 825, and *passim*. In the absence of any critique of Benedictus's thought, the major study remains the series of textual analyses by Seckel, "Studien zu Benedictus Levita," *Neues Archiv*, 1900, 1904, 1905, 1909 (2), 1910, 1914, 1915, 1916, continued by J. Juncker in *ZfRG*, K. A., 1934, 1935.

[14] Deuteronomy 27:17. The verse is cited in Ps.-Alexander, Ep. I, c. 1;

by the first three documents in his compilation: a forged enquiry speciously sent to Pope Damasus by Aurelius of Carthage requesting copies of the canons observed by the Roman Church, Damasus's alleged response commending to Aurelius the *"norma sanctorum canonum qui sunt spiritu dei conditi et totius mundi reverentia consecrati,"* and an *ordo* for the celebration of a synod. The canons were the law of the clergy, the *termini* set by the Fathers of the Church; the pope was their guardian, but councils were their authors. To be sure, Pseudo-Isidore was a more convinced advocate of papal prerogatives than Benedictus and Hincmar. He refers to the papal decreta *"in quibus pro culmine sedis apostolice non inpar conciliorum exstat auctoritas"*;[15] he distinguishes Rome as "the head of all churches," and claims for the bishop of Rome universal jurisdiction.[16] These premises had as corollaries that bishops of Rome had always been preserved from error by Divine Grace,[17] that they had ever been diligent guardians

---

Hinschius, *Decretales Pseudo-Isidorianae*, p. 95; Ps.-Victor, Ep. I, c. 6, p. 128; Ps.-Calixtus, Ep. II, c. 13, p. 139; Ps.-Fabius, Ep. II, c. 15, p. 163; Ps.-Eusebius, Ep. II, c. 13, p. 238; Julius, c. 11, p. 466; Siricius, c. 1, p. 524; and John, p. 695.

[15] Praefatio, c. 4, p. 18. Hincmar of Rheims, who, whatever his bias, was an excellent canonist, remarked of this passage, "Differentiam quoque inter epistolas quas collegit et sacros canones ex verbis beati Gelasii, quibus et sua verba interposuit, fecit." LV Capitula, c. 24, Migne PL. 126, 379. For more decided statements on the authority of papal decretals, see also, Ps.-Pius, Ep. I, c. 2, p. 117; Ps.-Victor, c. 6, p. 128; Ps.-Fabianus, Ep. I, c. 1, pp. 156f.

[16] Ps.-Eusebius, Ep. III, c. 15, p. 238, "propter universalem curam quae nobis propter privilegium ejusdem ecclesiae"; Ps.-Anacletus, Ep. III, cc. 29ff, pp. 82f; Ps.-Sixtus, Ep. II, cc. 5, 6, pp. 108f; Ps.-Dionysius, Ep. II, c. 2, pp. 195f, and *passim*.

[17] Ps.-Felix, Ep. II, c. 18, pp. 205f.

of the sanctions of the Fathers,[18] and that they had all been devoted to the ministry of the Divine Word and learned in matters of doctrine and ecclesiastical discipline.[19] Beyond this, Pseudo-Isidore's concept of papal authority also rested on the presupposition that, like all other bishops and archbishops,[20] the bishop of Rome issued his judgments after assiduous study of the canons and with the counsel and corroborative assent of other bishops.[21] Pseudo-Isidore also observed that the weapon of synodal trial and deposition was ready against popes who disdained to rule canonically and with the counsel of their brethren. Despite the honor in which he held Roman authority, the jurist included in his collection the request of Leo I that his actions be judged by a council, and records of synodal processes against Popes Sixtus, Vigilius, and Symmachus.[22]

[18] Ps.-Sixtus II, Ep. II, c. 7, p. 193; Ps.-Eusebius, Ep. III, c. 19, pp. 239f.

[19] Ps.-Clement, Ep. I, c. 19, p. 36. St. Peter is quoted as saying, "Erit autem ei grande solatium, quod post me non imperitus aliquis aut indoctus atque ignorans divini verbi ministerium, aecclesiastici ordinis disciplinam vel doctrinae regulam nesciens ceperit cathedram meam."

[20] Cf. the *salutationes* of the letters of Ps.-Victor, Epp. I, II, cc. I, 7, pp. 127, 129, "Victor Romanae ac universalis ecclaesiae archiepiscopus. . . ." and "Victor Romanae aecclesiae urbis archiepiscopus. . . ."

[21] Ps.-Eleutherius, c. 2, p. 125, "sicut ab apostolis eorumque successoribus multorum consensu episcoporum iam definitum est"; Ps.-Sixtus I, Ep. II, c. 4, p. 108, "a nobis et reliquis episcopis ceterisque sacerdotibus statutum est"; Ps.-Telesphorus, Ep. I, c. I, p. 109, "a nobis et a cunctis episcopis in hanc sanctam et apostolicam sedem congregatis statutum esse"; Ps.-Euticianus, Ep. II, c. 6, p. 211, "cum omnibus episcopis et sanctae Romanae atque universalis ecclesiae *utriusque ordinis* [!] fidelibus statuimus." See also Ps.-Calixtus, Ep. I, c. I, p. 135; Ps.-Felix, Ep. II, c. 8, p. 200; Ps.-Alexander, Ep. I, c. 6, p. 97.

[22] See pp. 603f, 562f, 628f, 675ff. It must be observed, however, that the exact contents of the Isidorian collection, before it was fused with the *Collectio Dionysiana-Hadriana,* or the *Hispana,* are unclear. We await the work of Professor Shafer Williams, which will elucidate this extraordinarily knotty problem.

The burden of governing the Church, therefore, fell not upon the bishop of Rome alone, but more broadly upon the episcopal order of which he was head. "Why is it unworthy to guard the precepts of the Church?" wrote Pseudo-Evaristus. "We all alike think and pronounce the same thing."[23] Pseudo-Anterus even disclaimed the power to set the measure for other bishops.[24] In the same tenor, Pseudo-Eleutherius wrote to the bishops of Gaul: "The universal Church has been committed *to you* by Christ Jesus so that you may labor for all and zealously care for others; but the brother who helps his brother shall be exalted, and the backslider shall be cast out."[25] The bishops are repeatedly described as the columns upon which the weight of the Church rests: "If you, who are the columns of the Church, begin to give way, the Holy Church which is ruled *by you* grows weak and falls."[26] All exercise the

[23] Ep. I, c. 2, p. 88.

[24] C. 6, pp. 154f, "Non est humilitatis meae neque mensure iudicare de ceteris et de ministris ecclesiarum sinistrum quippiam dicere."

[25] C. 6, p. 127.

[26] Ps.-Sixtus II, Ep. II, c. 4, p. 191; "Sic et vos qui columnae ecclesiae estis, si labefactari caeperitis, sancta aecclesia, que per vos regitur, tabescit et labitur." See also the letters of Felix, p. 697; Damasus (c. 8), p. 502; Pelagius II, p. 730; and Felix II (c. 4), p. 480. An important variation appears in the last citation: "Tu es enim, sicut divinum veraciter testatur eloquium, Petrus, et super fundamentum tuum aecclesiae columne, id est episcopi qui aecclaesiam sustinere et propriis humeris portare debent, tibi sunt confirmate tibique claves regni caelorum commisit atque ligare et solvere potestative que in terra et quae in caelis sunt, promulgavit." See also Ps.-Melchiades, Ep. I, c. 2, p. 243, and Ps.-Eusebius, Ep. III, c. 18, p. 239, "Sequentes in omnibusne apostolicam regulam et praedicantes omnia eius constituta ob custodiam episcoporum, qui columnae ecclesiae a deo dicti sunt, et ceterorum verorum sacerdotum firmantes arcana patrum statuta, statuimus iterum cum omnibus qui nobiscum sunt episcopis. . . ."

power of binding and loosing; all are vicars of Christ.[27] Diocesan and provincial administration, the ordination and trial of bishops, and all matters touching the interest of the episcopacy as a whole must be directed by synods or councils. Doctrine must be interpreted *"ex eruditione communi"*;[28] and articles of faith must be established by general councils.[29]

[27] Cf. Ps.-Eusebius, Ep. III, c. 17, p. 239. Ps.-Melchiades, Ep. I, c. 3, p. 243 distinguishes the bishop of Rome from other bishops by his privilege to judge episcopal cases, "et licet cunctorum par electio foret beato tamen Petro concessum est ut aliis praemineret eorumque quae ad quaerelam venirent causas et interrogationes prudenter disponeret."

[28] Ps.-Clement, Ep. v, c. 84, p. 66.

[29] Praefatio Isidori, c. 11, p. 20. Modern scholarship in general has taken two coordinate viewpoints toward Pseudo-Isidore: that he exalted the spiritual over the temporal power and that he championed the cause of papal monarchy. Dr. Ullmann's recent study is perhaps the most concise statement of this attitude, *The Growth of Papal Government* (pp. 180ff). See also E. H. Davenport, *The False Decretals* (London, 1916); C. H. Föste, *Die Reception Pseudo-Isidors unter Nikolaus I. und Hadrian II.*, Leipzig Diss. (1881); P. Funk, "Pseudo-Isidor gegen Heinrichs III. Kirchenhoheit," *Hist. JB*, 56 (1936), pp. 305ff; and G. Hartmann, *Der Primat des römischen Bischofs bei Pseudo-Isidor* (Stuttgart, 1930). Most notably, that position is registered by P. Fournier and G. Le Bras, in their *Histoire des collections canoniques en Occident*, I (Paris, 1931), pp. 145ff. See also M. Buchner, "Pseudoisidor und die Hofkapelle Karls des Kahlen," *Hist. JB*, 57 (1937), pp. 180-208. Two factors tend to modify the accepted position on Pseudo-Isidore's thought. The Pseudoisidorian compilation was intended as a book of discipline for clerical orders and does not touch at all upon the broader relationships of Church and State. Indeed, laymen appear in it rarely—civil officials far more rarely—and then only in the sacramental context of the Church, in which they would naturally be seen as spiritual subjects of the priesthood. The second is the importance Pseudo-Isidore gives conciliar government, which we have suggested in the text. For an excellent exposition of the Isidorian problem and a complete review of the relevant scholarly literature to 1905, see the article "Pseudoisidor" by E. Seckel in A. Hauck-J. J. Herzog, *Realencyklopädie für protestantische Theologie und Kirche*, 16 (Leipzig, 1905), pp. 265-307.

Thus, even Pseudo-Isidore, pro-papal jurist as he was, advocated a form of papal monarchy modified by conciliarist doctrine, a form which his contemporaries actually implemented in the numerous synods of the later ninth century.[30] One particular bishop, the Franks maintained, did not combine in his person the powers of all twelve Apostles; but all bishops were alike successors of the Apostles.[31] One bishop was not the sole *vicarius Dei* from whom all other bishops derived their powers; but rather all bishops received their powers directly from God, all were *vicarii Dei in Ecclesia.* The Church was governed by the episcopal corps; and any member of that order, even the most exalted, was subject to its universal laws and judgment.

B. HINCMAR OF RHEIMS

The fullest development of conciliarist thought appears in the writings of Hincmar of Rheims, an enthusiastic enemy of papal monism. When he became Archbishop of Rheims, in 845, Hincmar was about forty years old; he died in 882 still exercising the powers of his intellect and

[30] *Supra*, n. 3. See also, among numerous relevant legal citations MGH Cap. i, no. 178, pp. 366f; MGH Cap. ii, no. 189, p. 11; no. 293, c. 32, p. 406; no. 297, c. 7, p. 432. The compilation of A. Werminghoff indicates distinctly the Frankish tendency toward synodal government of the Church. "Verzeichnis der Akten fränkischer Synoden von 742-843," *Neues Archiv* 24 (1899), pp. 457-502, and for the years 843-918, *Neues Archiv* 26 (1901), pp. 607-678.

[31] E.g., Pseudo-Isidore; Ps.-Anacletus, Ep. iii, c. 28; Hinschius, *Decretales Pseudo-Isidorianae*, p. 82, "Episcopi vero domini apostolorum, presbiteri quoque septuaginta discipulorum locum tenent." See also the Epistola Synodus Carisiacensis, MGH Cap. ii, no. 297, c. 15, p. 441: ". . . sicut dictum est ab domino ecclesiae per prophetam: 'Pro patribus tuis nati sunt tibi filii,' id est pro apostolis creavit tibi episcopos qui te regant et doceant."

those of his office as vigorously as he had in the intricate political and doctrinal disputes of his first decade as metropolitan. Leaders in the second generation of the Carolingian Renaissance, such as Abbot Hilduin of St. Denis, disciplined Hincmar's native abilities, and the works which he later wrote in law and theology are among the greatest cultural achievements of his age.

In Hincmar's thought, there was no place for the papal monarchy, even though he acknowledged that the dignity of the Roman See was greater than that of any other. The Archbishop accepted Rome as "the oracle of divine law."[1] Through his words to St. Peter, Christ had estab-

[1] Ep. 11, Migne PL. 126, 81. The biography by Schrörs and the study by Lesne (see Bibliography) remain the most authoritative works on the the general activity of Hincmar. Two other general works, J. C. Prichard, *The Life and Times of Hincmar, Archbishop of Rheims* (Oxford, 1849), and G. C. Lee, "Hincmar: An Introduction to the Study of the Revolution in the Organization of the Church in the Ninth Century," *Papers of the American Society of Church History*, 8 (1897), pp. 231-260, have been superseded by more thorough and comprehensive studies. As for the writings of Hincmar himself, letters not published by Perels in the Monumenta edition or in the edition by Migne appear in C. Lambot, "L'Homélie du Pseudo-Jérôme sur l'assomption et l'évangile de la Nativité de Marie d'après une lettre inédite d'Hincmar," *Revue Bénédictine*, 46 (1934), pp. 265-282; A. Wilmart, "Distiques d'Hincmar sur l'Eucharistie, Un sermon oublié de S. Augustin sur le même sujet," *Revue Bénédictine*, 40 (1929), pp. 87-98; A. Wilmart, "Lettres de l'époque carolingienne," *Revue Bénédictine*, 34 (1922), pp. 234-245. On his use of sources, see F. Baix, "Les sources liturgiques de la *Vita Rimigii* de Hincmar," Miscellanea historica in honorem Alberti de Meyer, I (Louvain, 1946), pp. 211-227; O. Holder-Egger, "Zum Texte von Hincmars Schrift de villa Novilliaco," *Neues Archiv*, 23 (1898), pp. 196-198; V. Krause, "Hincmar von Reims der Verfasser der sogenannten Collectio de raptoribus im Capitular von Quierzy, 857," *ibid.*, 18 (1893), pp. 303-308; B. Krusch, "Reimser Remigius-Fälschungen," *ibid.*, 20 (1895), pp. 509-568; E. Perels, "Eine Denkschrift Hinkmars von Reims im Prozess Rothads von Soissons," *ibid.*, 44 (1922), pp. 43-100; E. Perels, "Hinkmar von Reims und die Bonifatiusbriefe," *ibid.*, 48

lished the Roman Church as "the first see, the mother and mistress of all churches throughout the world[2] and had imposed upon St. Peter and his successors the burdens of all.[3] Rome was to be consulted in all matters of dogma;[4] she might review the decisions of provincial and general councils[5] and impose forms of general observance upon all

---

(1930), pp. 156-160. F. X. Arnold, *Das Diözesanrecht nach den Schriften Hinkmars von Reims* (Vienna, 1935), and H. G. J. Beck, "Canonical Election to Suffragan Bishoprics According to Hincmar of Rheims," *Catholic Historical Review*, 43 (1957), pp. 137-159, discuss Hincmar's concept of ecclesiastical government, but the documentation in both works is slender. Several studies have been devoted to particular aspects of Hincmar's legal thought, without attempting a synthetic view. See M. Conrat (Cohn), "Über eine Quelle der römischrechtlichen Texte bei Hinkmar v. Rheims," *Neues Archiv*, 24 (1899), pp. 349-357; A. M. Gietl, "Hincmars collectio de ecclesiis et capellis," *Hist. JB.* 15 (1894), pp. 556-573; K. Hampe, "Zum Streite Hincmars von Reims mit seinen Vorgänger Ebo und dessen Anhängern," *Neues Archiv*, 23 (1898), pp. 180-195; M. Sdralek, *Hinkmars von Rheims kanonistisches Gutachten über die Ehescheidung des Königs Lothar II* (Freiburg i. B., 1881); S. Stein, "Lex Salica," *Speculum*, 22 (1947), pp. 113-134, 395-418, answered by J. M. Wallace-Hadrill, "Archbishop Hincmar and the Authorship of Lex Salica," *Tijdschrift voor Rechtsgeschiedenis*, 21 (1953), pp. 1-29, now reprinted in Wallace-Hadrill's, *The Long-Haired Kings*, New York and London, 1963; K. Weinzierl, "Erzbischof Hinkmar von Reims als Verfechter des geltenden Rechts," *Episcopus, Festschrift Kardinal von Faulhaber* (Regensburg, 1949); J. Weizäcker, "Hincmar und Pseudo-Isidor," *Zeitschrift für die historische Theologie*, 28 (1858), pp. 327ff. On the later effect of Hincmar's thought, see F. Thaner, "Hinkmar von Rheims und Bernald," *Neues Archiv*, 30 (1905), pp. 694-701, and A. Werminghoff, "Pseudo-Hinkmar," *Neues Archiv*, 30 (1905), pp. 471-472.

[2] LV Capitula, c. 45, Migne PL. 126, 456.

[3] *Ibid.*, c. 5, cols. 305f.

[4] De Divortio, Praefatio, Migne PL. 125, 623, "De omnibus dubiis vel obscuris quae ad rectae fidei tenorem vel pietatis dogmata pertinent, sancta Romana ecclesia, ut omnium ecclesiarum mater et magistra, nutrix ac doctrix, est consulenda."

[5] *Ibid.*, Responsio II, cols. 747f. Cf. MGH Epp. VIII, fasc. I, no. 160 a, c. 23, p. 132, "Sed ideo beatus Petrus, qui Christum vera fide confessus,

priests;[6] only the Apostolic See might summon general councils.[7]

Despite these powers, the bishop of Rome was still considered subject to the canons which the *assensus ecclesiae* had established as law.[8] The Church was governed "by many princes and many prelates of churches,"[9] not by one particular bishop. For all bishops held the same order,[10] all were vicars of Christ and successors of the Apostles.[11] All alike had received the power to bind and to loose.[12] The *privilegium Petri* did not confer the power of infallibility upon the successor of St. Peter; his pronouncements were binding and he himself was safe from synodal dep-

---

vero est amore secutus, specialiter claves regni caelorum et principatum iudiciariae potestatis accepit. . . ."

[6] MGH Epp. VIII, fasc. I, no. 108 b, p. 54. Cf. Ep. 52, Migne PL. 126, 271, "oportet nos hoc sequi quod ecclesia Romana custodit a qua principium sacrae institutionis nos accepisse dubium non est." See also Hincmar's response at the Synod of Troyes (878), Actio 2, Mansi XVII A, 346, and his ordination profession, MGH Epp. VIII, fasc. I, no. I, p. I.

[7] LV Capitula, c. 20, Migne PL. 126, 359.

[8] See below, pp. 91ff.

[9] De Divortio, Responsio I, Migne PL. 125, 746.

[10] Pro Ecclesiae Libertatum Defensione (hereafter cited as Pro Lib.) *ibid.*, col. 1059, "zelo universalis ecclesiae, quae domus Dei est, et sacri ordinis sacerdotalis, quod unum in omnibus episcopis est. . . ." Cf. Ad Episcopos Admonitio, c. 4, *ibid.*, col. 1009.

[11] De Divortio, Responsio 5, *ibid.*, col. 653, "Sed ideo has leges et illi Christi vicarii apostolorumque successores constituerunt et nos qualescunque ad vices illorum Dei presidentes ecclesiae. . . ."

[12] Ep. 8, Migne PL. 124, 894; Ep. 27, Migne PL. 126, 180f, 183; LV Capitula, c. 20, *ibid.*, col. 362, "Quae solvendi ac ligandi potestas, quamvis soli Petro data videatur a Domino, absque ulla tamen dubietate noscendum est quia et ceteris apostolis datur, ipso teste qui post passionis resurrectionisque suae triumphum apparens eis insufflavit, et dixit omnibus, 'Accipite Spiritum sanctum. . . .' Nec non etiam nunc in episcopis ac presbyteris omni ecclesiae officium idem committitur."

osition only so long as his judgments were in accord with the "laws established by the assent of the whole Church."[13] The pope did not promulgate laws, but merely commentaries on laws which were addressed to particular circumstances and whose applicability lapsed when those circumstances had passed.[14] Finally, Hincmar agreed that the pope might review synodal condemnations of bishops;[15] but that review could take place only after the accused had been tried canonically before a provincial synod, and it could proceed only in the metropolitan synod of the pope himself or in a synod presided over by his legates.[16] To all levels of episcopal administration, therefore, Hincmar applied the general rubric that "neither an archbishop without his suffragan bishop, nor suffragan bishops without the consent or order of their archbishops, should presume anything except what pertains to their own dioceses."[17] Pope, bishop, and priest were all subject to the *assensus ecclesiae* as ex-

---

[13] Ep. 8, Migne PL. 124, 883, 894ff. Cf. the decrees of the Synod of Fismes, c. 5, Migne PL. 125, 1076, "Anacletus papa . . . cum totius mundi sacerdotibus judicavit. . . ." See also, LV Capitula, cc. 43, 45, Ep. 30, c. 8, Migne PL. 126, 444f, 456, 193.

[14] LV Capitula, cc. 10, 25, Migne PL. 126, 318ff, 385f.

[15] MGH Epp. VIII, fasc. I, no. 160 b, c. I, p. 136.

[16] *Ibid.*, no. 160 a, c. 3, p. 123.

[17] See the letter of the Synod of Quierzy, MGH Cap. II, no. 297, c. I, p. 428, "sicut nec archiepiscopi sine coepiscopis, ita nec coepiscopi sine archiepiscoporum consensu vel jussu, nisi quae ad proprias pertinent parochias, debent praesumere. . . ." Cf. also LV Capitula, c. 15, Migne PL. 126, 333; Ep. 32, c. 8, *ibid.*, col. 234; and W. Gundlach ed., "Hincmars von Reims De ecclesiis et capellis," ZfKG, 10 (1889), p. 99. On local administration, see his letter to Nicholas I, Ep. 2, Migne PL. 126, 32, in regard to Rothad of Soissons: "Sed et alia, quae sui decessores ac praedecessores, caeterique fideles pro remedio animae suae eidem ecclesiae obtulerunt, ab eo sine consensu metropolitani ac coepiscoporum et sine oeconomi ac presbyterorum et diaconorum suae ecclesiae consensu pro libitu suo donata."

pressed in the canons and in synodal and conciliar decrees.

Although Hincmar of Rheims accepted the doctrine of Petrine primacy to some extent, the juristic structure of his conciliarism ran directly counter to papal monarchism. Fortunately for purposes of historical analysis, the Archbishop's doctrine conflicted with the papal within one closed context, the trial of Bishop Hincmar of Laon, so sharply as to provide a paradigm of conciliarist thought. Under accusation by his uncle and Metropolitan, Hincmar of Laon defended himself by claiming that the Church was a monarchical institution in which the pope held the right of original jurisdiction over all episcopal cases and exercised in his decretals the power of legislation. This attitude directly opposed two ecclesiological principles of the Archbishop: that the jurisdiction of the pope in processes against bishops was appellate and could be implemented only after trial and condemnation by a provincial synod, and that the power of ecclesiastical legislation resided only in the episcopal order as a whole.

The process against Bishop Hincmar of Laon casts the juristic aspects of Carolingian ecclesiology into high relief; for it was a dispute between a conciliarist and a papal monarchist, and it centered upon one point, the constitutive element of ecclesiastical law. Since the appeal of his case directly to Rome, bypassing his uncle's provincial synod, rested upon genuine and false decretals, the younger Hincmar was concerned to maintain that popes held legislative power in their own right; the Archbishop, whose counter-argument rested chiefly on canons—though he also employed papal decretals extensively—maintained that legislative power in the Church resided in councils. In order to understand clearly the importance of this distinction in ecclesiological terms, we must first review briefly Hincmar of Rheims's concepts of the Church and of the *lex ecclesiastica*.

When he wrote that "the Church is nothing else but the body of the faithful (*populus fidelis*), but the clergy is particularly known by this name,"[18] Pope John VIII stated an ecclesiological principle which occurs repeatedly in Hincmar's writings. In his early theological works and again late in his career during the process against his nephew, he wrote, "just as your mouth and your hand are members of one and the same body, so are priests and people members of one and the same Church."[19] Furthermore, he observed, "There is one kingdom, one dove of Christ—the Holy Church—abiding by the law of one Christendom, one kingdom and one Church, although the reins of government be managed by many princes of kingly power, and many prelates of churches."[20]

This general concept of the Church as the "Christian people," which Hincmar committed to the chastening power of kings in regal coronations,[21] was often superseded by a second and more hierocratic interpretation. For example, in the letter of the bishops of his province and that of Rouen to Louis the German (858), he repeated the conventional premise that God "disposed His kingdom,

[18] MGH Epp. vii, no. 5, p. 332.

[19] De Praedestinatione Diss. Post., Epilogue, c. i, Migne PL. 125, 420. lv Capitula, c. 48, Migne PL. 126, 478.

[20] De Divortio, Responsio i, Migne PL. 125, 746.

[21] Ordo Coronationis Hludowici Balbi, MGH Cap. ii, no. 304, p. 461. Cf. Ordo Coronationis Caroli ii, *ibid.*, no. 302, p. 457, "super populum suum constituere regem."

that is His Church, to be governed jointly by the pontifical authority and the royal power," but he continued to affirm that the Church had been committed to the bishops alone "to gain, augment, and govern," and that God had instituted bishops as the successors of the Apostles "to rule and to teach" kings.[22] During the process against his nephew, together with the broader interpretation, there appears this image of the "*templum sanctum in Domino*" as the episcopal hierarchy,[23] of the *Ecclesia* as the episcopacy[24] and as the *fraterna unanimitas* of the episcopal order.[25] The second construction was of fundamental importance to Hincmar's legal thought, for in his mind, the Church was a spiritual community comprising the priesthood and, only by extension, lay believers, a community whose law received its force and validity from the assent of the episcopal order as a whole.

For Hincmar, there were five means by which just and beneficial law[26] might be established in the Church: it

[22] Epistola Synodalis Carisiacensis (858), c. 15, MGH Cap. II, no. 297, pp. 440f.

[23] Lv Capitula, c. 35, Migne PL. 126, 420.

[24] Pro Lib., Migne PL. 125, 1053: "ne diutius haec irreverentia erga Dei ecclesiam maneat, et quantocius scandalum in episcopos excitatum competenti satisfactione sedetur."

[25] Lv Capitula, c. 48, Migne PL. 126, 482, interpolation in a citation from St. Augustine's Liber de Baptismo II, 12, "videlicet ad unanimitatem fraternam." Cf. Acta Synodi Duziacensis, c. 4, Mansi XVI, 666, "et fraternitatis nostrae unanimitate."

[26] In view of the punitive character which Hincmar attributed to law (De presbyteris criminosis, c. 24, Migne PL. 125, 1106; De Divortio, Responsio V, *ibid.*, 652; "De Ecclesiis et Capellis," ed. Gundlach, pp. 132f.), one must observe that he seems to have disregarded the possibility that some laws might be bad in themselves. To be sure, he was aware of the possibility; yet he referred to it specifically only once, in a brief quotation of St. Augustine's cryptic words to the effect that

might be written by the hand of God, set down by divine inspiration, "ordained through angels in the hand of His Mediator," established by common observance,[27] or decreed by an ecclesiastic.[28] These means correspond to the Decalogue (and, broadly, the Scriptures),[29] written ecclesiastical and secular law in general, and canons in particular,[30] cus-

---

one must persevere in the face of bad laws. (See the Concilium Valentinum III, c. 11, Mansi xv, 9, and Hincmar's Ad Episcopos Admonitio Altera, c. 16, Migne PL. 125, 1016.) Otherwise, with the exception of some hints that bad law could be corrected only by good, he was content to maintain that juridical decisions contrary to law were invalid. On the correction of bad law, see Pro Lib., Migne PL. 125, 1065; Ep. 15, Migne PL. 126, 95. Cf. Ep. 8, ibid., 66; "In domni apostolici epistolis continetur ut quae statuta sunt non ducat dissolvenda nisi sacris legibus inveniantur adversa. . . ." On the dissolution of illegal juridical decisions, see Pro Lib., Migne PL. 125, 1055; Ep. 8 (in the name of Charles the Bald to Hadrian II), Migne PL. 124, 894; De Presbyteris criminosis, c. 22, Migne PL. 125, 1104.

[27] "Quam non paganus indixit, non Christianus induxit."

[28] Ep. 8, Charles the Bald to Hadrian II, Migne PL. 124, 889.

[29] De Divortio, Responsio xii, Migne PL. 125, 700.

[30] Divine inspiration, according to Hincmar, motivated the promulgation both of canons and of secular edicts. For the canons, infra pp. 90ff. For the temporal laws, see De Divortio, Responsio v, Migne PL. 125, 653, "Christus, quoque, Dei virtus et Dei sapientia per se ipsam dicat: 'Ego sapientia habito in consilio et eruditis intersum cogitationibus; per me reges regnant et conditores legum justa decernunt; per me principes imperant et potentes decernunt justitiam.'" Similar citations of Proverbs 8:15 are frequent: e.g., Pro Lib., Migne PL. 125, 1052. Cf. the letter of Pope John VIII to Louis the German, MGH Epp. vii, no. 15, 281: "Sed et venerande Romane leges divinitus per ora piorum principum promulgate rerum eius prescriptionem nonnisi post centum annos admittunt." The reference to "angels in the hands of His Mediator" is cloudy, but probably refers to the promulgation of canons or to the general approval of the lex ecclesiastica by the priesthood. See lv Capitula, c. 25, Migne PL. 126, 385: "Et illas epistolas sanctorum et apostolicorum virorum diversis temporibus pro diversorum consolatione, sicut et beatus Gelasius dicit, a sede apostolica datas, et per eosdem Domini sacerdotes qui et angeli secundum Scripturam

tom (*consuetudo*), and papal decretals. In addition, Hincmar acknowledged an ill-defined *lex naturalis*.[31] With the exception of the canons, the promulgated forms of law were designed to accommodate the requirements of a specific age; and, while laws once issued remained laws forever, their legal relevance disappeared with the requirements they were designed to meet.[32] The legal character of the Scriptures and the *lex naturalis* need not detain us, since the Archbishop seldom employed Biblical literature except as a source for literary flourishes, and the *lex naturalis* appears rarely and in the most obscure of contexts.

---

appellantur ordinatas, cum beato Gelasio apostolico viro venerabiliter suscipiendas dico." The references are to Malachi 2:7, and Gelasius, Ep. xlii, 3, iii, De libris recipiendis, Thiel, *Epistolae Romanorum Pontificum*, pp. 457f.

[31] Cf. MGH Cap., ii, no. 297, Epistola Synodalis Carisiacensis, c. 2, p. 428. lv Cap., c. 20, Migne PL. 126, 354f, where "lex naturae" refers to the period before there were written laws.

[32] De Divortio, Responsio xii, Migne PL. 125, 699f. He also maintained, however, that secular laws and the decretals of popes were issued according to specific necessities and lost their effective vigor with the passing of those necessities. (See lv Capitula, c. 20, Migne PL. 126, col. 355. A specific example is cited *ibid*., c. 43, col. 446.) Therefore, Hincmar conceived of law, not as a corpus established for eternity in the remote past, but as one continually developing according to the requirements of a given age. New events could be met only with new establishments which were not contrary to "evangelical truth" or opposed "to the decrees of the Saints." (*Ibid*., c. 34, col. 419. Cf. Leo I, Ep. 16f; Jaffé 544 [320]; Migne PL. 54, 1202.) Cf. his references to the possibility that "new canons" might be established and to enactments by Popes Eugenius II and Leo IV and by Louis the Pious and Lothaire I as additions to the laws (Ep. 31, Migne PL. 126, 226), and his use of the Synod of Lestimes under St. Boniface, Ep. 22, Migne PL. 126, 142. See also De Divortio, Responsio v, Migne PL. 125, 652; "De Ecclesiis et Capellis," ed. Gundlach, pp. 107ff; Ep. 32, c. 23, Migne PL. 126, 241. His position on the correction of bad law would indicate such a concept of development. See also above, n. 26.

Of the remaining forms of law, *consuetudo* holds an anomalous position. Though Hincmar was referring specifically to royal laws, he could have applied the same statement to the *lex ecclesiastica* when he wrote, "The founders of laws have established and still establish laws not by the bare word, but in writing [*non nudo verbo sed scripto*], and they have confirmed and still confirm them by their subscription."[33] Typically, he adopted a written (Roman) law as his guide for the application of *consuetudo*, affirming that "that custom which does not impede the public good is to be kept in the place of law." At the same time, he questioned seriously the reliability of legal findings made according to it.[34] (The "ancient and customary laws" of kings and emperors to which he once referred were the written laws of the Roman emperors and the Frankish rulers.)[35] In pontifical and imperial administrative matters, however, he gave *consuetudo* an important, if generally prescribed, place. He considered respect for *consuetudo* useful particularly in managing

[33] Ep. 15, Migne PL. 126, 98.

[34] De Divortio, Responsio IX, Migne PL. 125, 679. Cod. Th. V, 20, 1 int. (Br. Th. V, 12, 1 int.) This passage is not cited in the valuable work by W. Boudriot, *Die altgermanische Religion in der amtlichen kirchlichen Literatur des Abendlandes vom 5. bis 11. Jhdt.*, Bonn, 1928, or by P. Krüger (T. Mommsen) ed., *Codex Theodosianus*, v. I (Berlin, 1905), p. ccxl, and M. Conrat (Cohn), *Geschichte der Quellen und Literatur des römischen Rechts im früheren Mittelalter*, 1 (Leipzig, 1891), p. 23f. n. 7. The same view is represented in Italo-Frankish law. See MGH Cap. 1, no. 95, c. 10, p. 201: "Placuit nobis inserere, ubi lex est, praecellat consuetudinem; et nulla consuetudo superponatur legi." *Ibid.*, no. 105, c. 22, p. 220: "Ut longa consuetudo, quae ad utilitatem publicam non impedit, pro lege servetur, et quae diu servatae sunt permaneant."

[35] Concilium Duziacense II, c. 5, Mansi XVII A, 292.

church property and in observing due privileges.[36] Even in these instances, however, Hincmar never distinguished the unwritten *consuetudo* clearly from that of formal constitutions. For example, he recalled that the *consuetudo* among the heathen which gave Alexandria status as a premier city (primatial in Christian times) "was afterwards confirmed by apostolic constitution";[37] and again, he referred to the "*lex antiquae consuetudinis* . . . found many times over in the sacred canons" by which the election of a metropolitan might be performed without consulting another metropolitan.[38] Therefore, he largely excluded the law of common observance, unconfirmed by canonical authority, from ecclesiastical practice. In temporal courts, the *consuetudo gentium* might be admitted only if the written secular laws were found insufficient. Even then, if the sanctions of custom were too cruel or did not conform to the principles of equity established by sacred authority, Hincmar required that custom be rejected, and that the case be taken to the presence of the king "so that together with those who know both laws [i.e., secular and ecclesiastical] and fear the establishments of God more than those of human laws, he may judge, he may decide, so as to preserve both when he can, but to preserve the justice of God when the earthly law

[36] See Hincmar of Rheims to Hincmar of Laon, Migne PL. 126, 542, 545. Pro Lib., Migne PL. 125, 1055.

[37] LV Capitula, c. 15, Migne PL. 126, 332, an interpolation into canon 6 Nicea I.

[38] LV Capitula, c. 15, and c. 26, cols. 331, 392. Cf. Hincmar of Rheims to Hadrian II, Migne PL. 126, 641f, and LV Capitula, c. 25, col. 385, "consuetudo quam catholica ecclesia habuit."

is rightly to be held in check."[39] In all instances, therefore, *consuetudo* must have the corroboration of "sacred authority" as expressed in the *lex scripta* before it could obtain the full force of law.

Consequently, the canons, decretals, and secular law composed the main body of the *lex ecclesiastica*. Of these, the canons held first importance, and the legal character of the other elements of the law must be seen with regard to them.

Above all, the canons were the distinctive law of the priesthood. As the Archbishop wrote, "The canons and the *regulae patrum* belong to priests in the same way as the law of Moses was also called the law of the Jews. . . . And, therefore, whoever is not a priest has no relationship to the canons."[40] Concerning the institution of canons, he affirmed, with a similar reference to the Mosaic code, "All establishments made by the priests of the Lord are eternal; for, like Moses, they receive their establishments from the divine oracle."[41] Indeed, no patristic tag was so ready to Hincmar's pen as the affirmation by Leo I that the canons were "established by the Holy Spirit and consecrated by the reverence of the whole world";[42] the power of the divine was always present in the canons, inspired

[39] De ordine palatii, c. 21, MGH Cap., II, pp. 524f. Cf. MGH Epp. VII, no. 52, c. 1, p. 304, "antiqua consuetudo legibus adiuvata. . . ." Kaufmann discounts this famous passage as evidence of the concept of equity. E. Kaufmann, *Aequitas Iudicium: Königsgericht und Billigkeit in der Rechtsordnung des frühen Mittelalters* (Frankfurt a. M., 1959), pp. 124f.

[40] LV Capitula, c. 32. Migne PL. 126, 414. Cf. Schrörs, *Hinkmar, Erzbischof von Reims* (Freiburg i. B., 1884), p. 401.

[41] Charles the Bald to Hadrian II, Ep. 8, Migne PL. 124, 892f.

[42] Leo I, Ep. 14 to Anastasius (Jaffé 411 [189]), c. 2. Migne PL. 54, 672.

by the Holy Spirit, the instruments of Christ,[43] "laws established for eternity."[44] In view of Hincmar's hierocratic construction of the Church as the priesthood, it is particularly important to observe that the actual constitutive element by which the priesthood, albeit divinely inspired, gave legal force to their canons was the "*assensus universalis ecclesiae*,"[45] the approbation of "all bishops throughout the whole world."[46] It was this constitutive element, this *assensus*, which preserved the unity of the *Ecclesia*, and which bound its members "in one dogma and one charity."[47] Between the canons of the Oecumenical Councils and those of other orthodox synods, Hincmar made no distinction in practice; he received the African canons with the same reverence as the Ephesene.[48] Alike, they derived "from the divine oracle"; alike, they were approved by the *assensus ecclesiae* and established as the unique and uniform law of the priesthood.

Against the measure of the canons the validity of papal enactments must be gauged. As we have observed in another context, the Archbishop disputed that papal

[43] Ep. 30, c. 22. Migne PL. 126, 202.

[44] See LV Capitula, c. 25, Migne PL. 126, 385f.

[45] *Ibid.*, c. 47, 465. Cf. Hincmar of Rheims to Hincmar of Laon, Migne PL. 126, 510, "ab ipsa prima sede atque ab omni ecclesia catholica comprobatos." Cf. Concilium Duziacense, Responsa episcoporum, Conclusio, Mansi XVI, 657, "Etsi imperatores Romanorum suas leges aeternas vel perpetuas appellaverunt, multo magis leges illae aeternae atque perpetuae sunt quae sunt sancto Spiritu promulgata."

[46] LV Capitula, c. 43, Migne PL. 126, 444.

[47] De Praedestinatione Diss. Post., Epilogus, c. 1, Migne PL. 125, 418f; LV Capitula, c. 48, Migne PL. 126, 477.

[48] *Ibid.*, c. 20, Migne PL. 126, 360f. Hincmar explicitly denied the possibility of conflict among the canons. De praedestinatione, Diss. Post., c. 37, Migne PL. 125, 413.

freedom to judge and approve the canons[49] which the younger Hincmar affirmed in exalting the papal decrees themselves to the status of canons.[50] For the Archbishop, the consent of the Apostolic See could never be given validly to any establishment contrary to the canons of Nicea;[51] indeed, the vigor of papal enactments derived from the fact that they were promulgated "*ex sacris canonibus.*"[52] So firm was he in this position, that he was charged before Pope John VIII at the Synod of Troyes (878) with "being unwilling to receive the authority of the decrees of the pontiffs of the Roman See." According to the historian Flodoard, he answered this charge with the equivocable promise "to receive and carefully to follow (as far as they are to be followed) the decretals of the Roman pontiffs received and approved by holy councils."[53] The very words of Hincmar's promise to obey any decree of the Roman Church, issued "according to the measure of the Holy Scriptures and the decrees of the holy canons,"[54] contain the same qualifications.

The popes, according to the Archbishop, did not promulgate laws; for, once subscribed and promulgated, laws remained binding forever,[55] and papal decretals were

[49] LV Capitula, c. 43, Migne PL. 126, 445ff. and in the argument to the same chapter, col. 285. See also n. 32 above, LV Capitula, c. 23, col. 368f, and c. 34, col. 420. Cf. Schrörs, *Hinkmar*, p. 405. The canons, Hincmar maintained, had their "proprium robur," apart from papal sanction. LV Capitula, c. 10, Migne PL. 126, 322.

[50] Ep. 1, Migne PL. 124, 984.

[51] Ep. 30, c. 8, Migne PL. 126, 193.

[52] This statement occurs with the greatest frequency in Hincmar's writings.

[53] Historia Remensis Ecclesiae III, 21, MGH SS. XIII, p. 515.

[54] Actio 2, Mansi XVII A, 346.

[55] De Divortio, Responsio XII, Migne PL. 125, 699f.

issued, not as abiding regulations, but as counsel for temporary conditions. Once the immediate circumstances which evoked a given decretal were past, the edict lost its legal relevance. Therefore, some of the decretals were incorporated into the canons, and so preserved their binding power;[56] others were altered for application to new circumstances; the rest slipped into desuetude.[57] Rather than promulgating laws, the papacy held the privilege of promulgating edicts about laws.[58] The basis of this right was, in the words of Leo I, the "*aequitas Petri*,"[59] which Christ,

[56] LV Capitula, argumentum to c. 21 in Hincmar's original redaction, Migne PL. 126, 283: "Qua ratione quaedam ex his quae in epistolis antiquorum apostolicae sedis pontificum scripta inveniuntur, a successoribus eorum usa non fuerint, et quaedam in decretis eorum posita et a conciliis inter canones sacros inveniuntur assumpta."

[57] LV Capitula, c. 20, Migne PL. 126, 355.

[58] *Ibid.*, c. 10, cols. 318ff. "Unde primum nobis sciendum est aliud esse promulgare sacros ordines et canonum disciplinas, aliud promulgare de sacris ordinibus et canonum disciplinis, sicut aliud est promulgare leges, et aliud promulgare de legibus. Promulgare autem leges, est leges condere; promulgare vero de legibus est de illis judicia sumere, et secundum illas judicare, earumque observationem et judicia omnibus intimare. . . . Qui scilicet episcopi et presbyteri in primordio nascentis ecclesiae et usque non ad parvum temporis progressum, uno nomine in singulis officiis vocabantur sicut in epistola Petri et in epistolis Joannis et in epistolis Pauli manifestatur. . . . Sed et reliqui per eos qui a Domino ad hoc constituti sunt ecclesiastici ordines promulgantur, eorum scilicet ministerio, Domino quod suum est exsequente. De sacris autem ordinibus promulgare est qui et quot sint et quales ac qualiter et a quibus vel quando sunt ordinandi, et quomodo ac quantum in singulis gradibus debeant ministrare, qualiter etiam ab ostiario usque ad summum sacerdotium quique valeant provehi. Et quae sint ex eis a sedis Romanae pontificibus promulgata, omnibus in ecclesiasticis dogmatibus exercitatis constat esse notissimum. . . ."

[59] Leo I, Sermo IV (III), Migne PL. 54, 151, J-L. 524, cited in Charles the Bald to Hadrian II, Ep. 8, Migne PL. 124, 893, and again, Ep. 32, c. 27, Migne PL. 126, 243. See F. Pringsheim, "Römische *aequitas* der christlichen Kaiser," *Acta Congressus Iuridici Internationalis*, v. I

in theory, bestowed upon St. Peter together with the power of binding and loosing. The power of binding and loosing, however, was given to all the Apostles, whom Peter represented, and consequently to all their successors, the bishops; and the privilege of judging definitively on the authority of the *aequitas Petri* remained with the successor of Peter only when his judgments proceeded from the *aequitas Petri*. That is, submitting to the precepts of the canons, the Apostolic See must issue its judgments in accordance with "what the assent of the universal Church has approved."[60] Judgments not so issued were to be regarded as invalidated by the *aequitas* itself, and as without effect.[61] Even when issued in perfect accord with the canons, however, papal decretals remained of value (*"maneant inconvulsa"*)[62] only as *promulgationes de legibus*, not as *promulgationes legum*.

Elements of secular law were received as part of the *lex ecclesiastica* through the force of the *assensus ecclesiae*.

(Rome, 1935), pp. 119-152, especially pp. 121f, 137f. Kirn limited his remarks to defining the words "aequitatis iudicium" in Hincmar's writings as "ein gerechtes Urteil," without attempting to determine the importance of the *aequitas Petri* in Hincmar's concept of canon law. P. Kirn, "Aequitatis Judicium von Leo dem Grossen bis auf Hinkmar von Reims," *ZfRG*, G. A. 52 (1932), pp. 53-64, esp. pp. 62ff.

[60] Cf. Gelasius I, Ep. 26, c. 3, Thiel, *Epistolae Romanorum Pontificum*, p. 395. Cited in Charles the Bald to Hadrian II, Ep. 8, Migne PL. 124, 893, and Hincmar, Ep. 32, c. 21, Migne PL. 126, 240. A devoted student of the works of Gregory I, Hincmar may have been influenced by the statement of that Pope (Reg. I, 5, MGH Epp., Regestrum Gregorii, 1, p. 36), "Cunctas vero quas praefata veneranda concilia personas respuunt, respuo, quas venerantur, amplector, *quia dum universali sunt consensu constituta*, se et non illa destruit, quisquis praesumit aut solvere, quos religant, aut ligare, quos solvunt."

[61] Migne PL. 124, 893f.

[62] *Ibid.*, col. 893.

Though all Christians were to be judged at the end of the world "not by Roman, or Salian, or Burgundian laws, but by divine and apostolic,"[63] the Church did not reject the laws of man as long as they were *christianae*.[64] Further, under the general rubric that "in a Christian kingdom, even the public [i.e., civil] laws must be Christian, in conformity and harmony with Christianity,"[65] Hincmar maintained that the *regulae sacrae* did not exclude from ecclesiastical judgments "the laws promulgated by emperors and kings for the Church and ecclesiastics and about the Church and ecclesiastics. . . . Rather, they order that, where they accord with the religious life of the Church, they are to be consulted jointly [with the canons] in trials, and that judgments are to be issued according to them."[66] Furthermore, he observed that temporal rulers frequently promulgated laws at the request of the Church and for its benefit.[67] In the reception itself, both the *aequitas Petri* and the *assensus ecclesiae* were instrumental: popes had judged Roman law "canonical" and had set it beside the canons as "laws by which the Church is governed and Christendom is ruled":[68] and the *regulae*, as expressions of

[63] De Divortio, Responsio V, Migne PL. 125, 658.

[64] *Ibid.*, Responsio XII, col. 695. Hincmar's meaning may be suggested by Cod. Th. XVI, 2, 16, which he cited in Pro Lib., Migne PL. 125, 1038: "In qualibet civitate, in quolibet oppido, vico, castello, municipio quicumque votum Christianae legis meritum eximiae singularisque virtutis omnibus intimaverit, securitate perpetua potiatur. Gaudere enim et gloriari ex fide semper volumus, scientes magis religionibus quam officiis et labore corporis vel sudore nostram rem publicam contineri."

[65] De Divortio, Responsio v, Migne PL. 125, 658.

[66] Concilium Duziacense I, Acta Synodi, c. 7, Mansi xvi, 668. Cf. LV Capitula, c. 27, Migne PL. 126, 395, "leges concordantes regulis."

[67] De Divortio, Responsio v, Migne PL. 125, 652f.

[68] *Ibid.*, Epistola Dedicatoria, MGH Epp. viii, fasc. i, no. 131 b, pp.

the *assensus ecclesiae*, approved the *leges imperatoriae*,[69] and themselves incorporated portions of imperial edicts.[70] Should this *assensus* be denied an imperial edict dealing with ecclesiastical matters, the edict itself must be considered void.[71]

Although Roman law appears to have been favored far more by the Church than other temporal laws—notably, the Frankish[72]—it is important to observe that even those titles of Roman law which did not "accord with the

---

70f; Hincmar of Rheims to Hincmar of Laon, Migne PL. 126, 559, "contra leges quas catholica et apostolica ecclesia ex antiquo servandas suscepit." Cf. the letter of Benedict III (Jaffé 2663, Migne PL. 129, 1001ff), where the same corroborative powers over secular laws is claimed specifically for the papacy. The remark of Professor Gaudemet, though referring to the early Christian Empire, is applicable here: "*Leges* et *canones* sont deux sources indépendantes, mais paralléles, et tendant aux mêmes fins," Compte rendu of B. Biondi, *Il diritto romano cristiano* (Milan, 1952-54), in the *Revue internationale des droits d'l'antiquité*, III, 1, 2 (1954/5), p. 417. See also F. G. Lardone, "Il diritto romano e i concilii," *Acta Congressus Iuridici Internationalis*, v. II (Rome, 1935), pp. 101-122, especially pp. 104, 120. On the general ignorance of Roman law in ninth-century Frankish Gaul, see C. G. Mor, "La Recezione del diritto romano nell collezioni canoniche de secoli IX-XI in Italia e oltr'Alpe," *ibid.*, v. II, pp. 296f, and J. Imbert, "Le droit romain dans les textes juridiques carolingiens," *Studi in onore di Pietro De Francisci*, vol. III (Milan, 1956), pp. 61-67. On the general problem, see H. E. Feine, "Vom Fortleben des römischen Rechts in der Kirche," *ZfRG*, K. A. 42 (1956), pp. 1-24.

[69] LV Capitula, c. 6, Migne PL. 126, 313. Cf. also the words "leges quas probat (*or* recipit) ecclesia," which occur with many of Hincmar's citations of Roman law: e.g., Pro Lib., Migne PL. 125, 1045, 1062f, LV Capitula, c. 30, Migne PL. 126, 411.

[70] LV Capitula, c. 43, col. 446.   [71] Ep. 15, Migne PL. 126, 96.

[72] In giving preference to Roman law, Hincmar was entirely in accord with the legal consensus of his time. See the Lex Ripuaria, c. LVIII, 1, MGH Legum v, p. 242, "Lex Romana quam ecclesia vivit," and MGH Cap. I, no. 168, c. I, p. 335. "Ut omnis ordo ecclesiarum secundum Romanam legem vivat." Cf. Benedictus Levita, Addit. IV, 160; Migne PL. 97, 909, "lex Romana, quae est omnium humanarum mater legum"; and MGH Cap. I, no. 179, c. 5, p. 369. See Appendix A.

religious life of the Church" were excluded from the *lex ecclesiastica*.[73]

An example of this exclusion occurred during the process against Hincmar of Laon. Before he was put in custody, the Bishop together with his clergy had signed an affirmation which declared that a *delator* should be punished either by the excision of his tongue or by decapitation.[74] Although this statement does not appear in Roman law in the precise wording rendered by the younger Hincmar, and although it does so appear in the collection of Benedictus Levita and (as Hincmar of Rheims knew)[75] in the *Collectio Angilramni*,[76] two sources with which the Bishop was quite familiar,[77] the Archbishop attributed it to the tenth book of the Theodosian Code (i.e., the *Lex Visigothorum*).[78] On this attribution, he denied that his nephew

[73] Frankish law was also subject to the same rubric. See De Divortio, Responsio VI, Migne PL. 125, 671, and the related letter to Hildegarius of Meaux, Ep. 25, Migne PL. 126, 170. At issue is the trial by ordeal. See also the Concilium Valentinum III, c. 11, Mansi, XV, 9: "Quia impia et Deo inimica et Christianae religioni nimis contraria, ex iniquissima ac detestabili constitutione quarumdam saecularium legum consuetudo. . . ."

[74] Schedula adversus Hincmarum, c. 25, Migne PL. 126, 607.

[75] LV Capitula, c. 24, Migne PL. 126, 377f.

[76] Benedictus Levita III, 360, Migne PL. 97, 843. See Seckel, "Studien zu Benedictus Levita: VIII," *Neues Archiv*, 40 (1915), p. 120; Hadrian I to Angilramnus (Jaffé 2447), c. 49, Migne PL. 96, 1061, and Hinschius, *Decretales Pseudo-Isidorianae*, c. 44, p. 765.

[77] On Hincmar's knowledge of Benedictus Levita, see below p. 103. On the Capitula Angilramni, see his Collectio II, Migne PL. 124, 1014, 1020, both citations of Capitula Angilramni, c. 11, printed in Hinschius, *Decretales Pseudo-Isidorianae*, p. 761. This citation also occurs in Benedictus Levita, Addit. IV, c. 17 (Migne PL. 97, 891). See W. Meyer, "Über Hincmars von Laon Auslese aus Pseudo-Isidor, Ingilram und aus Schreiben des Pabstes Nicolaus I," *Nachrichten von der kgl. Gesellschaft d. Wiss. zu Göttingen*, phil.-hist. Kl. (1912), pp. 223f.

[78] Schedula, c. 23, Migne PL. 126, 604.

could rightly use it as a juristic maxim, "since it is not suitable in ecclesiastical judgments of ecclesiastical ministers."[79] In subscribing to the sentence, his nephew had far exceeded the bounds of the episcopal office. The "avenging sword" was granted to the "judicial [i.e., secular] power" and not to ecclesiastical ministers; the office of the bishop was to forgive the penitent criminal, not to sentence him to death, and St. Ambrose had even written that if a priest spilt blood, he would lose his office before Christ and the Church. Consequently, according to "sacred authority," the law was suitable for the temporal power, but it was not "approved by the Church."[80]

For all the major components of the *lex ecclesiastica*, therefore, the *assensus ecclesiae* was the legally constitutive element; even those prescriptions of custom and of the papal decretals which had the full character of law received their force from being inscribed among the canons. Consequently, it was this same element of *assensus* which made of the priesthood "one kingdom and one Church, abiding by the law of one Christendom." It was the *assensus* which reserved "the bishop with his Church" to judgment according to the *lex ecclesiastica*, just as "men of all nations—even the Jews, the enemies of Christian law —are judged by the judgment of their own laws,"[81] and which guaranteed the liberties of the Church by making clergy a race apart and their law a law discrete from all others.

[79] *Ibid.*, c. 25, col. 607.
[80] *Ibid.*, c. 11, col. 578.
[81] Pro Lib., Migne PL. 125, 1055. Cf. MGH Cap. 1, no. 131, c. 6, p. 259, "Si Iudaeus aliquod maleficium contra christianam legem aut Christianum aliquem fecerit. . . ."

2. A Victory of Conciliarism: The Conflict of Hincmar of Rheims and Hincmar of Laon

Conciliarism was the predominant ecclesiological doctrine among the Frankish clergy, perhaps because great churchmen such as Hincmar of Rheims consciously fostered it in opposition to papal monism. Evidence of this counterdoctrine appears in nearly every extant pronouncement of the great ninth-century popes. It was the warrant used by John VIII and his predecessors in their consistent and vigorous efforts to vindicate Roman headship of the Church against arguments that supreme ecclesiastical powers were shared by all bishops, or by all metropolitans, and that these powers could rightly be exercised only by the whole body of the episcopacy. Consequently Frankish bishops and lower clergy who thought themselves ill-used and their privileges infringed by their immediate superiors—bishops or metropolitans—embraced the theological and juridical aspects of papal monism, defying diocesan or provincial jurisdiction and appealing their cases directly to the See of St. Peter.

The rivalry of these doctrines, and the temporary vindication of conciliarism in the Frankish context, is most clear in the trial of Hincmar of Laon. In order to sketch the lines of battle in this conflict, we shall have to review first the papal doctrines which Hincmar of Laon adopted.

+

Based on Christ's words to St. Peter (Matt. 16:17-19), the monarchical construction of the Church was common coin among papal theorists long before the ninth century. At the beginning of the period under review, Pope Hadrian I was repeating already well-worn concepts when he wrote that because of these words, St. Peter and his vicars, the Roman bishops, had acceded to the *principatus* of the entire Church, and the Roman Church had consequently become "the head of the whole world."[1] Rome became the guardian of the faith and the supreme ministrant of law not only in cases involving the episcopacy but also in all religious matters.[2]

Under Pope Nicholas I, these assertions of universal and plenary power within the ecclesiastical hierarchy received full expression, for the Photian dispute in the East and the trials of Rothad of Soissons and Hincmar of Laon in the West gave Nicholas ample opportunities to declare his hierocratic views with his characteristic union of the high-sounding phrase and the appropriate juristic principle. To his associate and biographer, Anastasius, Nicholas was the "rector and prince of the whole Church."[3] Nicholas's

[1] MGH Epp. v, no. 1, p. 3; no. 2, p. 6. See Appendix C.

[2] Gregory IV, MGH Epp. v, no. 14, p. 79: "Nulli dubium sit quod non solum pontificalis causatio, sed omnis sanctae religionis relatio ad sedem apostolicam quasi ad capud ecclesiarum debet referri et inde normam sumere unde sumpsit exordium. . . ." Cf. *ibid.*, no. 14, pp. 73f. See also the ninth-century work wrongly called Homelia Leonis IV, Migne PL. 115, 675: "Nos quidem quamvis indigni, locum Aaron tenemus; vos autem Eleazari et Ithamar. Nos vice duodecim apostolorum fungimur; vos ad formam septuaginta discipulorum estis. Nos vero pastores vestri sumus; vos autem pastores animarum vobis commissarum." (See P. W. Finsterwalder, "Das sogennannte Homelia Leonis IV. und ihre Bedeutung für Hinkmars Capitula und Reginos Inquisitio," ZfRG, K.A. 27 [1938], pp. 639-664.) To be sure, popes continued to address other bishops as "*fratres*," but the equality implicit in that term did not represent a uniform attitude. Cf. Gregory IV to the Frankish bishops, MGH Epp. v, no. 17, p. 228: "Romano pontifici scribentes contrariis eum in prefacione nominibus appellastis, fratrem videlicet et papam, dum congruencius esset solam ei paternam reverenciam exhibere."

[3] Liber Pontificalis, Vita Nicolai, c. 41, ed Duchesne, v. ii, p. 159.

own language is no less exalted. As the Bishop of the
Roman See, to whom the care of the Lord's whole flock
in every part of the world was committed,[4] he declared
that in the Church he was established prince over all the
earth.[5] His authority transcended the boundaries of the
two empires;[6] it reached to the very ends of the earth,[7]
and comprehended territorial as well as spiritual dominion.[8] By virtue of the commission to St. Peter, he maintained that he could judge of all members of the priestly
order, establish laws within the Church, and issue general
decrees and judgments.[9] Rome was the ultimate repository
of ecclesiastical discipline and law,[10] the source of episcopal
power,[11] the arbiter of synods and councils.[12] But Nicho-

---

Cf. MGH Epp. vi, no. 82, p. 433, "Principatum divinae potestatis, quem
omnium conditor electis suis apostolis largitus est, super solidam
fidem apostolorum principis, Petri videlicet, soliditatem constituens.
. . ."

[4] MGH Epp. vi, no. 5, p. 271. Cf. *ibid.*, no. 88, p. 477.

[5] *Ibid.*, nos. 29, 71, 88, pp. 296, 392, 475.

[6] Cf. the report of Anastasius on the fourth Council of Constantinople
(869), Mansi xvi, 9: "quod ad utriusque imperii unitatem, immo totius
Christi ecclesiae libertatem pertinere procul dubio credebatur precipue
summi pontificii vestri querebatur assensus." The letter was sent to
Hadrian II. Cf. Anastasius, Praefatio Historiae Ecclesiasticae, Migne
PG. 108, 1187f, and the letter Anastasius wrote to Basil I in the name
of Louis II, MGH Epp. vii, p. 387: "Unum est enim imperium Patris
et Filii et Spiritus Sancti, cuius pars est ecclesia constituta in terris,
quam tamen Deus nec per te solum nec per me tantum gubernari dis-
posuit. . . ."

[7] Migne PL. 119, 890, "a finibus terrae, ut ita dicam. . . ." Nicholas
refers to Gaul.

[8] See Anastasius's letter to Hadrian II, Mansi xvi, 10, and the Liber
Pontificalis, Vita Adriani II, c. 53, ed. Duchesne, v. ii, p. 183.

[9] Cf. MGH Epp. vi, no. 18, c. 2, p. 285; no. 29, p. 296; no. 31, p. 300.
[10] *Ibid.*, no. 88, pp. 480f.
[11] *Ibid.*, no. 18, c. 3, p. 285; no. 99, c. 73, p. 593.
[12] *Ibid.*, no. 29, p. 296.

las's contribution to the theory of ecclesiastical administration was more than a sharpening of familiar claims; he implemented them so vigorously that two bishops whom he had condemned declared, "He is making himself emperor of all the world."[13]

Hincmar of Laon invoked the juristic aspects of this doctrine in his defense. His argument rested chiefly upon the principle that papal decretals were laws in themselves, whether or not they were confirmed by councils. Indeed, he would have accepted unreservedly the statement made by his champion, Pope Hadrian II, in 869: "Those who do not shrink from disparaging St. Peter and his successors or from invidiously spurning the *decreta* they have issued through the Holy Spirit are undoubted blasphemers against the Holy Spirit."[14] Unfortunately, the extant writings of the younger Hincmar are insufficient for a comprehensive analysis of his legal thought. Like his uncle, he construed the *Ecclesia* as the body governed by the *lex ecclesiastica*, the priesthood, or, more particularly,

[13] Praefatio ad episcopos regni Lotharii, Migne PL. 121, 379. Cf. Liber Pontificalis, Vita Nicolai I, c. 41, ed. Duchesne, v. II, p. 159; Regino of Prüm, Chronicon (a. 868), MGH SS. I, p. 579. Cf. Haimo of Halberstadt, Expositio in II. Cor. 1:23, Migne PL. 117, 611: " 'Non quasi dominamur fidei vestrae,' sicut imperatores quia unius fidei jam sumus vos et nos. . . ."

[14] F. Maassen, "Eine Rede des Papstes Hadrian II vom Jahre 869," *SB. der Ak. der Wiss. zu Wien*, phil.-hist. Kl., 72 (1872), p. 541: "Hi nimirum dum beato Petro eiusque successoribus derogare atque ipsorum decreta sancto spiritu edita invidiose contemnere non metuunt, proculdubio in spiritum sanctum blasphemare videntur." Cf. the very suggestive article by T. Klauser, "Die liturgischen Austauschbeziehungen zwischen der römischen und fränkisch-deutschen Kirche vom achten bis zum elften Jahrhundert," *Hist. JB*, 53 (1933), pp. 169-189.

the episcopal hierarchy—a kingdom united in one heart and one spirit.[15] Again, like his uncle, he construed the *lex ecclesiastica* as consisting of several elements, though he nowhere said precisely what those elements were. His demonstrable unfamiliarity with Roman law eliminates that source from consideration,[16] and, while he cited Frankish law authoritatively, he consulted it, as did the Archbishop, on administrative matters peculiar to the Frankish Church and not on matters of general ecclesiastical discipline.[17] One may therefore conclude that secular laws were of only tangential importance in his legal system.[18] Further, though he did not discount the legal relevance of the Scriptures, he did not consult or refer to them

[15] Ep. 8, Migne PL. 124, 1067. Cf. *ibid.*, cols. 1052f.

[16] For example, he grossly misattributed Cod. Th. xvi, 2, 31, xvi, 2, 34, which his uncle rightly attributed in Pro Lib. (to which the Bishop was referring), to the collection of Benedictus Levita (Benedictus Levita, ii, 116, 389; Migne PL. 97, 763, 795). On this text, see Seckel, "Benedictus Levita Studien: vii," *Neues Archiv*, 34 (1909), p. 363.

[17] His citations of Frankish law appear to have been taken uniformly from Benedictus Levita. See Ep. 3, Migne PL. 124, 998, "ut sine auctoritate ... expellantur," = Benedictus Levita, i, 87 (Migne PL. 97, 713), *Ansegisus* i, 84 (*MGH* Cap. i, pp. 406f); *ibid.*, "De his qui ... sustineant," = Benedictus Levita, i, 98; cols. 713f, "De ordinatione servorum ... forma servanda est" = *ibid.*, 210 (cols. 726f), Ansegisus i, 88 (p. 406), with variations. In the printed version of Hincmar's letter, the words "laici de familia . . . et de his quos" are omitted toward the end of the citation between the words "agendum est quos" and "praepositi canonicorum." In letter 8 (col. 1036): "Quaecunque a singulis . . . arbitrio saeculari" = Benedictus Levita ii, 111 (col. 763), with variants; "Synodali decreto ... anathemate feriatur" = *ibid*. iii, 207 (col. 824); "De viris Deo ... attributa facultas" = *ibid.*, 199 (col. 823); "Si quis ... ultiones mereri" = *ibid.*, ii, 115, and ii, 406 (cols. 763, 798), with variants.

[18] On the other hand, he is said to have used "legales sententias catholicorum imperatorum" in one of his compilations, no longer extant. Hincmar of Rheims, lv Capitula, c. 30, Migne PL. 126, 411.

as a legal source; and the *lex naturalis* does not appear at all in his writings. If his limited literary remains are not deceptive, the other legal sources mentioned by the Archbishop—the canons, *consuetudo*, and papal decrees—were accepted also by his nephew, but with distinct changes. The Bishop confused the finely drawn distinctions of *assensus ecclesiae* and *aequitas Petri*; he judged that the canons owed their binding force to papal approval;[19] he gave papal decretals the name of "canons";[20] and finally, he exalted *consuetudo*, the *consuetudo* transmitted to Rome by the Fathers and preserved and interpreted without deviaton or error by the popes, as the element of unity in the *regnum ecclesiae*.[21] *Auctoritas Petri* assumed the character both of the *assensus* and of the *aequitas*, and the legally constitutive oligarchy in the theories of Hincmar of Rheims found a counterpart in the legally constitutive monarchy of his nephew.[22]

[19] Enlighteningly enough, Hincmar of Rheims quoted as his nephew's own words an excerpt from a letter of Nicholas I to Photius which the bishop included in his Collectio II: "Decretalia quae a sanctis pontificibus primae sedis Romanae ecclesiae sunt instituta cujus auctoritate atque sanctione omnes synodi et sancta concilia roborantur et stabilitatem sumunt, cur vos non habere vel observari [Nicholas, "observare"] dicitis nisi quia vestrae ordinationi contradicunt." LV Capitula, c. 24, Migne PL. 126, 382; Hincmar of Laon, Collectio II, Migne PL. 124, 1022; Nicholas I, MGH Epp. VI, no. 86, p. 450.

[20] See Hincmar of Laon, Ep. I, Migne PL. 124, 984; LV Capitula, c. 43, Migne PL. 126, 444, 446, 448.

[21] Ep. 8, Migne PL. 124, 1067.

[22] One cannot determine whether Hincmar of Laon held to these theories throughout his episcopal career or whether he formed them rather late in it, when Pope Hadrian showed him the way by taking parts of the Pseudo-Isidorian decretals into the papal arsenal. (In his address cited above [n. I], Hadrian quoted numerous Pseudo-Isidorian letters also used by Hincmar in his *Collectiones*: Ps.-Alexander,

In the eyes of his uncle, Hincmar of Laon disengaged himself from the Church, construed as the episcopacy, one body, one kingdom, under the one law of the canons. Within this theoretical context, the Archbishop saw the

---

Ep. 1 [Hadrian, c. 4, p. 545; Hincmar, c. 7, Migne PL. 124, 1001], Ps.-Sixtus II, Ep. 11 [Hadrian, c. 5, p. 547; Hincmar, c. 5, cols. 1003f], Ps.-Anacletus [Hadrian, c. 4, p. 547; Hincmar, cc. 2, 3, 4, col. 1005], Ps.-Zephyrinus [Hadrian, Ep. 1, c. 2, p. 547; Hincmar, Ep. 11, cc. 11, 12, col. 1007], Ps.-Calixtus [Hadrian, Ep. 1, cc. 5, 6, p. 547; Hincmar, Ep. 11, c. 13, cols. 984f, 1005], Ps.-Eusebius, Ep. 11 [Hadrian, cc. 12, 13, 14, p. 553; Hincmar, cc. 11, 12, 13, 14, cols. 1006f], Ps.-Julius, Ep. 1 [Hadrian, cc. 5, 6, 8, pp. 550f; Hincmar, cc. 6, 8, col. 996], *ibid*., Ep. 11 [Hadrian, cc. 11, 13, 15, pp. 551f; Hincmar, cc. 11, 12, 13-17, 19, cols. 1007-1012, 996f, 1005]. There are also several letters cited by Hincmar, but not by Hadrian [Ps.-Victor, Ps.-Lucius, Celestine, Sixtus III], and many citations in Hadrian's speech not found in Hincmar.) One can determine, however, that in the early period of the controversy, before he was imprisoned and his actions were submitted to synodal review, he contented himself largely with a defense which fell within the theoretical framework of his uncle: that is, he defended his contested actions on the basis of the canons. Against the ninth canon of Antioch, which his uncle claimed as warrant for interposition by the metropolitan, the Bishop of Laon cited the twenty-fourth and twenty-fifth canons of the same Council, with the purpose of excluding that interposition. According to those canons, "The bishop may have the power to dispense ecclesiastical goods to the poor, with the greatest reverence and fear of God," and, "Let the goods of the Church be guarded with all care and knowledge; . . . for they are to be dispensed according to the judgment and the power of the bishop to whom are committed the people and the souls congregated within the church." (Ep. 8, Migne PL. 124, 1028.) Without disputing the validity of the canons, the Archbishop rejected this defense on the ground that his nephew had administered his church "with unseemly irreverence," while the canons prescribed administration "with the greatest reverence and fear of God." (Migne PL. 126, 525.) Further, since his nephew resisted his admonitions and refused to restore "reverent" ecclesiastical government in the diocese of Laon, "he rose up brazenly against the holy canons and secured the pronouncement of canonical sentence against himself." (Responsa episcoporum, conclusio, Mansi xvi, 657. Cf. Flodoard, Historia Remensis Ecclesiae, iii, 22, MGH SS. xiii, p. 519.)

dispute with his nephew as "schism from the sacred canons, schism in the Church."[23]

Throughout the conflict the Archbishop maintained that the canons allowed him, as metropolitan, juridical supremacy throughout his province and the right of free interposition in the administrative affairs of his suffragans. The ninth canon of the Council of Antioch was the test passage for this position: "Through every region, the bishops should know that the metropolitan bishop has the care of the entire province, and that consequently anyone anywhere who is known to have *negotia* may come to the metropolis."[24] Twice, Hincmar of Laon obligated himself by oaths which his uncle interpreted as tokens of submission to this principle. The first was rendered before his ordination to the see of Laon, in the presence of his ordainers, representatives of the churches of Rheims and Laon, and "other men of a different order." The text of this oath is not preserved; but it is recorded that "he too entered a subscription in his own hand, just as—according to the custom of the church of Rheims—those who are about to be ordained bishops are wont to subscribe, after the profession of the catholic faith, [an affirmation] of their obedience toward the metropolis of Rheims, according to the *sacrae regulae*."[25] The second oath was

[23] lv Capitula, c. 47, Migne PL. 126, 469. Cf. De ordine palatii, c. 7, MGH Cap. ii, p. 520, and Admonitio pro Carlomanno, c. 4, Migne PL. 125, 1010.

[24] There are eight distinct citations of this canon in the lv Capitula alone: c. 2, cols. 295, 298; c. 17, col. 344; c. 26, col. 392; c. 28, col. 397; c. 29, col. 405; c. 35, col. 422; c. 47, col. 469.

[25] Schedula, c. 9, Migne PL. 126, 575; Acta Synodi, c. 9, Mansi xvi, 673, sentence of Adventius; lv Capitula, Praef., Migne PL. 126, 292, where Hincmar of Rheims stated that the oath included a promise of

rendered at the Synod of Attigny, where the Bishop was to account for delinquencies in his administration. There, he declared, "according to the holy canons and the decrees of the Apostolic See promulgated on the basis of the holy canons (*ex sacris canonibus*), I shall be obedient to the privilege of Hincmar, metropolitan of the province of the church of Rheims, as far as I know and am able."[26] Still, this second oath (which was submitted to the younger Hincmar himself for correction, and in which he promised his obedience personally to his aging uncle and not officially to the metropolis)[27] seems to have been very much like the first. In both, the Bishop promised obedience to the metropolitan privileges ordained by the canons. In his uncle's eyes, he consequently submitted to the principle of free juristic interposition by the metropolitan.

When the younger Hincmar denied that principle during the conflict, his denial was interpreted by his uncle as "schism from the sacred canons." Nor did the support of his clergy strengthen him legally, for their agreement was in direct opposition to the divinely inspired establishments of the orthodox *assensus*. "If one separates himself

---

obedience to the metropolitan and to the metropolis, and a general promise "in living, teaching and judging" to observe the precepts of the canons and the admonitions of Gregory the Great's Pastoral Rule.

[26] Hincmar of Laon, Collectio I, Migne PL. 124, 999; Schedula, cc. 13, 33, Migne PL. 126, 583, 624f. Cf. Responsa, c. 10, Mansi xvi, 654; and Hincmar of Rheims to Hincmar of Laon, Migne PL. 126, 502. Hincmar of Laon rendered an additional affirmation of obedience in avoiding simony, which does not appear to have been given as a formal profession and subscription. LV Capitula, c. 35, Migne PL. 126, 424.

[27] Proclamatio regis, c. 5, Mansi xvi, 580; Schedula, c. 33, Migne PL. 126, 624f; Hincmar of Laon, Collectio I, Migne PL. 124, 999.

from the Church in regard to ecclesiastical dogmas, whoever assents to his action cannot deny that he also is schismatic. And even if all priests and the whole world should assent, damnation would encompass those assenting."[28] Furthermore, as a consequence of his schism, the Bishop of Laon had severed himself not only from the *lex ecclesiastica*, but also from the episcopal order. By the violation of his formal *professiones et subscriptiones*,[29] by his disobedience toward his ecclesiastical superiors,[30] and by his rejection of the canons, he had cast himself from the episcopacy and made himself, according to the civil and ecclesiastical laws, schismatic from the orthodox Church.[31]

There were three principal instances where these positions conflicted and where the extent of the canonical obedience which the younger Hincmar had undertaken by oath came into question: the Bishop's promulgation of an edict on the proper juridical procedure to be followed against clerics; his sweeping use of the power of excommunication; and his appeal of the process against him to Rome.[32]

---

[28] LV Capitula, c. 36, Migne PL. 126, 433, and c. 48, col. 478. Hincmar of Rheims to Hincmar of Laon, *ibid.*, col. 526.

[29] *Ibid.*, Praefatio, c. 32, cols. 292, 414. Cf. Council of Carthage I, c. 13, Mansi III, 697.

[30] LV Capitula, c. 47, col. 468, canon 5 Antioch.

[31] LV Capitula, c. 4, col. 300: referring to himself, but with an obvious reference to his nephew's action, Hincmar wrote, "et si sacros canones et decreta catholicae ecclesiae incenderem et abdicarem, me procul dubio non solum ab episcopatu ipse dejicerem, verum et ab ecclesia catholica divisum et alienum, id est schismaticum et anathematizatum publicis et ecclesiasticis legibus efficerem. . . ." Cf. Acta Synodi, c. 6, Mansi XVI, 667.

[32] I omit lesser instances of defiance, such as the acceptance of an abbacy and palatine administration in the province of Tours without the consent of his metropolitan or of the Archbishop of Tours and his

Before he himself was brought before a synod to answer for his administration of the spiritual and temporal affairs of his see, the Bishop of Laon became alarmed by the anger of Charles the Bald which his treatment of royal tenants had aroused. Hincmar believed that that anger was in part due to the counsel of his uncle; and, after attempting to placate Charles by rendering him an oath of loyalty, he issued a statement of principle directed both toward the King and toward his uncle. As to secular intervention in the trial of bishops, he declared that bishops were reserved to the judgment of God, and could not be condemned by "human examination." As a threat against his uncle, he proclaimed that an informer should be punished by the amputation of his tongue or by decapitation.[33] This edict, subscribed by Hincmar of Laon himself together with his clergy, met vigorous resistance from the Archbishop on three counts: first, in promulgating a sentence of physical death for informers, the Bishop had usurped the office of the secular ruler;[34] second, he had dared to prescribe that sentence by inference against his Metropolitan;[35] and, last, he had presumed to pronounce on a matter of general importance to the priesthood, "although," wrote

---

refusal to join in the excommunication of the rebelling Carloman in 870/871.

[33] See LV Capitula, c. 7, Migne PL. 126, 314; Schedula, c. 11, *ibid.*, 576. The same words occur three times in the Pseudo-Isidorian collection, Ps.-Alexander, Ep. 1, c. 7, Hinschius, *Decretales Pseudo-Isidorianae*, p. 98; Ps.-Sixtus II, Ep. 11, c. 7, p. 193; and the letter of Julius I "Decuerat vos," c. 19, p. 474.

[34] Acta Synodi, c. 9, Mansi XVI, 674.

[35] LV Capitula, c. 4, Migne PL. 126, 301, "contra me"; Schedula, c. 23, *ibid.*, col. 603, "me episcopum episcopi delatorem." See also Mansi XV, 645, "delator esse voluisti."

his Metropolitan, "the statutes of the Church teach that without me you can decree nothing which pertains to the general observance of all the priests of the Lord."[36] Thus, by subscribing to statements contrary to the truth revealed in the Gospels, to apostolic authority, and to the decrees of councils, all issued with the assent of the Universal Church and confirmed by papal authority, the Bishop had, in the judgment of his Metropolitan, separated himself from the Church committed to him and from the communion of orthodox priests. By forcing his clergy to subscribe with him, he had plunged them all with him into the heresy of schism.[37]

After he failed to overcome the anger of his King and the censure of his Metropolitan, the younger Hincmar was summoned before the Synod of Verberie to answer the charges against him. Fearing what might befall him as a result of the enquiry—he later wrote that he believed his uncle had advised the King "to bring men strong and skillful enough to capture such a brute"[38]—he assembled his clergy and people before setting out for the synod. He announced to them his suspicion that, "although right [*jus*] and the laws of the canons command by precept that the bishop may order the property of his Church by dispensing it to whomever he may wish and however he wishes," that power would be taken from him. He therefore placed his own diocese under provisional interdict, to take effect if permission to take his case to Rome personally were denied him at the synod or if he were placed in

[36] LV Capitula, c. 36, Migne PL. 126, 428.

[37] *Ibid.*, c. 47, cols. 467ff.

[38] Schedula, c. 23, Migne PL. 126, 602f. The simile is to "the indomitable unicorn." *Ibid.*, c. 24, col. 605.

custody, and to remain binding until he himself should speak to his people again in his see or send them letters from Rome.[39] Though turbulent, the Synod of Verberie passed without adversity for the Bishop; but the interdict took effect shortly after when, without synodal sanction, Charles the Bald did in fact place him under custody.[40] Charles and his supporters later maintained that he had restrained "that insolent bishop . . . so that he might be corrected and not fall from his position."[41] But Hincmar was not "corrected," and he sent messengers to announce to his people that the provisional interdict was to take effect.[42]

Denied all sacraments, the people and clergy of Laon appealed to the Archbishop of Rheims for assistance; and, when his nephew refused after three admonitions "to loose this ban of impiety," the elder Hincmar himself declared the interdict void and the church of Laon absolved of it.[43] The younger Hincmar protested vehemently that his uncle had no right to loose the ban he had imposed. In response, the Archbishop declared that the ban was not an excommunication but merely a curse deriving more from vindictive wrath than from "the judgment of justice."[44] Further, "according to the *regulae* and laws," he had "the power by the metropolitan authority, to correct what [the Bishop] presumed to do contrary to the canons"[45] and to declare void all the enactments of his nephew that he

---

[39] Hincmar of Rheims to Hincmar of Laon, Migne PL. 126, 515f.

[40] *Ibid.* See also LV Capitula, c. 8, Migne PL. 126, 315.

[41] Acta Synodi, c. 6, Mansi XVI, 667.

[42] Hincmar of Rheims to Hincmar of Laon, Migne PL. 126, 515.

[43] Acta Synodi, c. 7, Mansi XVI, 667f, LV Capitula, cc. 30, 33, cols. 307f, 416.

[44] *Ibid.*, c. 30, cols. 407f.

[45] *Ibid.*, c. 33, col. 416.

found "contrary to the precepts of the Gospel and opposed to the decrees of the saints.[46] The canons of Antioch, which the Bishop had cited in his defense, wrote the Archbishop, delegated to the bishop only the powers to govern his church with reverence and to ordain priests and deacons; "beyond this, let them not attempt to do anything without the counsel of their metropolitan."[47]

If, as Hincmar of Rheims explicitly said, his nephew adopted the interdict as a means of self protection[48] it fell far short of its purpose. His final effort defiantly to escape the judgment of his uncle succeeded no better. Summoned again to answer charges against him before the Synod of Attigny, the younger Hincmar sought to reconcile himself to Charles and to his metropolitan by submitting promises of obedience to them. His promises were received, and Charles and the elder Hincmar exchanged the kiss of peace with him. He had, however, asked his uncle to appoint judges to decide the causes pending against him, and, when their first decisions were uniformly on the side of his plaintiffs, he fled from the synod. Soon afterwards, "without the knowledge of his Metropolitan and without canonical and episcopal judgment," he submitted to the judgment of a secular court sitting in the presence of Charles himself.[49] When it became apparent that his uncle would not accept the judgments of that court,[50] the Bishop sent to his uncle a formal appeal of his case to Rome.

[46] Hincmar of Rheims to Hincmar of Laon, Migne PL. 126, 526.

[47] *Ibid.*, col. 524.

[48] Schedula, c. 31, Migne PL. 126, 623. See *ibid.*, c. 28, col. 624, where Hincmar of Laon's objection that he acted on the precedents of his uncle and of popes is refuted.

[49] Schedula, c. 19, Migne PL. 126, 594.   [50] *Loc.cit.*

Thus Hincmar violated one of the principal juristic tenets of the elder Hincmar: that initial jurisdiction in the trial of a bishop lay unalterably with the metropolitan synod of his diocese. Furthermore, the form of the appeal was decisive in the legalistic mind of the Archbishop; it was written and subscribed, "a little work [*pitaciolum*] put together without any regard for right and subscribed with his own hand, contrary in every way to his aforementioned profession [of Attigny]." The formal subscription which the Bishop had added to his appeal, wrote his uncle, overturned the profession just rendered, though by that first subscription "he had destroyed the insolence of past disobedience, and had built anew by promising and subscribing future obedience, according to the holy canons, toward the privilege of his metropolis." By the subscription to his appeal, contrary to the "privilege of his metropolis," the Bishop lapsed into his former insolence; and by contravening the earlier subscription, he had, according to the canons, deprived himself of his orders. It was as though he had subscribed the appeal with the words, "I, Hincmar, going against my profession and subscription, have voluntarily stripped myself of office." Further, by this illicit subscription and the earlier one he had entered with his edict, he had proved himself not a Christian and had set himself under the anathema.[51]

At this final breach, Hincmar of Laon's defense rested entirely upon his attribution of legislative power to the bishop of Rome. Papal decretals established, he maintained, that no trials of bishops might be judged definitively without the decision of the Roman See;[52] and, further, if an ac-

[51] Schedula, c. 17, Migne PL. 126, 589.
[52] E.g., Migne PL. 124, 998.

cused bishop mistrusted the judgment of his metropolitan and his fellow suffragans, he might appeal his case directly to Rome without submitting to adjudication by his provincial synod.[53] He was vigorously supported in this position by Pope Hadrian II, who threatened Charles the Bald with excommunication as a tyrant, perjurer, and despoiler of ecclesiastical lands for his actions toward the Bishop, and declared the process against the younger Hincmar void.[54] The case, wrote Hadrian, must be removed to Rome for judgment according to the *privilegium Petri*.[55]

In response to the papal demands, Charles threatened, in a letter written by Hincmar of Rheims, to depose Hadrian in synodal trial.[56] But the conflict of the papal and the conciliar position was not consummated; for the physical weakness of the Pope and his early death prevented the conduct of the trial according to the principles of the papal monarchy and allowed the elder Hincmar to vindicate his ecclesiological principles. Since Hincmar of Laon refused to "recognize the limits and measure set for [him] by God in the sacred canons,"[57] and presumed without the counsel of his Metropolitan, to issue a declaration touching the general observance of the priesthood, to suspend his clergy from their duties of his own accord, and finally, to deny the juridical privilege of his Metropolitan, he effected his own "schism from the canons, schism in the Church." By his professions of obedience to his Metropolitan "according to the sacred canons," he had joined his

---

[53] *Ibid.*, 992, 993, 994, 999.
[54] MGH Epp. VI, no. 34, pp. 738ff.
[55] Migne PL. 124, 894.
[56] *Ibid.*, cols. 895f.
[57] LV Capitula, c. 18, Migne PL. 126, 350.

personal assent to the *assensus ecclesiae* by which the canons and other components were constituted elements of the *lex ecclesiastica*; he had entered that *fraterna unitas* which made of the clergy "one kingdom and one Church"; he took for his own the peculiar law of the "bishop with his church." But later, by his subscriptions to his edict, his appeal to Rome, and by the interdict he issued, he was accounted a disrupter of the *assensus ecclesiae*, one outside the *fraterna unitas*, and an enemy of the common, unifying *lex ecclesiastica*. He had deposed himself; he had set himself outside the *templum sanctum in Domino*. The final, synodal judgment which Hincmar of Rheims ultimately won, therefore, condemned not only the Bishop of Laon but also by implication the ecclesiological doctrine he had advocated. Sustained by the power of Hincmar of Rheims, conciliarism had been vindicated.

CHAPTER IV · THE CHALLENGE
OF ROYAL SUPREMACY

1. The Dualistic View of Royal Power

CONCILIARIST ecclesiology was endangered by papal monism, but even more, among the Franks, by a flaw in dualistic political thought. The Frankish clergy had countered the doctrine of royal monism with the doctrine that the ecclesiastical and the civil powers were discrete and that each was supreme in its own jurisdiction. The legal competences of the two offices, however, could not be sharply divided, and the ensuing juristic confusion allowed the royal power to threaten the very liberties which the dualists had sought to guarantee. Some scholars have maintained that the very great authority which Carolingian kings claimed and exercised in ecclesiastical affairs derived from a quasi-sacerdotal character of the royal office and that those rulers were, in a real sense, "theocratic kings" and heads of the Church. It is hoped that the following discussion will show that this interpretation neglects to distinguish sufficiently between what was divinely sanctioned and what was genuinely divine, and that the royal office in the ninth century was not considered ecclesiastical in nature, powers, or purpose, although writers commonly acknowledged that it might serve the interests of the Church.

Dualism and royal monism coincided exactly in construing the nature of kingly authority in wholly secular terms; they differed only in defining the degree to which that authority might be exercised in ecclesiastical matters.

To the minds of ninth-century writers, the king was the promulgator and the avenger of laws, the bestower and guarantor of legal privileges and immunities, and the defender of civil order. Since his obligations of juristic defense extended to the spiritual estate as well as to the temporal, he must intervene when necessary in the legal and disciplinary affairs of the clergy, even to the extent of promulgating edicts in purely ecclesiastical matters and of enforcing the deposition of seditious bishops. This intervention did not, however, infer a sacerdotal character to the king; nor, through his special duties toward the priesthood, was the juridical integrity of the royal office conversely absorbed by and subordinated to the juristic structure of that order. Like the episcopal, the royal ministry remained a separate office, or *dignitas*.[1] However decisive the effects of royal action in clerical affairs, the warrant for the action itself remained wholly secular: the ruler's exercise of *potestas mundana* in the name of law. In the chapters which follow, we shall indicate that this, rather than any "theocratic" principles, determined the character

[1] H. X. Arquillière (*L'Augustinisme politique*, 2d ed. Paris, 1955, pp. 172f, 179 and *passim*) finds in the term "regium ministerium" an indication of subservience to the ecclesiastical hierarchy. A more general interpretation of the term, however, is warranted by its interchangeability with *"regia dignitas"* (Ep. 8, Charles the Bald to Hadrian II, Migne PL. 124, 881ff), and by the use of the equivalent phrase "episcopale ministerium." When Hincmar of Laon, for example, threatened to implement his "ministerium" by excommunicating Charles the Bald and his followers (Migne PL. 126, 495) he clearly meant that he would exercise the powers of his office, not that he would perform any service. The meaning *ministerium = dignitas* is, of course, quite old. Cf. Cod. Th., xii, 1, 121 and xvi, 5, 13, ed. Mommsen-Krüger, v. I$_2$, pp. 692, 860, and Tertullian, Apologeticus, c. 39, Migne PL. I, 532. (On the general problem, see E. H. Kantorowicz, *The King's Two Bodies* [Princeton, 1957], pp. 383ff, 445 n. 422.)

Frankish authors attributed to the royal office in theory and directed the rôles Carolingian kings actually assumed in the affairs of the Church.

Frankish theorists based their temporal interpretation of the royal office chiefly on three premises derived from patristic sources: that the royal power was gained through popular election or divine dispensation, rather than through ecclesiastical offices; that the first duty of the king was to enforce the law in human affairs (ecclesiastical law as well as civil, in a Christian state); and that the means for the performance of the royal ministry was armed terror, an instrument foreign to the priesthood. Of supreme importance was the statement of Isidore of Seville that, in consequence of original sin, God imposed the punishment of servitude to sin upon the human race. To repress the consequent disorders, princes and kings were elected in order to force their people by terror to refrain from wrongdoing and to subject them by laws to right living. Sometimes, he wrote, temporal princes were found within the Church. Those rulers were particularly bound to accomplish "through the terror of discipline" what the priest could not bring about "through the preaching of doctrine" and to perform the service of defense for which Christ had commended the Church to them.[2] Pope Gregory I also maintained that human government was a consequence of sin, and he saw in fear of the secular ruler a corrective

[2] Sententiae III, 47, 1; 51, 4-6. Migne PL. 83, 717, 723. The second passage was quoted by the Council of Paris (829), MGH Conc. II, no. 50, c. 2(56), p. 652. See F. Kern, *Gottesgnadentum und Widerstandsrecht*, 2d ed., by R. Buchner (Münster, 1954), p. 124, n. 269.

for "those living wickedly."[3] Anticipating Isidore and Gregory on the origin of civil government, Augustine had already defined the relationship of the royal office to human affairs more concretely than they did. The government of temporal matters which rulers held and which required the obedience of the Church in dealings of this world[4] was directed to the maintenance of peace,[5] to securing the tranquil enjoyment of property tenure through the preservation of law.[6]

These principles about the origin and purpose of civil authority were critical to ninth-century thought. In Augustinian terms, the Church remained Jerusalem, and worldly power Babylon:[7] the two cities were separate but of mutual benefit in this world. Hincmar of Rheims records the position that every earthly kingdom was gained by wars and increased by victories, rather than by ecclesiastical offices,[8] and that the duty of the king was to repel enemies and to repress and punish the seditious, while that of the bishop

[3] Moralia in Job, XXI, 15 (11), 22, 23. Migne PL. 76, 203f. See Hincmar of Rheims, LV Capitula, c. 14, Migne PL. 126, 327f.

[4] Expositio quarumdam Propositionum ex Epistola ad Romanos, Migne PL. 35, 2083, c. 72.

[5] De Civitate Dei, XIX, 26.

[6] Tractatus VI in Johannis Evangel. 25, 26, Migne PL. 35, 1437.

[7] See Hincmar's interpolation in his citation of De Civitate Dei, XIX, c. 26: "scilicet Hierusalem, hoc est ecclesia, et Babylon, quae est mundana potestas." Ad Episcopos et Proceres, Migne PL. 125, 984, c. XLI.

[8] Ep. 27 to Hadrian II, Migne PL. 126, 180, "et dicunt saecularem scripturam dicere, quia omne regnum saeculi hujus bellis quaeritur, victoriis propagatur, et non apostolici vel episcoporum excommunicationibus obtinetur, et Scripturam divinam proponunt dicere, 'Quia Domini est regnum per quem reges regnant et cui voluerit dat illud,' ministerio angelorum et hominum."

was to administer the sacraments.[9] Following his master, Alcuin,[10] Rhabanus Maurus conceived the royal *dignitas* as having been discovered "by human invention," in contrast to the priestly *dignitas*, which was instituted by divine authority.[11] The royal office prepared men's bodies for death; the priestly nourished their souls to life.[12] Of the two, only the priestly would be found in the Eternal Kingdom.[13]

[9] Concilium Duziacense I, Responsa Episcoporum, c. 3, Mansi XVI, 646. Cf. Walafrid Strabo, De Exordiis, MGH Cap. II, p. 480, c. 6, "reges et sacerdotes . . . qui motibus corporis imperant et spiritales hostias immolant Deo. . . ."

[10] De Rhetorica, ed. C. Hahn, *Rhetores Latini minores* (Leipzig, 1863), pp. 525f. As Professor Wallach has discovered, this passage was taken from Cicero's De Inventione I, 2. Wallach, *Alcuin and Charlemagne*, p. 6, n. 1.

[11] Cf. Hincmar of Rheims to Louis III, Ep. 19, Migne PL. 126, 113: "Christus, a quo legitimus omnis episcopatus cepit exordium et omnis principatus accepit provectum. . . ."

[12] Epp. Fuld. Frag. MGH Epp. v, c. 23, p. 528: "Duae dignitates atque potestates inter homines constitutae reperiuntur. Una ex humana inventione reperta, hoc est imperialis atque regalis. Altera vero ex divina auctoritate instituta, hoc est sacerdotalis. Quarum una hominum corpora parat ad mortem, altera animas nutrit ad vitam." In epistola ad Brunwardum abbatem: "Regalem potestatem non ex divina sed humana auctoritate esse somniat. . . ." Cf. Alcuin to Aethelhard of Canterbury, MGH Epp. IV; no. 17, p. 48: "Divisa est potestas saecularis et potestas spiritalis; illa portat gladium mortis in manu, haec clavem vitae in lingua." And in a later letter to the same prelate (*ibid.*, no. 255, p. 413): "Divisa est sacerdotalis atque regalis potentia. Illa portat clavem in lingua caelestis regni, iste gladium ad vindictam reorum. Sed multo praestantior potestas quae vivificat, quam illa quam occidit. . . ." Cf. Hincmar of Rheims, Schedula, c. 11, Migne PL. 126, 578. In his De Divortio Lotharii (Migne PL. 125, 772, Responsio VII), Hincmar also distinguishes between the *medicinalis mucro,* of the bishops, which is used to preserve the sound members from the unsound, and the *gladium judiciale* of kings, used "to destroy the wicked from the earth."

[13] Rhabanus Maurus, Enarrationes in Epp. Pauli, VII, 13, Migne PL. 111,

Rhabanus's own disciple, Haimo of Halberstadt, differing somewhat from his master, affords the most concise definition of the royal duties: "The king," he wrote, "is a minister of God; that is, he has been established by God for your benefit, by terror and assistance to guard and protect you, lest you be killed by your enemy and lest others snatch away your property." When the human race had become bestial and, "after the fashion of wild animals," had begun to rage against itself, God set rulers over the *bestiales homines* to repress the fierceness of their spirits by terror. In his own day, wrote Haimo, the end of the civil power remained simply to prevent those who wished to do evil from doing it.[14]

For ninth-century authors, as for the Fathers, terror continued to be the instrument of the royal ministry, the restraint of those who rode roughshod over laws "as brute and unreasonable animals."[15] The ministry of terror was not to be used wantonly, but in accordance with legal precepts.[16] Nor was it granted to any save to the king

---

1560. Rhabanus is quoting St. Augustine, Expositio quarumdem Propositionum, Migne PL. 35, 2083 c. 72. Cf. the letter of Charlemagne to Elipandus, sent from the Synod of Frankfurt (794), MGH Conc. I, no. 19F, p. 160: "Huius vero civitatis ipse Dei verus et proprius filius, Deus verus, homo verus, Jesus Christus, dominus noster, regali praesidet potentia. . . ."

[14] Expositio in Rom. 13: 1-4, Migne PL. 117, 478ff.

[15] Ad Regem de Coercendo Raptu Viduarum, Migne PL. 125, 1019, c. 4. See also Hincmar's De Divortio, *ibid.*, col. 738, Responsio XXI; his letter to Charles the Bald, MGH Epp. VIII, fasc. 1, no. 126, p. 65; and the Capitulary of Quierzy (873), MGH Cap. II, no. 278, c. 7, p. 345.

[16] *Timor Dei* on the part of the ruler was also supposed to guide his actions. See Ratramnus, Contra Graecorum opposita, IV, 6, Migne PL. 121, 331; *Sedulii Scotti Liber de Rectoribus Christianis*, ed. S. Hellmann, p. 80, c. 18; Hincmar, De Ordine Palatii, MGH Cap. II, c. 2, p. 518.

alone[17] and, by his delegation, to inferior officers of the
respublica. The clergy were prohibited from sharing it.[18]
Smaragdus urged that the royal terror be used to purify
the Church and to extirpate pride, wrath, violence,
lust, greed, and cruelty.[19] On a less moralistic level, other
writers saw fear of the king simply as an element sustain-
ing public order. Amalarius of Metz and Florus of Lyon,
for example, both deplored the decay *"timoris regum et
legum"* in their time and the consequent juridical and
civil confusion.[20]

Cf. the Synod of Ver (844) MGH Cap. II, no. 291, c. 6, p. 385: "De
raptoribus autem id nobis videtur optimum, ut, quoniam ecclesiasticam
excommunicationem parvipendunt, secularium legum terreantur auster-
itate," and Pope Stephen V to Bishop Liutward of Vercelli (886), MGH
Epp. VII, no. 6, p. 336: "Non autem sine causa gladium portat rex,
vindex est enim contra omnes iniquos ut terrore conprimat quos nequit
corrigere monitis salubribus."

[17] Relatio Episcoporum, MGH Cap. II, no. 196, c. 9, p. 38.

[18] E.g., MGH Cap. I, no. 19, c. 2, p. 45.

[19] Via Regia, Migne PL. 102, 958, c. 18. See M. L. W. Laistner, "The
Date and the Recipient of Smaragdus' *Via Regia*," *Speculum*, 3 (1928),
pp. 392-397, who maintained that the *Via Regia* was written between
813 and 816 for Louis the Pious, and J. Scharf, "Studien zu Smaragdus
und Jonas," *Deutsches Archiv*, 17 (1961), pp. 333-384, who argues that
it was written between 817 and 826, for Pippin I, of Aquitaine.

[20] Amalarius to Count Matfred, MGH Epp. V, no. 10, p. 202. For a
general biography of Amalarius, see J. A. Cabaniss, *Amalarius of Metz*
(Amsterdam, 1954). Florus, Querela de Divisione Imperii, MGH Poet.
Lat. II, p. 560, vv. 14, 16, 27, 36. See also Epitaphium Arsenii, II,
c. 6, MGH SS. II, p. 550: "Iudices non nisi venale aliquid agunt,
populus imperialibus non suffragatur officiis, auctoritas non viget praela-
torum quoniam imperialis et regum deperiit, . . ." and *Jonas d'Orléans
et son "De Institutione Regia,"* ed. J. Reviron, cc. 4, 11, pp. 145f, 168f.
In addition, see the admonitory letter presented to a West Frankish
"Charles" in the later ninth century: "Iudices pravos viriliter atque
severe corripite . . . ut qui mali sunt regalem timeant auctoritatem,
teneant legem et rationem, boni vero . . . ament fidem et miseri-
cordiam." E. Dümmler, "Ermahnungschreiben," *Neues Archiv*, 13

The relationship these writers saw between the execution of law and the function of royal power received expression in the liturgical thought of Hincmar of Rheims, who ascribed to the sceptre, "the sign of royal power," parallel symbolism to the book of law given Hebrew kings at their coronation "so that they might know that they ought to rule themselves, correct the wicked and direct the good in the path of righteousness according to it."[21] The sceptre, therefore, symbolized both the concept of the king as the executor of the law and that of the king as its avenger; it was the emblem of the office through which he was "to repress the evil by his terror and to exalt the well-meaning and the poor by his authority."[22]

In his work, *De Regis Persona et Regio Ministerio*, Hincmar brings together these diverse characteristics to describe the king, "the prince and lord of the earth" (*praef.*). The royal power was bestowed, not ecclesiastically, but divinely. Since God Himself brought good kings to government

---

(1887), pp. 195f, and the similar emphasis in the letter of the bishops of Charles the Bald to Louis the German (MGH Cap. II, no. 297, c. 12, p. 436): "Curate ut mali, si non propter Deum, vel propter timorem vestrum malum agere metuant."

[21] De Ordine Palatii, c. 5, MGH Cap. II, p. 519, and *ibid.*, no. 304, p. 461.

[22] Ad Episcopos, Admonitio altera, Migne PL. 125, 1015, c. 13. Cf. his Pro Lib., Migne PL. 125, 1056: ". . . pronuntio quia nunc lex Domini irreprehensibilis nostris infelicibus et periculosissimis temporibus tantum vigorem non habet reverentia divinitatis sicut antequam nomen Christi in honore per universum orbem fieret, leges Romanae habebant timore imperatoris." See Ps. 18:8. See also, the De Divortio, Migne PL. 125, 754, Responsio v; "cuius [regis] ministerium est agere ut illa [capitula legalia] observentur . . ." and his Schedula, Migne PL. 126, 627, c. 34, where he affirms that violation of the laws is contrary to the royal ministry.

and allowed wicked rulers to reign, the kingship commanded the obedience of subjects whether the king were personally good or evil (cc. 1, 2). Hincmar construed the royal duties in an exclusively secular light: he held that they were simply to guarantee the earthly tranquility of his subjects by the establishment and execution of law. The chapters in the second and third sections of the *De Regis Persona* (cc. 19-29, 29-33), which Hincmar added to the early synodal letter that was the basis of his work, illustrate clearly his position. All of those additions support the major premise that "either the people must keep the just and promulgated laws, or the prince must vindicate the laws justly and reasonably in every way" (c. 27). The king must act according to the laws (c. 27) and fulfill the office God has given him as avenger of divine wrath (c. 26). He must execute justice against sinners and overt malefactors (cc. 20, 22, 25), shunning their company and denying them undeserved mercy (c. 21), at the same time giving them time for repentance (c. 28). The unrepentant must be punished, even if they are members of the royal family (cc. 28, 29. Cf. cc. 30, 31, 33). In his first section, adopting the chapters of the synodal letter almost without change, Hincmar described as a divine service the duty of the king to promulgate laws and to secure obedience to them.[23]

The accession of the king depended upon divine dispensation rather than upon human election; the performance of the royal ministry depended upon the character of the

[23] Migne PL. 125, 833ff. See G. Laehr, "Ein karolingischer Konzilsbrief und der Fürstenspiegel Hincmars von Reims," *Neues Archiv*, 50 (1935), pp. 106ff.

king; the length of his reign, even should he be evil or negligent, was determined by the judgment of God. Although he owed some duties to the Church, those responsibilities were fundamentally extra-ecclesiastical; for the Church had no specific power to delegate them, to supervise their exercise, or to withdraw them. The royal ministry was the ministry of the *dominus terrae*, and it was external to the "spiritual republic" of the Church.

+

In a lapidary sentence, Hincmar of Rheims wrote that the office of the king was "to fight and to promulgate laws."[24] Together with the two other primary jurists of his age, Pseudo-Isidore and Benedictus Levita, the Archbishop saw a close relationship between the two duties, for they considered both armed force and the coercive power of civil laws useful to the defense of the Church. Yet, just as they thought the warrior-king external to ecclesiastical order, so they also viewed the king in his legislative functions toward the Church as one who, though entirely excluded from the priesthood, supported it by his peculiar juridical authority.

As the Pseudo-Isidorian Decretals themselves purport to derive from the period before the establishment of the Christian Empire, they contain little on the duties of the prince in the Church. Pseudo-Isidore, however, does affirm that temporal rulers should be *"cooperatores legis Dei"*;[25]

[24] Ad episcopos admonitio altera, c. 2, Migne PL. 125, 1009; De officiis, *ibid.*, 1088.

[25] Ps.-Clement, Ep. 1, c. 39, Hinschius, *Decretales Pseudo-Isidorianae*, p. 43.

and the description of Constantine's actions at the Council of Nicea and the Constantinian Donation, which he added to his compilation, elucidate his meaning. As we have already observed, Constantine declined to judge bishops accused at Nicea, "for God has given you as gods to us," and he left the juridical matters of the Council to his bishops. He himself merely confirmed the conciliar resolution.[26] In the Donation, the imperial "cooperation" took the form of the bestowal of honors and governmental powers upon the Bishop of Rome and the confirmation of that transfer under the threat of anathema.[27] Further, the documents from the Conciliar Epoch which follow the False Decretals in many Pseudo-Isidorian collections quite patently describe the figure of the temporal ruler as the corroborator and enforcer of conciliar decrees; but they also show that he took no part in the synodal deliberations which shaped those decrees.[28] In Pseudo-Isidore's terms, therefore, the prince was wholly a *"cooperator legis Dei,"* and not a *"doctor legis Dei."* His ministry extended to promulgating and enforcing ecclesiastical edicts, but not to composing or deliberating upon them.

Unlike Pseudo-Isidore's letters and decrees, all of which derive or allegedly derive from ecclesiastical authorities (with the exception of the Donation of Constantine), the forgeries of Benedictus Levita purport almost entirely to be edicts of Frankish synods and general assemblies issued under the royal authority. Consequently, the "Benedictine"

[26] Hinschius, *Decretales Pseudo-Isidorianae*, pp. 256f.

[27] *Ibid.*, pp. 249ff.

[28] See, for example, the records of the Council of Chalcedon, Hinschius, *Decretales Pseudo-Isidorianae*, pp. 284ff, and those of the third Synod of Toledo, *ibid.*, pp. 354ff.

concept of the royal office and its relationship to ecclesiastical law is somewhat better defined than the Isidorian. Benedictus repeated the conventional thought that the first characteristic of kingship was the duty of punishment and defense. The king, he wrote, bore the "sword of God,"[29] and was divinely charged to exercise his powers "for the terror of many . . . for the vengeance of God."[30] He cites the statement of Isidore of Seville that the princely power exists within the Church for the enforcement of ecclesiastical discipline and to attain through terror what the priest could not attain through doctrinal pronouncements.[31] The chief duties of the king, consequently, were to repress the wicked and seditious, [32] to grant military defense to the Church through his own action[33] or through advocates and *defensores* whom he delegated,[34] and, finally, to see to the administration of justice.[35] As for royal intervention in ecclesiastical processes, Benedictus adduces the familiar image of Constantine at Nicea and the words of Valentinian to his bishops: "Your cause is above us. Therefore, discuss your cases among yourselves, since you are above us."[36]

[29] II, 432, Migne PL. 97, 802.

[30] I, 332, col. 745.

[31] Addit. II, 24, col. 869. Cf. I, 375, col. 751.

[32] I, 26, col. 707. Cf. III, 422, col. 851: "per potestates exteras adducantur, id est per judices saeculares."

[33] III, 33, 392, cols. 805, 847f.

[34] See Benedictus's excerpts from the Council of Paris (829) on this point; Addit. II, 25-28, cols. 869ff.

[35] II, 219, Addit. IV, 115, cols. 774, 904.

[36] II, 403, col. 797. Cf. another response of Valentinian as in Addit. IV, 3, cols. 887f: "Mihi quidem, cum unus de populo sum, fas non est talia perscrutari; verum sacerdotes, quibus haec cura est, apud semetipsos congregentur, ubi voluerint."

As Benedictus wrote in his introductory verses, the issuance of laws "*pro utilitate ecclesiae*" was one way in which the foremost duty of the king was exercised:

> Namque patrant multi funestas spe rapinas,
> Nonnulli violant templa dicata Deo;
> Sunt alii scelerum fedati labe suorum,
> Fistula quos omnes commemorare nequit.
> Sed cohibet[37] tales legum censura sacrarum
> Decretisque vetat ista patrare piis.[38]

Despite the great number of ecclesiastical matters dealt with by Benedictus and the relative formlessness of his work, he clearly meant the function of legislative defense to be implemented for the preservation of ecclesiastical immunities and clerical privileges—especially that of trial before an ecclesiastical court—and for the enforcement of discipline within the priestly order. He implied no powers to pronounce on matters of faith and doctrine. Even the disciplinary edicts which Benedictus included were made to fall under the general limitations already observed: that new law must not violate the purpose of old;[39] that to be legally valid enactments must be approved by the counsel of subjects;[40] and, finally, that "the law of emperors is not above the law of God, but under it."[41] The purpose of royal legislation in ecclesiastical affairs, then, was to enforce privileges and canonical precepts already established,

---

[37] Charles the Bald.

[38] Col. 702.

[39] See II, 322, 324, 391, cols. 783, 796.

[40] Praefatio, col. 701. See also the caption to Addit. IV, col. 887, and II, 383, 370f, 366, I, 392f, 36, and *passim*, cols. 795, 790f, 787f, 752f, 708f.

[41] Addit. III, 18, col. 874.

to defend order, and to preserve discipline. The royal legislator touched ecclesiastical, but not sacred, things in his
enactments; his power to terrorize, not the episcopal
power to teach, confirmed his edicts.

The same principles occurred in the thought of Hincmar
of Rheims. The promulgation of laws, an attribute peculiar
to kingship,[42] was specifically intended "to coerce and
punish the wicked."[43] "Read the sixteenth book of Roman
law [i.e., the Theodosian Code], read the decretals of
Damasus, scan the letters of Leo and other pontiffs sent to
emperors in regard to divers councils, turn through the
edicts of the emperors on heretics, promulgated at the
petition of bishops, study the *capitula* of our Caesars, and
you will find of what great profit the severity of laws has
been and continues to be, not only to the serenity of the
Church, but also to desired peace and cherished tranquility
of all Christendom." The law was for the wicked, not for
the just.[44]

Among his contemporaries Hincmar was aware to an
extraordinary degree of the place which Roman imperial
law held in ecclesiastical regulations; and his concept of
the proper legal functions of his own kings was largely
formed by his view of the relations between Roman law

[42] De Regis Persona, c. 16, Migne PL. 125, 844.

[43] De presbyteris criminosis, c. 24, Migne PL. 125, 1106. In De
coerdendo raptu viduarum, c. 18 (*ibid.*, 1031), he suggests that enactments "a fidelibus et ministris regni Christi principibus" contrary to
law violate the royal office.

[44] MGH Epp. VIII, fasc. 1, no. 135, pp. 84f. Cf. De Divortio, Quaestio
VI, Migne PL. 125, 757. See also "De ecclesiis et capellis," ed. W. Gundlach, *ZfKG*, p. 132: "Si nostri alios, per quos nobis iter fuerit, depraedari
temptaverint, et iram Dei et malum nomen et offensam principis incur-
ramus et ea, quae perpere acta fuerint, per legem emendare cogamur."

and the canons. Looking back to the patristic Church, he wrote that, in times of ecclesiastical necessity, the Church (i.e., the episcopacy) was accustomed to petition emperors for beneficial laws, and emperors were accustomed to promulgate them "to re-enforce and supplement the canons."[45]

A close relationship consequently emerged between the canons and Roman law, and portions of each were excerpted and used in the other; Roman law stood as canonical in ecclesiastical processes.[46] Even more generally, in civil affairs, bishops were subject to civil law.[47] The Roman law established ecclesiastical immunities,[48] prescribed the juridical procedure followed by the clergy,[49] and established the lines of regular discipline in the clergy.[50] But in Hincmar's eyes the intervention of "earlier princes" in ecclesiastical legislation went no further than purely disciplinary matters. It was customary, he wrote, "as often as some novelty in the orthodox faith or in the divine religion emerged, for it to be referred by the judgment [*sententia*] of the prince to the counsel of bishops. And then the vicars of Christ, our God, the prelates of His holy Church, decreed to be believed, followed, held and preached by all what was to be believed, followed, held and preached, according to their judgment, to the authority of the Holy

[45] De Divortio, Responsio v, Migne PL. 125, 652. Cf. De Praedestinatione Diss. Post., c. 37, and Pro Lib., Migne PL. 125, 401, 1048; and LV Capitula, c. 43, Migne PL. 126, 446.

[46] MGH Epp. VIII, fasc. I, no. 160 b, c. 8, p. 138.

[47] De Ecclesiis, *ibid.*, no. 108 a, p. 53; De Divortio, Responsio VI, Migne PL. 125, 687f; Ep. 24, Migne PL. 126, 157f; Charles the Bald, Ep. 8, Migne PL. 124, 892.

[48] Ep. 15, Migne PL. 126, 95.

[49] De Divortio, Responsio v, Migne PL. 125, 652f.

[50] Schedula, c. 35, Migne PL. 126, 633.

Scriptures, to the doctrine of orthodox masters and canonical authority, and to the decretals of the Roman pontiffs. . . ."[51] Hincmar held, therefore, that points of doctrine were outside the competence of imperial (and royal) legislators, whose promulgations in ecclesiastical matters he interpreted as simple corroborations of the canons.

Hincmar approached Frankish law with a similar attitude; but he considered that law more a safeguard against the civil disorders of his day than a support of ecclesiastical discipline. Promulgated, not arbitrarily, but with the counsel and assent of those affected,[52] Frankish ecclesiastical law, like the Roman, must answer the necessities of the clergy.[53] Like all civil laws in Christian states, it was subject to the measure of divine law.[54] The difference in his attitudes toward the two laws, however, may be shown by referring to the excerpts from Frankish law in the decree issued by the Synod of Fismes, which Hincmar himself almost certainly composed. Instead of the prescriptions of juristic procedure and the establishments of privilege familiar in Hincmar's citations from Roman law, one finds prohibitions of public violence, guarantees of ecclesiastical property tenure, and confirmations of episcopal authority over the lower clergy. The part of the legislator, however, was the same in both codes: his pro-

[51] MGH Epp. VIII, fasc. 1, no. 131 b, pp. 70f.

[52] De Ordine Palatii, c. 8, MGH Cap. II, p. 520. In matters of ecclesiastical discipline, Hincmar seems to have wished royal legislation to be bound quite closely by this limitation. See De presbyteris criminosis, cc. 1-4, 16, Migne PL. 125, 1093ff, 1101.

[53] De Divortio, Responsio V, Migne PL. 125, 652f; "De ecclesiis et capellis," ed. Gundlach, pp. 107ff.

[54] De Divortio, Responsio XII, col. 695; De Ordine Palatii, c. 21, MGH Cap. II, pp. 524f.

mulgations were issued "*pro utilitate ecclesiae*"; and, not entering into the area of spiritual government, he fulfilled the second function of royal office, "to promulgate laws."

✝

Indeed, the distinction between the kingship and the episcopacy drawn by the jurists is perhaps most obvious in their limits upon the power of the kings to legislate in ecclesiastical matters. Frankish theorists acknowledged legislation, or the promulgation of laws, as being a characteristic royal function; and they construed the exercise of that function in ecclesiastical matters, not as the arrogation of sacerdotal powers by the king, but rather as the implementation of a proper attribute of kingship in the service of the Church. Ratramnus of Corbie distinguished it as such when he wrote, "According to the testimony of the Prophet, Christ is described as king and priest: 'The Lord is our law-giver; the Lord is our King' (Isa. 33:22). And again: 'Thou mayst break them with a rod of iron' (Ps. 2:9). But that He is a priest, the Father testifies to the Son, saying: 'Thou art a priest forever after the order of Melchisedech' (Ps. 109:4)."[55] In short, Ratramnus credited legislation to the king and not to the priest; and, as we shall see, he thought the king's legislative powers in ecclesiastical matters to be sharply limited.

The restrictions he prescribed were principally those commonly advocated by his contemporaries. For example, it was a general premise that temporal laws were to be issued for the stability and defense of the Church and her

[55] Contra Graecorum Opposita iv, 5, Migne PL. 121, 324.

ministers, for the sake of common peace and justice, and for the tranquility of the realm.[56] In particular, ecclesiastical constitutions must be enacted to answer necessities of the Church.[57] New laws must be issued with regard for the old and especially for canons and synodal decrees, for Scriptural precepts, and for the general tenets of Christianity.[58]

Ratramnus and his contemporaries also prescribed one major limitation specifically on the enactment of law. To achieve legal validity, an act appears to have required twofold assent: the constitutive assent of a synod or general assembly at the framing of the laws, and the informal assent of the community at their promulgation.[59] Of these, the first was of course the more important; Charles the Bald referred to it when he affirmed that laws were established by the *"consensus populi et constitutio regis"* and affirmed that kings and bishops, with the consent of the community of the royal vassals, had established laws for the

[56] Capitula Pistensia (869), MGH Cap. II, no. 275, c. 3, p. 334.

[57] See the Annales Einhardi, a. 819, MGH SS. I, p. 205; Louis the Pious's Prooemium Generale for the enactments to which Einhard refers, MGH Cap. I, no. 137, p. 274; and Ansegisus, I, Praefatio, MGH Cap. I, p. 397.

[58] See the confirmation of Charles the Bald to St. Columba at Sens (847), DC II, no. 102, p. 273; the letter of the Synod of Troyes (867), Mansi xv, 790 ("Multi quippe reges et principes synodalibus decretis colla subdiderunt."); the Synod of Touzy (860), Mansi xv, 570f; *Jonas d'Orléans et son "De Institutione Regia,"* c. 11, ed. Reviron, p. 165; the letter of Sigwald of Aquileia to Charlemagne, MGH Epp. IV, no. 8, p. 505; and that of Agobard of Lyon to Nibridius of Narbonne, MGH Epp. v, no. 9, p. 200.

[59] See Charlemagne's Capitulare legibus additum (803), MGH Cap. I, no. 39, p. 113; the Constitutio Carisiacensis de Moneta (861), no. 271, p. 302; the Capitula Pistensia (862), c. 2, *ibid.*, no. 272, p. 307; and the Edictum Pistense (864), c. 3, *ibid.*, no. 273, p. 311.

state of the Church and the welfare of the kingdom.[60] From the days of Charlemagne, this element of assent, particularly the assent of bishops, was regarded as necessary for making valid establishments in ecclesiastical matters. Kathvulf, for example, while maintaining that Charles was a vicar of God "over all His members" and that bishops, as vicars of Christ, stood in the second place to him, urged Charlemagne "to establish the law of God over the people of God" through common counsel with his bishops.[61] In the same tenor the Synod of Mainz (813) left the review of ecclesiastical legislation entirely to the clergy.[62] As the capitularies of Louis the Pious and the numerous establishments of Charles the Bald show, this limitation remained effective throughout the ninth century.[63]

Ratramnus' work, *Contra Graecorum Opposita*, illustrates succinctly the importance of these limitations in Frankish thought. In 867, Pope Nicholas I, contesting the advancement of Photius as patriarch of Constantinople, received a letter from the Byzantine Emperors Michael and Basil in which the Emperors disparaged the Roman profession of the Filioque doctrine and disciplinary practices of the Western Church—among them, fasting on the Sabbath and clerical celibacy.[64] Nicholas appealed to the

[60] Edictum Pistense (864), c. 6, MGH Cap. II, no. 273, p. 313. Cap. Pistensia (862), *ibid.*, no. 272, c. 1, p. 303. Cf. *ibid.*, no. 275, c. 3, p. 334, no. 272, c. 2, p. 307, "regia et synodalia."

[61] MGH Epp. IV, no. 7, p. 503.

[62] MGH Conc. I, no. 26, p. 259. Cf. the Concilium Aquisgranense (802), no. 29, p. 230.

[63] E.g., Conventus Suessionensis (853), c. 7, MGH Cap. II, no. 258 A, p. 266.

[64] See the letter of Nicholas, MGH Epp. VI, no. 100, pp. 603f, sections of which are repeated by Hincmar of Rheims, Annales Bertiniani (a. 867), MGH in usum scholarum, p. 89, Ep. 14, Migne PL. 126, 93f,

Frankish clergy for support, and his summons brought
forth the treatise of Ratramnus, together with others by
Aeneas of Paris and Odo of Beauvais. Ratramnus' central
objection was that the Emperors had declared on points of
dogma without episcopal counsel and had required Nicholas's legates either to endorse their declarations or to suffer
anathematization. "We see," he wrote, "laymen going contrary to all ecclesiastical rules, and imposing decrees upon
the Faithful. Those who may not establish statutes on any
matter of ecclesiastical law without the counsel of bishops
strive to constitute laws of Faith. And then, according to
their decrees, some are received into communion and others
are removed from it."[65] In doing so, "they usurp the headship of the Church for themselves and take for themselves
the loftiness of the Apostles . . . wishing to set the throne
of their office above the stars of Heaven (that is, to sur-
pass the whole company of the saints) and to usurp the
veneration due patriarchs to the end that they may become
counterparts of Christ in the whole church subject to
them." Neither patristic authority nor ecclesiastical or
human law granted them this power "to alter *leges ecclesiasticas*."[66] Christ had granted the power of binding and
loosing and had committed the offices of teaching and
baptizing to the Apostles, not to "the Emperors of the
Greeks."[67] The Emperors had contravened all law—the
laws of Scripture, of the Fathers, and "their own laws,"
the edicts of previous emperors—by pronouncing upon

---

and by Ratramnus, Contra Graecorum Opposita, I, I, Migne PL. 121,
225ff.

[65] II, I, Migne PL. 121, 243.

[66] IV, 8, ibid., col. 335.   [67] II, I, *ibid.*, col. 243.

matters of Faith and of ecclesiastical discipline without taking the judgment of bishops in council. Indeed, they had both lapsed into error and become doubly criminous as *"transgressores tam divini et humani juris quam ecclesiasticae constitutionis."*[68]

These concepts of Ratramnus indicate the general tenor of Frankish dualism, which held that the natures of the royal and the episcopal offices were quite different and that their jurisdictions were correspondingly separate. In Church affairs, even the characteristic legislative powers of the king might be exercised legitimately only when confirmed by proper ecclesiastical authority. Babylon had no arbitrary jurisdiction in the affairs of Jerusalem.

2. Royal Intervention in Ecclesiastical Affairs

The warrant for royal direction of Church affairs under the great Charles was, as we have seen, the king's supremacy over all elements in the civil state. It was the same under his descendants; but the juristic thought of the later period modified the royal monism of the earlier. Differing in degree rather than in substance from the doctrine that preceded them, political thinkers in the epoch after Charlemagne continued to acknowledge the king as supreme in secular matters and as exercising in them legal authority over the clergy. In adopting this position, dualists modified it by raising to the level of a legal principle one premise already acknowledged in the time of Charlemagne: that the king was not head of the Church, or, in other words, that the royal office was outside the Church and that the

[68] IV, 6, *ibid.*, col. 330.

species of power it held was non-ecclesiastical. In this way, Frankish authors accentuated the social dualism we have observed as existing within Charlemagne's political monism and attempted to establish it as a political as well as a social doctrine.

Yet, political dualism was a fragile intellectual structure, too much at variance with political reality to survive intact. That doctrine was not sufficient to obliterate monistic practice; and there was constant tension between the dualistic ideal of two governments and the often blurred lines of jurisdiction which actually separated ecclesiastical rule from secular. In many cases, the distinction between "civil" and "ecclesiastical" was difficult; for example, it was not clear whether a case involving enfeoffment of a bishop by his king should be tried in a secular court according to royal law, or in synod, according to the canons. In this section we shall examine the warrant claimed by Charlemagne's successors for intervening in some critical ecclesiastical affairs, and, in the next, we shall indicate how dualistic ecclesiology and dualistic political thought conflicted.

Frankish rulers after Charlemagne exercised considerable influence in Church administration, much as he had done. This was their prerogative, not for any "theocratic" reasons, but by virtue of the temporal claims of the ruler over all his subjects, clerical and lay. Vested by his father with the imperial title and charged with exercising his government both over clergy and over laity,[1] Louis

---

[1] Chronicon Moissiacense (a. 813), MGH SS. i, pp. 310f; Thegan, Vita Hludowici, c. 6, MGH SS. ii, p. 591. Louis even briefly adopted his father's title "Romanum regens imperium, serenissimus augustus," MGH Cap. i, no. 132, pp. 267f.

the Pious claimed the rôle of a good shepherd having charge of Church and people.[2] In his view, the cohesive element in the state was the royal ministry, the greatest part of which abided in the king's person while civil officers and bishops alike shared it in discharging their civil duties.[3] As the representative of God, Louis received the adoration of his subjects.[4] The ruler both of the Church and of the Empire,[5] "the rector of all Christian religion in so far as it pertains to men,"[6] he strove to root out heretical beliefs by instructing others in the true Faith.[7] He was the lawgiver of the clergy,[8] the bestower of bishoprics,[9] and the censor of bishops,[10] with whom he claimed similar

[2] Astronomus, Vita Ludovici, c. 62, MGH SS. ii, p. 646.

[3] MGH Cap. i, no. 150, pp. 303f.

[4] Synod of Paris (825), MGH Conc. ii, no. 44, p. 529, commenting on a text of Gregory the Great: "Sed ne nos non necessaria ignorantia id non intelligendo diutius torqueat, sensus eiusdem sententiae talis est: Nos quidem ante ipsam non prosternimur quasi ante divinitatem, sed illum adoramus et cetera. Quod tale est, acsi regi in throno sedenti dicas: Nos quidem, o rex, non quasi ante divinitatem ante te prosternimur, sed illum adoramus, quem per imaginem tuam, quia homo es, dominum Iesum Christum hominem recordamur natum aut passum vel in throno sedentem cuius imitator es tu sedens in throno."

[5] Ermoldus Nigellius, In Honorem Ludovici, ii, 416: MGH Poet. Lat. ii, p. 36, "ecclesiam imperiumque regit." See also MGH Conc. ii, no. 52, p. 683.

[6] MGH Epp. v, no. 7, p. 258.

[7] MGH Epp. v, no. 32, pp. 353f.

[8] MGH Cap. i, no. 137, p. 274; no. 169 A, pp. 339f. On this point as represented early in the reign of Louis the Pious, see J. Semmler, "Reichsidee und kirchliche Gesetzgebung," ZfKG, 71 (1960), pp. 37-65, and, on the general problem, F. L. Ganshof, Recherches sur les capitulaires (Paris, 1958), esp. pp. 89ff.

[9] See below, p. 157f.

[10] MGH Cap. ii, no. 187, pp. 8f; Annales q.d. Einhardi (a. 821), MGH SS. i, p. 208; Thegan, Vita Ludovici, c. 56, MGH SS. ii, pp. 602f. Even the pope was not immune, Epitaphium Arsenii, ii, 17, MGH SS. ii, pp. 564f.

footing *"in servitio Dei."*[11] Indeed, his actions in ecclesiastical affairs dominated his attention so greatly that one biographer wrote, "His works declare him, not merely a king, but rather more, a bishop."[12]

The sons of Louis the Pious made similar assertions. Like their father, they considered their palace "sacred";[13] at the beginning of their official documents, they set the chrismon, the sign of orthodoxy and of divinely granted understanding.[14] They too disposed of bishoprics, censured prelates and directed them in the conduct of the episcopal ministry,[15] summoned synods,[16] and sat among bishops at the trials of higher clergy.[17]

In all this, however, they arrogated no spiritual authority. Within the framework of Germanic practice, they were implementing the Gelasian statement that, in civil matters, bishops were subject to civil law. According to the terms of Germanic tenure, bishops received the lands of their churches by royal cession; in return, they owed their kings definite services, and in times of common civil

[11] Rimbert, Vita S. Anskarii, c. 25, MGH SS. II, p. 710.

[12] Astronomus, Vita Ludovici, c. 19, MGH SS. II, p. 616.

[13] E.g., Hincmar of Rheims, De coercendis militum rapinis, Migne PL. 125, 953: "In palatio vestro quod sacrum appellari et esse debet...."

[14] Hincmar, MGH Epp. VIII, fasc. I, no. 141, p. 109.

[15] Concilium Ticinense (855), Mansi XV, 19f. See especially the letter sent by Charles the Bald to Hincmar of Laon on behalf of the clergy and people of that see. Hincmar, LV Capitula, c. 51, Migne PL. 126, 487f.

[16] See the comment of Lupus of Ferrières, MGH Epp. VI, no. 78, p. 71: "Sacris domini regis non sum evocatus. Propterea ad conventum non veni."

[17] E.g., Ratbod of Soissons, Libellus Proclamationis, Migne PL. 119, 749; Hincmar of Rheims, De Praedestinatione, dissertatio posterior, c. 36, Migne PL. 125, 387ff.

necessity the lands of their churches could even be expropriated by the temporal power to provide for general defense.[18] Kings did not impose these services—to counsel,[19] to provide the king with *hospitalitas* on his journeys,[20] to pay taxes,[21] to supply the royal army with soldiers, and to render military service in person[22]—because they held genuine ecclesiastical authority. Rather, they required them as the simple due of an enfeoffed subject to his king.[23] The king was the head of civil society, and bishops, as members of that society, owed him their obedience; but this relationship did not extend to spiritual matters.

In ecclesiastical affairs, one of the most critical powers of the king was that of summoning synods, for those assemblies were the principal *fora* of Church discipline. It was commonly accepted that kings might summon and attend synods and, upon review, give their decrees the sanction of civil law. The authority to convene synods, however, was clearly based upon territorial dominion and the possession of coercive power. Charlemagne, for example, as the *dominus terrae*, sent forth his summons for the Synod of Frankfurt (794) "through the divers provinces subject to the governance of his kingdom."[24] Such

[18] On the general problem, see E. Lesne, *Histoire de la propriété ecclésiastique en France*, v. II, fasc. 2 (Lille and Paris, 1926), pp. 382ff.

[19] Hincmar, Ad Episcopos, c. 32, Migne PL. 125, 978f.

[20] Hincmar, Ep. 27, Migne PL. 126, 183f.

[21] Hincmar, De Fide Carolo Servanda, c. 38, Migne PL. 125, 981.

[22] Hincmar, Ep. 39, Migne PL. 126, 260.

[23] MGH Cap. II, no. 275, c. 3, p. 337; no. 260, c. 10, pp. 273f; no. 300, c. 6, pp. 451f. Hincmar, Pro Lib., Migne PL. 125, 1050f.

[24] Libellus Sacrosyllabus, MGH Conc. I, no. 19 D, pp. 130f. Certainly, one may not question the authority of the royal summons. See above, note 16.

an action was beyond the power of any of his clergy, for metropolitans could legitimately summon synods only for their own provinces. Since the authority of the king extended over all the metropolitan provinces in his realm, he was competent to convene general assemblies from them all, even though his jurisdiction was only temporal. Charles the Bald exercised his royal powers in this way when Archbishop Herard of Tours and Bishop Actard of Nantes, after summoning the ravagers of the ecclesiastical goods of Nantes to juridical hearings without success, prevailed upon him to convene his whole clergy "to amend these affairs."[25]

The presence of kings in synods is likewise to be explained in terms of worldly power: Charles the Bald attended the Synod of Soissons "so that he might demonstrate by his devotion that he was a son of the Church, and also show, by the royal power, if the occasion should arise, that he was her protector."[26] Finally, the power of the king to review synodal decrees affected, not their character as synodal decrees, but their position in the law of the kingdom. The rejected canons of the Synod of Meaux-Paris, to which we have already referred, remained synodal decrees, but without legal effect in the eyes of the civil government.

[25] Chronicon Namnetense, c. 15, ed. R. Merlet (Paris, 1896), pp. 50f.
[26] Conventus Seusonniense (853), c. 1, MGH Cap. II, no. 258, p. 263. Cf. the letter of Nicholas I to the Emperor Michael (865), MGH Epp. VI, no. 88, p. 470: "Dicite, quaesumus, ubinam legistis imperatores antecessores vestros in synodalibus conventibus interfuisse, nisi forsitan in quibus de fide tractatum est, quae universalis est, quae omnium communis est. . . ." At the Synod of Ponthion (876) Charles, interestingly enough, did not attend the hearing of clerical cases. Annales Bertiniani (a. 876), MGH in usum schol., p. 129.

The rôle of the king in his synods, therefore, remained that of the *cooperator Dei*.[27] Like Constantine at Nicea, he might summon councils, sit in them, address his bishops, and confirm their decisions; but judgment remained in the hands of the episcopacy.[28] Sedulius Scottus provides a clear image of this relationship between king and synod. God, he wrote, wished the king to be "His vicar in the governance of His Church," so that he might guard the proper relations of subject and superior. In performing that duty, the king must enable his bishops to perform their offices fully, yielding them the support of his earthly power and allowing them to hold annual synods "where ecclesiastical rights and business may be discussed justly and lawfully."[29] The ruler himself was not to act in any ecclesiastical affairs before receiving the pertinent synodal decisions; for such matters "ought not to be investigated except by synodal assemblies, or resolved except by canonical sanctions."[30] Then, he might fulfill the synodal decrees, following the examples of Valentinian, Constantine, Jovian, and the two Theodosiuses "who pleased the Omnipotent in so far as, through the inspiration of the Lord, they submitted the royal purple, the sceptre, and the height of the imperial dignity to divine precepts and canonical establishments. . . ."[31]

In the trial of clerics, which proceeded in synods, the

[27] Concilium Moguntinum (847), MGH Cap. II, no. 249, p. 184.

[28] See Hinschius, *Decretales Pseudo-Isidorianae*, p. 256, Cassiodorus, Historia Tripartita, I, 20, II, 2, 5, 77, Rufinus, Historia Ecclesiastica I, 2, 6.

[29] *Sedulii Scotti Liber de Rectoribus Christianis*, c. 19, ed. S. Hellmann, pp. 86f.

[30] *Ibid.*, c. II, p. 51.   [31] *Ibid.*, c. II, p. 52.

same denial of jurisdictional hegemony to the temporal ruler is obvious; rather than formulating episcopal sentences, the king executed them. To be sure, the intellectual background of this aspect of dualistic thought was temporal absolutism. The author of the *Gesta* of the bishops of Le Mans recorded that, as an act of vengeance, Pippin the Short arbitrarily blinded Bishop Gauziolenus.[32] But, subsequently, when "wisdom began to increase and canonical authority began to be closely studied, according to the command of Charles the most glorious king of the Franks,"[33] the more formal system of synodal trial was introduced. Charlemagne himself seems never to have violated that system; rather, he appears to have insisted upon it in the purgations of Pope Leo III[34] and Peter of Verdun,[35] and in the deposition of Joseph of Le Mans.[36]

That is not to say that the episcopacy was free from royal censure after the days of Pippin. Pope Leo IV invited the Emperor Louis II to correct his delinquencies;[37] Louis himself, following the example of his grandfather and namesake,[38] instituted an examination into the "habits, conversation, and actions" of his bishops.[39] And Charles the Bald threatened bishops who abused the power of

[32] Gesta Episcoporum Cenomannensium, c. 17, Mabillon, *Analecta*, p. 288.

[33] *Ibid.*

[34] See Wallach, *Alcuin and Charlemagne,* p. 23.

[35] Synodus Francofurdense (794), Capitula, c. 9, MGH Conc. i, no. 19G, p. 167.

[36] Gesta Episcoporum Cenomannensium, c. 20, Mabillon, *Analecta*, p. 291.

[37] MGH Epp. v, no. 40, p. 607.

[38] Capitula de Missis Instruendis (829), MGH Cap. ii, no. 187, pp. 8f.

[39] Concilium Ticinense (855), Mansi xv, 19f.

excommunication with "synodal judgment and [his] royal power."[40] At the same time, jurists of the ninth century were concerned to prevent the temporal ruler from "descending from the imperial throne and ascending the episcopal cathedra" to sit in formal judgment over bishops.[41]

This tendency is well expressed in the letter *De Jure Appellationum*, which Hincmar sent to Pope John VIII in the name of Charles the Bald. With regard to ecclesiastical process, Hincmar represents the king only as the establisher of law. In the midst of a land from which the full reception of Roman and canon law had previously been barred by civil turmoil, he writes, Charlemagne had introduced those laws and guaranteed that the juridical procedure they required be honored in the trials of clerics. Subsequently, observance of these regulations lapsed, and new precepts contradicting the old appeared, specious establishments of the Apostolic See. Attempting to reestablish and confirm the establishments of his grandfather, Charles the Bald himself played the part of a *"conditor legum."*[42] In the actual trial of clergy, however, he claimed no part. To the contrary, he cited Constantine's refusal to judge his bishops. The trial procedure which Hincmar described in his letter is correspondingly that of trial by provincial synods, with the right of appeal to Rome reserved.[43]

[40] Capitulum Septimannicum (844), c. 8, MGH Cap. II, no. 255, pp. 257f. Cf. Capitula Pistensia (869), cc. 6, 7, *ibid.*, no. 275, p. 334; Conventus apud Confluentes (860), *ibid.*, no. 242, pp. 155f; MGH DK III, no. 125, p. 201.

[41] MGH Epp. VI, no. 88, p. 469.

[42] Ep. 32, cc. 1-3, Migne PL. 126, 231ff.

[43] *Ibid.*, cc. 7, 19, cols. 234, 239f.

In the time of Louis the Pious, Charles's father, the canonical trial of bishops by bishops appears to have been uniformly preserved.[44] The bishops of Milan, Cremona, Orléans, and Amiens, who were leaders in the revolt of 830, were all deposed by their fellow bishops, rather than by secular judgment.[45] Ebo of Rheims, who officiated at Louis' penance and excommunication in 834, was also brought before synodal judgment. The records for the earlier depositions are completely insufficient to establish the character Louis assumed in them. In the trial of Ebo, however, the Emperor's part is well known: he presented an accusation against the Archbishop and then, on the request of the accused, withdrew from the hearing. At the conclusion of the process, Ebo presented his written confession to the synod, which, in turn, gave it to Louis.[46] There can certainly be no question that these depositions were political measures, or that they were brought about principally by the temporal power. But the part formally assumed by the Emperor in them was negligible.[47]

Because of the difference in the character of the ruler, the ecclesiastical processes during the reign of Charles the Bald present a more varied picture. In some cases, the integrity of the canonical process was preserved. In the trials of Rothad of Soissons and of the Rheims clerics,

---

[44] See, however, the example of Fortunatus of Grado, who fled from trial "ad palatium." Annales q.d. Einhardi, a. 821, MGH SS. ii, p. 208.

[45] Astronomus, Vita Ludovici, c. 30, MGH SS. i, p. 623; Thegan, Vita Ludovici, c. 37, MGH SS. ii, p. 598.

[46] MGH SS. xiii, pp. 472f.

[47] One may compare the process instituted against bishops loyal to Charles the Bald by Nomenoë in his revolt against the Frankish King. See the Chronicon Namnetense, c. 11, ed. Merlet, pp. 36-39.

which were matters of provincial discipline touching the royal interests but peripherally,[48] Charles was content to allow the canons to take their course. His actions during the trial of Rothad are not fully known. According to the testimony of Rothad himself, the King summoned the synod which tried him, sat in it, and professed that he was utterly bound by its decision.[49] His part in the trial of the Rheims clerics is better defined. The Synod of Soissons (853), which judged the case, met by royal command. Despite the annalistic report that Charles "presided" there,[50] the records of the synod itself affirm that Hincmar of Rheims, Wenilo of Sens, and Almaric of Tours were presidents[51] and that Charles "humbly" took his seat among the bishops to act as a son and defender of the Church.[52] In the course of the hearing, he was merely an auditor and a reviewer of evidence.[53] At the conclusion of the synod, submitting to the laws of the canons,[54] he acted as a recommender of sentence, stating that since the clerics had entered false charges, they should be deprived of communion, according to the letter of canonical authority. Moreover, he added, ecclesiastical law prohibited them from holding Church offices. He asked that "through the indulgence of the synod, a more humane

[48] The fate of Wulfhad, the leader of the Rheims clerics and later Bishop of Bourges, was of considerable interest to Charles. See below, p. 156f.

[49] Libellus Rothadi, Migne PL. 119, 747, 749. Cf. Nicholas I, Sermo, ibid., col. 891.

[50] Annales Bertiniani (a. 853), MGH in usum schol., pp. 42f.

[51] MGH Cap. II, no. 258, p. 264.

[52] Ibid., pp. 263f.

[53] Mansi XIV, Actio II, III, cols. 985f.

[54] Hincmar of Rheims, De Praedestinatione, c. 36, Migne PL. 125, 392.

sentence might be passed allowing them communion." The bishops accepted his proposal; and finally, "with the assent and favor of the most Christian and glorious King, Lord Charles," the acts of the synod were read and were subscribed "by the hands of all." Significantly, Charles himself did not sign the synodal decree.[55]

In civil cases which touched the royal interests more directly, Charles tended to intervene himself rather than to await the course of canonical judgment. The process he instituted against Wenilo of Sens is, of course, an exception to this rule. Wenilo was charged with infidelity and perjury against his King in joining forces with Louis the German when he invaded Charles's lands in 858. Urgently needing the support of his episcopacy, Charles conformed completely to canonical precepts in his attempt to avenge the wrong done him. He entered written charges against the Archbishop at the Synod of Savonnières (859)[56] and chose four bishops as *judices electi* to judge the case.[57] Shortly thereafter, Wenilo reconciled himself to the King, avoiding formal trial. Charles's actions in this case were clearly a bid for ecclesiastical assistance at a time of extraordinary necessity.

The cases of Bishops Samuel of Toulouse and Hincmar of Laon, however, illustrate Charles's preference for civil action against bishops in civil matters. After Charles had assassinated Bernard of Septimania with his own hand, Samuel gave the body of the murdered count liturgical burial in his church and erected a monument to his

[55] Mansi xiv, Actio 8, col. 988.
[56] MGH Cap. ii, no. 299, pp. 448f.
[57] Remigius of Lyon, Wenilo of Rouen, Herard of Tours, and Rudolf of Bourges; Mansi xv, 530.

memory. Charles was enraged, and despite the protests of his bishops that his sentence contravened ecclesiastical law, he enforced his principle that bishops must be tried by royal and lay jurisdiction in matters pertaining to royal privileges and the laws of the kingdom. Samuel was consequently forced before the royal vicar and subjected to his sentence.[58] As already described, Charles made a similar attempt in the process against Hincmar of Laon to subject a bishop to secular jurisdiction without reference to canonical procedure.

These processes, however, do not suggest any arrogation of spiritual authority by Charles. Indeed, his own defense of the action against Samuel specifically defines it as a civil process in a civil matter; and his charges against Hincmar similarly were that he had imperiled the strength of the royal militia by his deprivations and, further, that he had worked actively against public order. The punishment of Samuel did not involve his deposition or touch his spiritual office in any way. Likewise, though they aroused the protests of the canonically learned, the temporal proceedings against Hincmar did not impinge upon his spiritual government. Indeed, in the definitive synodal process which superseded those proceedings and ended in Hincmar's deposition, Charles appeared as one of two principal accusers[59] and as a witness, but he assumed no jurisdictional powers.[60] Ultimately, therefore, he

[58] Narratio de morte Bernardi, Bouquet VII, p. 287.

[59] Hincmar of Rheims was the other.

[60] Cf. his part as an auditor, at Hincmar's own request, in the hearings conducted at Attigny. See Hincmar of Laon, Ep. 8, Migne PL. 124, 1030ff.

did not "sin against his ministry"[61] by presuming to judge and punish the Bishop; and Hincmar was blinded by the civil authorities only after the episcopal order itself had rejected him.

The warrant for the king's instituting civil action against bishops was the same as that for his intervening openly and decisively in episcopal elections: his role as *dominus terrae*. Quite clearly, the bishoprics, which Charlemagne's contemporaries thought lay in the power of God and the king,[62] continued to be so conceived under his successors. Indeed, so firmly established was the royal privilege to participate in episcopal accessions that even Hincmar of Rheims, whose strong championship of free and canonical elections is well known, found it necessary to apologize to Louis the German for having ordained Bertulf of Trier without his consent; he had not acted, he wrote, "in contempt of you or with infidelity toward you."[63]

There was no question that the spiritual ministry of the episcopacy was bestowed, not by secular action, but through the sacramental consecration, and that consequently the assumption of pastoral government depended

[61] Hincmar of Rheims, Schedula, c. 24, Mansi xiv, 617.

[62] See the Monk of St. Gall, Gesta Caroli, i, 5, MGH SS. ii, p. 733.

[63] Ep. 41, Migne PL. 126, 262. Charles's appointment of Bertulf to Trier was clearly both a reward for Bertulf's relative, Adventius of Metz, who had secured Lotharingia for Charles at the death of Lothaire II (869), and a measure to establish his own authority in the disputed lands. See Flodoard, Historia Remensis Ecclesiae III, 21, MGH SS. xiii, p. 516, and the Gesta Trevirorum, c. 27, MGH SS. viii, p. 165. His attempt to secure Cologne by a similar installation failed. See below, pp. 154ff. In the division of the middle kingdom (870), both Trier and Cologne fell to Louis the German. MGH Cap. ii, no. 251, p. 193.

ultimately upon the offices of spiritual rather than temporal princes.[64] On the other hand, the character of bishops as sharers in the royal ministry, as territorial governors responsible for services in the temporal as well as the spiritual *respublica*,[65] permitted kings to oversee their inception of government by ordering the election, reviewing its results, and investing the *electus* with the temporalities of the see.[66] Thus secularly conceived, the royal nomination of bishops might bring one "to the height of the episcopal title," but not to the full exercise of the episcopal office; joint and corroborative offices of the Church were still required. The royal action, therefore, remained only one component of the episcopal accession, and its union with the sacramental offices was an expres-

[64] See Hincmar of Rheims, Ep. 33, c. 4, Migne PL. 126, 248: "Et Odacrus invasor vacantis ecclesiae . . . per saecularem potestatem prius res et facultatem ipsius ecclesiae vacantis obtinuit, ut saltu quoquomodo ad altitudinem episcopalis nominis perveniret et sacerdos non esse, sed dici tantummodo inaniter concupivit. Non attendens, quia sic ab ipso Christo summo pontifice ac rege regum sunt distincta potestatum officia ut spiritalis actio a carnalibus distaret incursibus et militantes Deo minime se negotiis saecularibus implicarent, ac vicissim non illi rebus divinis praesidere viderentur, qui essent negotiis saecularibus implicati." See also Hincmar's, LV Capitula, c. 16, Migne PL. 126, 337: "per cujus manus impositionem Dei judicio te in illa sede residere cognosco." The order issued Lupus of Châlons by Charles the Bald for the administration of sacraments in the pastorless diocese of Rheims does not necessarily imply spiritual administration on the part of the king. Flodoard III, 11, MGH SS. XIII, p. 486.

[65] Cf. the letter of the Synod of Fismes to Louis III, Hincmar of Rheims, Ep. 19, Migne PL. 126, 110; and the letters of the church of Sens to Hilduin and the Empress Judith (829/9). MGH Epp. V, no. 13, pp. 285ff.

[66] See G. Ehrenforth, "Hinkmar von Rheims und Ludwig III von Westfranken," ZfKG, 44 (1925), pp. 65ff.

sion of the "*foedus concordiae*" between kingship and episcopacy to which we shall return.[67]

Numerous justifications were offered for the nomination to a spiritual office by the secular power. Charlemagne saw in it the implementation of the divine will;[68] and Florus of Lyon saw the establishment of peace and harmony between the *potestas mundana* and the episcopacy.[69] A more fundamental justification, however, was offered by the position of the king as the *princeps terrae*.[70] One of the Carolingian formulae commanding the ordination of a bishop states this position unequivocably: "Since after God, the government of all earthly things [*cuncta terrena*] remains in the royal power, it behooves us to take sound counsel to the end that men who clearly appear worthy of governing the places of the saints be established guardians over them. . . ."[71] The writings of the most dedicated champions of ecclesiastical liberties affirm the same standpoint. Hincmar of Rheims, for example, wrote

[67] The words occur in the letter of Wenilo of Sens to Amulo of Lyons, cited above, which was written in the year of the Cologne agreement, or shortly after. MGH Epp. vi, no. 81, p. 73: "ut cum eo tale foedus concordiae ineatis, ut ubicumque ecclesiasticae utilitati in portione regni divinitus sibi collata vestrae auctoritatis dispositione in re tanta cupit [Charles] consulere, unanimitate vestri consensus continuo adiuvetur."

[68] E. Munding ed., *Texte und Arbeiten herausgegeben durch die Erzabtei Beuron*, I, Abt. Heft 6 (Beuron, 1920), p. 4.

[69] De electionibus episcoporum, c. 4, Migne PL. 119, 13. But Florus adds, "Unde graviter quilibet princeps delinquit si hoc suo beneficio largiri posse existimat, quod sola divina gratia dispensat. . . ."

[70] Hincmar of Rheims, Ad Episcopos, Admonitio Altera, c. 5, Migne PL. 125, 1010, and the related passage in De Ordine Palatii, c. 9, MGH Cap. ii, p. 520.

[71] Marculfi Formul. Aev. Karol., no. 14. MGH Formulae, p. 119.

that episcopacies and monasteries were *beneficia regis*, which God had commended to the king "to defend and to commend to suitable managers [*dispensatoribus*]."[72] And Wala, while maintaining that "Christ should hold the goods of churches like another commonwealth" distinct from the temporal *respublica*, affirmed that the office of the king was to see that those goods be committed to faithful and wise administrators.[73]

From this fundamental justification, three others derived: royal intervention was warranted in answering the spiritual need of a widowed church, in the event of an unsuccessful election which imperiled the welfare of a church, and in circumstances of public necessity. The Synod of Paris (829) imposed upon Louis the Pious the duty of seeing that "good pastors and rectors" were established in the episcopal office, for the preservation of ecclesiastical vigor and the avoidance of spiritual detriment to the Church.[74] And the Synod of Thionville (844), followed by that of Meaux-Paris (845/6) similarly urged the Frankish kings to consider the dangers in store for a church without a bishop and to name bishops for vacant

---

[72] "De ecclesiis et capellis," ed. W. Gundlach, *ZfKG*, 10 (1899), p. 108. Cf. the letter of the Synod of Fismes to Louis III, Migne PL. 126, 110: "Facultates ecclesiae, quas ad defendendum et tuendum vobis Dominus *commendavit*," and similar passages in Pro Lib., Migne PL. 125, 1054, and Ep. 21, Migne PL. 126, 128. When Louis III pressed this concept to its logical conclusion, however, he came into conflict with the archbishop. See Hincmar's letter to the king, Ep. 19, c. 4, Migne PL. 126, 112: "Sunt qui dicunt, ut audivi, quia res ecclesiasticae episcopiorum in vestra sint potestate ut cuicunque volueritis eas donetis." Ehrenforth, "Hinkmar von Rheims und Ludwig III von Westfranken," p. 83, has "episcoporum."

[73] Epitaphium Arsenii, II, 2, MGH SS. II, p. 548.

[74] MGH Cap., II, no. 196, c. 2, p. 48.

churches "without delay and according to canonical authority."[75] The Synod of Ver (844), concerned by the disorders suffered by the churches of Orléans and Rheims during their episcopal vacancies, petitioned Charles to permit the accession of Hagius, "a priest of your palace," to the first see, as he had already been ordained by Wenilo of Sens, and to allow the vacant church at Rheims to proceed to an election.[76]

During the reign of Louis the Pious, *visitatores* announced to episcopal electors the power of the King to nominate in the event of an unsuccessful election. If the electors should advance someone who had connived to gain the see through wickedness, the *visitatores* would not consent to his election, but would report their action to the Emperor. "And he will be able to give [the episcopacy] under whatever circumstances [*undecumque*] and to whatever cleric he wishes, without any danger, and with the license of the canons."[77] In the same tenor, the Synod of Valence (855), protesting against the accession of "*indiscussi et inexaminati scientiaeque literarum pene ignari*" to the episcopacy, declared that if it became necessary to prevent the installation of such a person, the metropolitan over the see in question should "approach

[75] MGH Cap. ii, no. 227, c. 2, p. 114. The Synod of Meaux-Paris, however, deleted sections of this chapter, among them the important phrase "aut episcopos a Deo datos et" from the petition that "sine dilatione iuxta auctoritatem canonicam aut episcopos a Deo datos et a vobis regulariter designatos et gratia sancti Spiritus consecratos accipiant (ecclesiae)." *Ibid.*, no. 293, c. 8, p. 399.

[76] MGH Cap. ii, no. 291, c. 10, p. 385. Cf. the letters of Pope Leo IV on behalf of the Church of Rieti: MGH Epp. v, nos. 19, 21, pp. 597f.

[77] MGH Formulae, no. 1, p. 551.

the Imperial Clemency . . . so that the glorious Emperor may honor the Church of God with a worthy minister."[78]

This power was of course capable of broad interpretation, allowing as it did for the judgment of the validity of the election and the qualifications of the *electus* by the king. Two sources from the reign of Louis the German, however, indicate that it was not unconditional. In a form letter preserved in the St. Gall collection, Louis claimed the right of nomination only should canonical procedure fail to advance a worthy candidate: If the electors should promote a person disqualified by servile origin, civil commitments, or personal failings, "we may exert the royal power, and, according to the wisdom divinely given us, establish a bishop for the Church of God who will both know how to rule the Church canonically and suffice to bear [*occurrere*] our service. . . ."[79] The second source shows how this principle was put into practice.

Regino of Prüm records that Louis observed these qualifications in the elevation of Willebert of Cologne. On the death of Lothaire II, Charles the Bald attempted to secure his claims in Lotharingia by establishing his cleric Hilduin in the vacant see of Cologne. Without resorting to canonical election, Charles had most of the people of Cologne render oaths of fealty to Hilduin, and

[78] Mansi xv, 7, c. 7. Cf. Hincmar of Rheims, De Praedestinatione, c. 36, Migne PL. 125, 383. The accession of Ebo is an example of the use of this power. See the letter of Charles the Bald to Nicholas I, Migne PL. 124, 871f. Hincmar of Rheims, however, represents the position that the power to reject unsuitable candidates lay initially with the metropolitan and his suffragans. See Ep. 39, Migne PL. 126, 260.

[79] MGH Formulae, no. 1, p. 396.

commanded the Bishop of Tongres to ordain him to the Title of St. Peter in Cologne. Before Hilduin could be duly consecrated and installed, Louis the German, also claiming the lands of his dead nephew, sent Archbishop Leutbert of Mainz and five other bishops to Cologne to contravene the "election" of Hilduin and to consecrate another in the vacant see. To the representatives of the clergy and people of Cologne, whom he met at Touzy, Leutbert announced "on behalf of the King that they should take counsel among themselves and elect a prelate from their own flock at once, and that he had been sent to consecrate immediately whomever they should decide by common counsel was to be advanced." To the objections of the legates that Hilduin already claimed their fealty, Leutbert answered: "If you spurn the election granted you by the King, the King has the discretion and the power to give you as bishop whomever he wishes. Know in all certainty that in three days you will have a bishop other than Hilduin." Under these conditions, the envoys elected Willebert, and Leutbert together with his fellow bishops consecrated him and surreptitiously installed him in Cologne. Charles was forced to withdraw the claims of Hilduin.[80] Louis' own statement that "we have canonically elected and advanced [Hilduin] to the aforesaid metropolis with the consent of the clergy and people" suggests that he assumed a more decisive role in Willebert's choice than Regino gives him. In any event, he did not formally prefer his choice to the exclusion of canonical election; and he claimed as warrant for his interven-

[80] Regino of Prüm, Chronicon (a. 869), MGH SS. I, pp. 581f.

tion, not spiritual powers, but "secular terror and discipline."[81]

The justification of royal nomination in circumstances of public necessity was most clearly stated in a letter by Wenilo of Sens to Amulo of Lyon. Requesting Amulo to consecrate two royal nominees, Wenilo urged his episcopal colleague in the name of Charles the Bald not to think it boldness that bishops, especially those for the more distinguished sees, should be chosen from the royal palace. For in the time of Pippin, Pope Zacharias had taken cognizance of "the necessity of this realm" and had consented to such intervention "lest through the simplicity of pontiffs" temporal adversity should harm the Church.[82]

Necessity, which also authorized the temporal power to assume control over the disposition of ecclesiastical property,[83] was specifically the defense Charles the Bald offered for his wholly arbitrary promotion of Wulfhad to the see of Bourges. While the validity of Wulfhad's clerical orders was still in question before the Synod of Soissons (866), Charles committed the see of Bourges to him and secured his almost clandestine consecration.[84] Charles's statement that he had acted upon the counsel of all his bishops and vassals and of the archdiocese of Bourges was patently gratuitous.[85] But there is no reason to doubt his

[81] MGH Epp. vi, no. 6, p. 248.   [82] *Ibid.*, no. 81, p. 73.

[83] See the Concilium Aquisgranense (836), MGH Conc. ii, no. 56, p. 722, and the Synodus apud Theodonis Villam (844), MGH Cap. ii, no. 227, c. 5, p. 115.

[84] Annales Bertiniani (866), MGH in usum schol., p. 83. Since he was an enemy of Wulfhad, Hincmar's comments are perhaps uncharitable. Cf. the letter of Charles the Bald to Nicholas I, Ep. 4, Migne PL. 124, 870.

[85] Mansi xv, 708f.

affirmation that Wulfhad had been installed "under the urgent necessity of this kingdom." Bourges, he wrote, was much afflicted by pagan invasions, the crimes of "wicked Christians," and the "unstable character of its people." Moreover, Charles's son, Charles of Provence, to whom the government of that area had been committed, was young and epileptic and required strong counsellors. Wulfhad, who had proven himself vigorous, upright, and faithful in all things advantageous to the elder Charles, and who had been the tutor of the younger, was therefore advanced for the repression of civil disorder and for the defense of the royal interests.[86]

No warrant for nominating to the episcopacy, therefore, attributed spiritual powers to the Carolingian king or allowed him to claim headship of the Church as later rulers did. Indeed, the grounds of his intervention in episcopal accessions were all rigorously construed in terms of his secular office as territorial lord and defender of order, and warranted by the requirements of "secular terror and discipline."

Further, the manner in which temporalities were conferred indicates the purely secular character of the king's action. Of the four instances in the period under review in which the temporalities were apparently bestowed symbolically *per baculum*, two throw very little light on the meaning of the royal action. Indeed, the confused nature of the text in which the earliest of those instances is recorded allows one to wonder whether the investiture of Aldricus of Le Mans was performed by Archbishop

[86] Ep. 5, Migne PL. 124, 874.

Landramnus of Tours with his own staff in conjunction
with another constitutive act by Louis the Pious, or by
Louis alone, using the Archbishop's stave.[87] Again, a later
chronicler merely records, without exposition, that Charles
the Fat conferred the pastoral staff upon Herifred *cum
summa reverentia* and sent him to be ordained Bishop of
Auxerre.[88]

The two other instances (both pertaining to the see of
Hamburg) are more illuminating. The anonymous
biographer of St. Rimbert relates that Rimbert was
elected unanimously by clergy and people, and was then
conducted by Bishop Theodoric of Minden and Abbot
Adalgar of Corbie to the presence of Louis the German.
"And, received honorably by him, he acquired the *do-
minium* of the bishopric through the usual commendation
of the pontifical stave." His consecration followed.[89] The
second instance is the accession of Rimbert's successor,
Adalgar. Rimbert was allowed to install Adalgar as his
successor; his choice was confirmed by canonical election,
and *per manus acceptionem* Adalgar became "the king's
man."[90] After Rimbert's death, Adalgar received the pas-

[87] Gesta Aldrici, c. 1, MGH SS. xv, p. 309.

[88] Gesta Episcoporum Antissiodorensium, 1, 41, Migne PL. 138, 255.

[89] MGH SS. ii, c. 11, p. 770. Cf. *ibid.*, c. 21, p. 774: "unde aput
gloriosum primo regem Hludowicum, quo commodante episcopatum
accepit." See also Regino's description of the attempted installation of
Hilduin at Cologne (Chronicon, a. 869, MGH SS. i, p. 582): "omnes-
que pene manibus datis eius dominationem susceptam haberent (the
people of Cologne) . . . ."

[90] Vita S. Rimberti, c. 21, MGH SS. ii, p. 774. The biographer adds,
"ac sancta synodo haec omnia roborante." Lesne, *Histoire de la propriété
ecclésiastique en France*, v. II, p. 83 n. 3, does not mention the investiture of Adalgar.

toral stave from Louis the German.[91] The investiture of Adalgar obviously confirmed arrangements concluded before Rimbert died; that is, his right to the episcopal succession and his liege obligations toward the King. The words with which Rimbert's biographer described his subject's investiture support the conclusion that these instances of commendation were fundamentally examples of feudal submission rather than of the transmission of spiritual authority. Adam of Bremen's additional remarks that Rimbert and Adalgar received pallia from Rome emphasize that point.[92] In any case, investiture *per baculum* by the king was not an integral part of the rite of consecration, as was the bestowal of the pastoral stave by bishops;[93] a wholly non-sacramental act, it occurred rather in a place other than that of the episcopal consecration and some days or weeks before (as in the cases of Aldricus,

[91] Adam of Bremen, Gesta Hammaburg. Eccles. Pontiff. I, 37, MGH SS. VII, p. 298.

[92] *Ibid.*, I, 37, 48, pp. 297, 301.

[93] On the bestowal of ring and staff by consecrating bishops, see Hincmar of Rheims, Epp. 29, 38, Migne PL. 126, 188, 257f. The lack of a sacramental character in the royal bestowal of temporalities, at least as performed by Louis the German, is indicated in the letter of Gozbald of Würzburg to Pope Gregory IV, which asks ecclesiastical confirmation of the King's cession. The letter is printed by E. Dümmler, "Karolingische Miscellen," in *Forschungen zur deutschen Geschichte*, 6 (1866), pp. 121f. See also O. Meyer, "Zum Rechte der Besetzung der bischöflichen Stühle im Karolingerreich," *ZfRG.* K. A., 24 (1935), pp. 331ff. The investiture with temporalities was part of nomination to the episcopacy, which corresponded to canonical election (cf. the letter of Hincmar of Rheims to his suffragans, Ep. 33, Migne PL. 126, 245f, where the clergy and people of a widowed church are to elect the "futurus episcopus," and the Gesta Episcoporum Antissiodensium, I, 40, Migne PL. 138, 253, "Uribaldus . . . a Ludowico gloriosisimo ac semper Augusto [actually, Louis the Stammerer] huic civitati futurus directus est episcopus. . . .)." See above, note 64.

Herifred, and Rimbert) or after the consecration (as in the case of Adalgar).

Temporal subjection of the *electus* to his king marked other episcopal accessions not known to have been marked by formal investiture *per baculum*. There is no evidence for such acts of submission before the death of Louis the Pious, though the acceptance of Otger by the clergy and people of Mainz suggests a liege relationship between Otger and Louis. "We know," they wrote, "that he is faithful, well-disposed, humbly subject, and duly favorable toward you in all things. . . ."[94] The institution, however, is evident under Louis' descendants. We have already alluded to the commendations of Rimbert and Adalgar to Louis the German. It is not clear whether Herifred, a cleric employed in the palace of Charles the Fat and therefore probably bound by oath to Charles before his accession to Auxerre, assumed a further obligation at his advancement. Under the West Frankish rulers at the end of the century, one knows that Louis the Stammerer rewarded the *famulatus* of his cleric Wibald with the see of Auxerre,[95] and that his son, Louis III, attempted to establish his "vassal," Odacre, in Beauvais.[96]

The practice, however, is most fully attested for the reign of Charles the Bald. Wulfhad of Bourges was "*fidelis ministerialis noster*";[97] the church of Chartres was "commended" to Burchard;[98] and the Breton bishops deposed by Nomenoë during his insurrection are suggestively re-

[94] MGH Epp. v, no. 18, p. 325.
[95] Gesta Episcoporum Antissiodorensium, 1, 40, Migne PL. 138, 253.
[96] Ep. 19, c. 8, Migne PL. 126, 115f.
[97] Charles the Bald to Nicholas I, Ep. 3, Migne PL. 124, 867.
[98] Visio Audradi, Bouquet vii, p. 291.

corded to have been preferred *"manu Francorum regia,"* and to have been deposed "for their fidelity" to Charles.[99] The complaint Charles entered against Wenilo of Sens in 859 is particularly important as it indicates that the "free clerics" attached to the royal service (from among whom, as we have already observed, bishops were regularly chosen) were usually bound to the king by an oath of fealty. Charles explicitly states that Wenilo was so bound and adds the example of "his relative, my cleric named Tottold, who commended himself to me and promised his fidelity by oath."[100] From this evidence, we may infer that other prelates who were advanced from the royal service—for example, Willebert of Châlons-sur-Marne,[101] Aeneas of Paris,[102] Bernus (nominated to Autun), and Gottschalk of Chalons[103]—were similarly obligated.

The text of their supposed oaths is unfortunately unknown; but it was probably similar to the one Charles required of Hincmar of Laon, which was, in essence, rendered Louis the Stammerer in 877 by all his bishops: "I [promise] to be faithful and obedient now and hereafter to my lord *senior* Charles, according to my ministry, as a man ought rightly to be faithful to his lord and a bishop to his king."[104] Documents deriving from the ad-

[99] Chronicon Namnetense, ed. Merlet, cc. 11, 12, pp. 32f, 40f. Cf. Gesta Aldrici, MGH SS. xv, p. 326.

[100] Liber Proclamationis, cc. 1, 13, MGH Cap. ii, no. 300, pp. 451ff. See also the letter of Remigius of Lyon to Wulfhad, Mansi xv, 530: "Imputat [Charles] quod cum jurejurando fidei a vobis accepto Senonum praesulatum vobis largitus sit. . . ."

[101] Mansi xv, 861ff.

[102] MGH Epp. vi, no. 98, pp. 86f.

[103] *Ibid.*, no. 81, pp. 73f.

[104] Hincmar of Rheims, Schedula c. 10, Migne PL. 126, 575f.

vancement of Bernarius as Bishop of Grenoble illustrate the
high value which Charles set on the terms of fealty represented by this oath. At this time the three rulers, Louis
II, Lothaire II, and Charles, issued separate letters to Archbishop Ado of Vienne for Bernarius's consecration. In the
letters of Lothaire II, whose cleric Bernarius was, the
electus is called "our vassal" (*fidelis noster*);[105] and in that
of Louis II, he is referred to as "*eundem clericum nobis
fore fidelem.*"[106] The absence of these terms, with their
suggestions of feudal relationships, from Charles's letter
may explain the distinct contrast between it and the other
two commands. Louis and Lothaire both crisply commanded the fulfillment of the consecration. But Charles
urged caution, admonishing Ado to examine the candidate
before his ordination carefully so as to see that he was
canonically qualified for the episcopacy, and he warned
the prelate that negligence in that duty would incur
divine censure.[107]

Neither the oaths of episcopal *electi*, therefore, nor the
actions of the kings who received them impute a sacerdotal
or quasi-sacerdotal character to the royal functions. They
rather suggest only the conclusion of the relationship between vassal and lord, between the recipient of a benefice
and its grantor; and one may conclude that they represent
merely the exercise of those offices of defense and territorial

[105] MGH Epp. vi, no. 23, 2, p. 176.

[106] *Ibid.*, no. 23, 1, p. 176.

[107] *Ibid.*, no. 23, 3, p. 176. "Vos enim sictis inde satis canonicam
auctoritatem: quicquid enim ibi neglectum fuerit, vobis sine dubio a
Domino imputabitur, qui disponere et ordinare, etiamsi dilectus nepos
noster in alia intendens praeterit, ne populus Dei pastori carens ober-
raret. . . ."

dominion commonly ascribed to kings in the Carolingian period.

Despite its purely temporal basis, the exercise of the royal competence in clerical affairs has been interpreted as "royal sacerdotalism." Particularly, this interpretation has been applied to the summoning of synods by the king and his participation in them, to his actions in the trial and condemnation of clerics, to his intervention in episcopal elections, and to his legislation in ecclesiastical matters. Yet, whatever their effects in the "spiritual republic," these actions were not construed as manifestations of spiritual authority on the part of the ruler. Rather, they were seen as an effluence of his roles as defender of law and as the lord of the earth. Even his more patently arbitrary actions —as, for example, the completely uncanonical nomination to a vacant episcopacy—were justified as being necessary for the welfare of the state. The only powers delegated to the king in respect of synods were to summon them and to review and confirm their decrees with a view toward giving them effect in temporal courts. In the trial and condemnation of clerics, he held no canonical authority, and in the processes themselves he was able to assume only the part of the accuser, not that of the judge. His power to intervene in episcopal elections derived, not from a spiritual embellishment of the royal office, but from the dual character of the episcopacy as an office of temporal as well as spiritual responsibility and from the dominion of the king over ecclesiastical as well as secular lands. Finally, "legislation" in ecclesiastical affairs, as well as in temporal, was not an autonomous or arbitrary act on the part of the king. Indeed, the king did not legislate at all;

rather, he promulgated laws to which he and his subjects had agreed in common, according to the necessities of the time. Equally important, the religious legislation of the Carolingians did not purport to be canons or articles of faith, but merely confirmations or corroborations of canons. Neither his actions in ecclesiastical matters, therefore, nor the legal grounds for them brought to the Frankish king any but the temporal qualities attributed to him by contemporary theorists. Without attributing a priestly or episcopal character to the king, dualists could well ascribe to him such great powers in ecclesiastical affairs that dualistic theory might, under some circumstances, warrant the reality of royal monism.

3. Response to the Challenge: The Conflict of Charles the Bald and Hincmar of Laon

The trial of Bishop Hincmar of Laon, instructive as it is in the dimension of ecclesiology, is of equal value in the area of Church-State relations, for it illustrates both the purely secular warrant for royal intervention in ecclesiastical affairs and, more broadly, the tensions within the political dualism of Frankish jurists. According to that dualistic view, as we have suggested, the Church and the temporal commonwealth were institutionally discrete. In terms of ecclesiastical law, temporal authorities were *potestates exterae*, as regards legislation and discipline within the Church; they were excluded from the juridical affairs of the episcopacy. At the same time, however, they were charged with the sacred duty of preserving the vigor of the canons through the chastisement of the wicked. Once put to the test, as it was in the process against Hincmar of Laon, the practical impossibilities of this legistic structure became apparent.

Its implicit contradictions can be seen most clearly in the context of the historical events which we have already described. On the petition of the younger Hincmar, Charles the Bald restored the villa Pauliacus to the church of Laon, from which it had long been alienated. Within six months, Charles petitioned Hincmar to cede tenure of that same property to him; and, contrary to the canons, the Bishop executed this realienation of ecclesiastical property without counsel of his metropolitan and his fellow bishops. Charles in turn bestowed the holding anew upon his vassal "Norman" (or "a Northman"?), who had held them before the restitution to Laon.[1] Soon afterwards, Hincmar resumed control over these holdings by violence,[2] and "Norman's" complaint was joined to earlier accusations that the Bishop had expelled other vassals of Charles from their benefices without just cause.[3] According to the younger Hincmar, Charles had commended a considerable number of men to him, and at the same time, had promised to give his see additional resources for their future support. These promises, however, went unfulfilled; and the resources of Laon were so heavily taxed that Hincmar could not continue to render Charles *temporale obsequium* by supporting the men commended to him and at the same time provide for the necessities of his see. The Bishop maintained, in addition, that Charles granted goods of his

[1] Migne PL. 126, 504. Cf. Mansi xvi, 650f.
[2] Migne PL. 126, 502, 504.   [3] *Ibid.*

church to men who refused any service to Laon, and who in fact worked actively to the detriment of himself and his church. Therefore, when the men of the King claimed from Hincmar the benefices Charles had bestowed upon them in his diocese, he declared himself unable to satisfy their demands.[4]

Hincmar resorted militantly to the position that "right and the laws of the canons command by precept that the bishop may order the property of his Church by dispensing it to whomever he may wish and however he wishes." This claim, which brought him into conflict with his uncle,[5] led also to the intrusion of the *potestas extera* into the system of ecclesiastical legal theory.

The trial of Hincmar shows that the dualist principles that royal and episcopal government were independent of each other, and that bishops were subject to kings in temporal matters, were incompatible and that the right, or even the obligation, of the king to punish all criminals subverted the doctrine of the legal integrity of the clergy. Hincmar was charged with one major crime: that he had perjured himself of his oath of loyalty to his King through disobedience, calumny, and rebellion. If, as the dualists maintained, the bishop must be subject to his king in civil matters, might the temporal power violate the legal privileges of the episcopacy in prosecuting a seditious prelate? The King's oaths to preserve the *lex canonica*[6] and the

---

[4] Hincmar of Laon to Hincmar of Rheims, Ep. 8, Migne PL. 124, 1027ff; Hincmar of Rheims to Hincmar of Laon, Migne PL. 126, 494.

[5] Migne PL. 126, 495, cc. 4, 5.

[6] Pro Lib., Migne PL. 125, 1041; Synodus Bellovacensis, MGH Cap. ii, no. 292, pp. 387f.

"law and justice suitable to each man,"[7] which Hincmar of Rheims cited in defense of his exclusion of temporal power from ecclesiastical processes, implied, not a passive attitude toward the canons, but the active defense of their vigor; and the royal duty of protecting the goods of the Church allowed the entrance of that power into ecclesiastical affairs when the interests of the Church were in danger.

Charles moved according to these principles, reasoning that the purpose of the royal office was to maintain civil order and to punish malefactors and that, as one guilty of political crimes, Hincmar was liable to civil punishment. On the complaints of his dispossessed vassals, Charles summoned and at length brought Hincmar to judgment before a secular court; for he was still determined, just as he had been thirty years earlier in the trial of Bishop Samuel of Toulouse, "that he would not suffer bishops to be examined outside of the royal and lay jurisdiction in matters pertaining to regalian rights and to the laws of the kingdom."[8] To Charles, this forceful intervention seemed appropriate, for the younger Hincmar had perjured himself of two oaths "to be faithful and obedient now and from this hour onwards to [his] lord *senior* Charles, according to [his] ministry, as a man ought rightly to be faithful to his lord and a bishop, to his king."[9]

[7] Migne PL. 125, 1042; Promissio Carisiacensis, MGH Cap. ii, no. 261, p. 296. Despite the involvement in uncanonical proceedings of all parties to the alienation of the villa Pauliacus, only Hincmar of Laon suffered censure for it. See Schedula, cc. 15, 27, Migne PL. 126, 585, 611, and Hincmar of Rheims, Ep. 27, Migne PL. 126, 184.

[8] Bouquet, vii, p. 287.

[9] See *supra* p. 161, and Schedula, c. 10, Migne PL. 126, 525f, and F. Lot, "Le serment de fidèlité à l'époque franque," *Revue Belge de philologie et d'histoire*, 12 (1933), p. 579.

Moreover, Charles believed that his sacred office as the *corrector iniquorum* required him to act "to the correction" of the "insolent bishop."[10]

The acts by which Hincmar perjured himself, indeed, necessitated the taking of civil measures against him. It was, Charles said, a new and dreadful thing "for a bishop in a peaceful realm to stand with a military force against a king to prevent his execution of the laws."[11] In forcibly obstructing Charles's enquiries into his vassals' protests against Hincmar, and consequently in hindering the performance of the royal duty "to do justice according to the law,"[12] Hincmar exceeded the canonical limits of his office. By this "sedition," moreover, he transgressed the secular component of the *lex ecclesiastica*, "those laws for which the Church petitioned the princes of the earth to serve its own purposes."[13] Those laws prescribed the punishment of civil violence by the secular power, and, on a higher level, patristic authority charged that power with punishing the wicked as a sacred duty. Accordingly, the Bishop's own wrongdoing invited the legitimate intervention of the *potestas extera* against him,[14] "for it is the part of the royal power to repel enemies and to suppress or punish the seditious."[15]

The other charges against the Bishop of Laon were likewise civil in nature: that, before the Roman Curia, he had

---

[10] Acta Synodi, c. 6, Mansi xvi, 666f. Cf. Annales Bertiniani (a. 871), "Hincmaris Laudunensis nomine tantum episcopum, homo insolentiae singularis."

[11] Proclamatio Regis, c. 6, Mansi xvi, 581.

[12] Acta Synodi, c. 4, col. 662f.

[13] Responsa Episcoporum, c. 11, Mansi xvi, 655f.

[14] Cf. *ibid.*, c. 3, col. 645f.

[15] *Ibid.*, col. 646.

calumniously accused his King of usurping ecclesiastical properties;[16] that he had conspired with Lothaire II to desert his own King;[17] and that he had abetted men unfaithful to Charles to escape his judgment "so that they could not be bound according to the laws or freed or judged by law."[18] The Bishop had risen against the King, the guarantor of property tenure and individual rights;[19] in doing so, he had sinned against Christ Himself.[20] Therefore, according to Roman law and the canons, he had deprived himself of office as a perjurer,[21] calumniator, and rebel, and he had also made himself liable to punishment by the temporal power.

The grounds for royal intervention against Hincmar deserve particular attention for they define the temporal concept of office which motivated Charles in that process and in the others which we have already mentioned. In the letters he sent Pope Hadrian II concerning Hincmar's trial, Charles stated most lucidly the dualistic concepts which directed his actions.

When the King took action to correct "that insolent Bishop,"[22] Hincmar secretly entered charges against him before the papal court. Hadrian II thereupon sent a vigorously worded letter to Charles in which he

[16] *Ibid.*, cc. 6-8, col. 651-653.

[17] *Ibid.*, cc. 3, 11, col. 645f, 655f; Acta Synodi, c. 6. cols. 666f.

[18] Responsa, c. 12, *ibid.*, col. 656.

[19] *Ibid.*, c. 10, col. 654f. See Augustine, Tractatus VI in Johannis Evangelium (Migne PL. 35, 1437), cited also in this controversy in Pro Lib., Migne PL. 125, 1052, and Ep. 8, Charles the Bald to Hadrian II, Migne PL. 124, 886.

[20] Responsa, c. 12, Mansi XVI, 656.

[21] *Ibid.*, c. 10, col. 654f.

[22] Acta Synodi, c. 6, *ibid.*, 667.

denounced the Frankish king as a "perjurer, tyrant, and usurper of ecclesiastical property," threatened him with excommunication, commanded him to enable Hincmar to take his case personally to Rome, and committed the lands of the church of Laon to Charles for safekeeping until the conclusion of the case.[23]

Two concepts predominate in Charles's strong response: the separateness of the royal from the episcopal office, and the purely temporal warrant for the exercise of the royal ministry. His accession to the royal office, wrote Charles, was "through the grace of God, by paternal and avital succession";[24] and the example of Saul and David together with other scriptural precepts demanded reverence toward the king even should he be "already cast aside by the Lord."[25] Thus tacitly denying the power of the clergy to create and to remove kings, Charles further drew a fine distinction between the powers of temporal and spiritual offices. As Pope Gelasius I wrote, Christ so ordered the world that Christian princes required the services of pontiffs to attain eternal life, and pontiffs required those of secular officials in temporal affairs. Neither should the prince intrude into sacred matters nor the bishop into worldly. "'Every pontiff,' said the Apostle, 'taken from among men, is established for the sake of men in things pertaining to God, that he may offer both gifts and sacrifices for sins (Hebr. 5:1)' that is, not only for his people,

[23] The text of Charles's letter shows that this letter of Hadrian was more strongly worded than that of 868, in which the holdings of Laon were also committed to the care of Charles and Hincmar; MGH Epp. VI, no. 14, 15, pp. 715f.

[24] Ep. 8, Migne PL. 124, 881.

[25] *Ibid.*, col. 883.

but also for his own sins, since he is set about with infirmity. And the office of the king is to dispatch the business of the kingdom. . . ."[26]

In the terms of this division between the competence of the royal office, which extended to all worldly affairs, and that of the episcopacy, which extended primarily to the sacramental, Hadrian had assumed for himself undue powers by presuming to judge a case of perjury and infidelity to a king.[27] "According to [his] royal ministry,"[28] Charles professed himself willing to submit to the priesthood in its sacramental functions;[29] but should Hadrian continue to disparage the royal ministry and to "usurp" functions rightly pertaining to it,[30] he would force Charles to intervene against him.[31]

In Charles's eyes, Hadrian had discredited the royal office in each of its major roles: legislative, administrative, and punitive. By transgressing the limits of his office, he had dishonored the emperors who, as *conditores legum*, had established ecclesiastical privileges, and particularly those of the Roman Church;[32] by commanding Charles to act as the guardian of the ecclesiastical properties of Laon, he had vilified the role of the king as "lord of the earth"; and by ordering him to support Hincmar in his journey to Rome, he had subverted the duties of the king as the punisher of the wicked, the executor of law, and the guardian of civil order.

For Charles, the last two points were of the greatest importance: the essence of the royal office consisted in

[26] *Ibid.*, 892.　　[27] Ep. 7, *ibid.*, 879.
[28] Ep. 8, *ibid.*, 894.　　　[29] *Ibid.*, 891.　　　[30] Ep. 7, col. 877.
[31] Ep. 8, col. 894ff.　　[32] *Ibid.*, 891.

territorial dominance and in punition. That Hadrian should appoint Charles as trustee of the Laon holdings aroused the King, "since we kings of the Franks, born of a royal house, have hitherto been reckoned, not overseers for bishops, but lords of the earth." Though Leo of Bourges had said that kings and emperors had granted juridical privileges to bishops, he had not said that secular rulers were the bailiffs of bishops; and St. Augustine affirmed that property tenure was guaranteed by the legal functions of kings, not that by episcopal command kings were village functionaries. Christ himself rendered His tax to Caesar, "and the Apostle wished kings to be served, he wished kings to be honored, and not cast under foot."[33] In his eyes, Hincmar had been regularly and synodically condemned.[34] The Bishop's deposition was complete; and Hadrian's commission of the lands of his church to Charles, "until he may return to his own," was futile. For Charles, as the *dominus terrae*, assured Hadrian, "that as long as God preserves us in the governance of the kingdom, Hincmar will not have the bishopric of Laon under his rule."[35]

In criminal processes, the royal duties to preserve law and to repress civil disorder were closely related to territorial dominion. Popes, Charles wrote, had admonished "the lords and princes of the earth" to preserve imperial and royal laws "unchanged and unbroken." The obliga-

---

[33] Ep. 7, col. 878, Ep. 8, col. 886. Cf. Gesta Episcoporum Cenomannensium, c. 17, Mabillon, *Analecta*, p. 289, where Abraham the *"vicedominus"* of the dead Bishop Gauziolenus supervises the temporalities of Le Mans, and MGH Epp. v, no. 9, p. 113.

[34] Ep. 8, col. 889.

[35] Ep. 7, col. 880.

tion to discharge this duty was reinforced by the fact that bishops and even popes had bound themselves to observe the civil law.[36] Hincmar had conspired "against the public security and quiet"[37] even after his condemnation and consequently had required the intervention of the royal power against him. Hadrian's command that the process be renewed in Rome and that Charles assist Hincmar in attending it perverted the royal ministry. It is surely a new sort of law, the King declared, that a ruler must yield his support to a profligate malefactor; for no law established in the accepted manners ever "commanded me to be a fosterer of a condemned and anathematized criminal. For I am a king established by God, set off from others by a two-edged sword—the punisher of evildoers and the defender of the innocent—for the punishment of the wicked and for the praise of them that do well, as the Apostle says."[38] It is the part of the royal ministry, not to assist the criminous and seditious, but rather to see that the vigor of the laws is preserved. Scriptural, patristic, and legal authority appointed the king as the avenger of wrongdoing to whom bishops were subjects in matters of public discipline.[39] And should even the Bishop of Rome persist in wrongful judgments and violations of the limits of his office, he would force the temporal power to move his deposition.[40]

[36] Ep. 8, cols. 891f.
[37] *Ibid.*, 886. The phrase, "contra custodiam publicam et quietem," is taken from Cod. Th. XVI, 2, 3, 5, cited in Ep. 8, col. 890.
[38] *Ibid.*, 889. Cf. col. 886.   [39] *Ibid.*, 893.
[40] Charles refers obliquely to the process in the Fifth Ecumenical Council against Theodore, and cites the letter of Gregory I to the Eastern Patriarchs, Reg. v, 41, MGH Epp. Regestrum Gregorii, I, pp. 331ff.

Far from conceiving of his office as subordinate to episcopal direction or as a part of the jurisdictional apparatus of the clergy, Charles maintained rather the fundamental separation of the civil office from ecclesiastical ministrations; indeed, he imagined the superiority of the royal over the episcopal ministry in matters of civil order and generally in all temporal affairs. His accession to the kingship was assured "by the grace of God" and hereditary succession; should he prove unworthy of his office, he was still to be regarded with the honor and reverence due the divinely established king and not to be reviled or censured. The same integrity of the kingship prevailed also in the royal functions. For Charles explicitly stated that the kings were the "lords of the earth" not the subalterns of bishops; and he threatened to exercise his punitive ministry against even the Bishop of Rome, the head of the episcopal order. In these royal letters, as in the writings of the Fathers, the area of the king's activities remained the temporal world; the warrant for his functions, the public security; his instrument, armed punishment. All these elements and the earthly dominance upon which they were based were beyond the episcopal ministry— whose hegemony in spiritual affairs was, however, uncontested—and peculiar to the office of the *dominus terrae*.

Aroused by the report of Charles's civil process against his nephew,[41] Hincmar of Rheims composed a series of three memoranda to the King in which, from the point of view of the *lex ecclesiastica*, the royal power is an extralegal element. Charles, he wrote, had exceeded his minis-

[41] Hincmar of Rheims to Hadrian II, Migne PL. 126, 643. The reference is to Hincmar of Laon's Schedula, Migne PL. 124, 1025ff.

try;[42] he had demeaned the royal office by his irreverence toward the Church of God;[43] and thus he fell liable to the punishment which Uzziah brought upon himself when "he stretched forth the hand of presumption against the priestly ministry."[44] Since the time of Constantine, secular rulers had not even legislated *de episcopis*;[45] moreover, the Christian Roman emperors—including the Arian Constantius II—and, after them, the Frankish rulers, had upheld the legislative and juridical integrity of the clergy by law and had bound their own princely power to obey and honor that integrity.[46] Consequently, it was not the place of a king publicly to recriminate against a bishop, to summon him before a secular court, to sequester the revenues of his Church, and to muster laymen and clerics holding benefices of the accused before the royal presence.[47] The property of the Church was committed to the bishop to be administered, and to the royal power only to be defended.[48] Royal intervention in the administrative affairs of the clergy—including its juridical matters —violated the legal integrity of the clergy, fulfilling the Scriptural prediction, " 'And the priest shall be as the people,' set apart by no discrete law from the commons."[49]

[42] Pro Lib., Migne PL. 125, 1050.

[43] *Ibid.*, col. 1053.   [44] *Ibid.*, col. 1058.

[45] Cf. LV Capitula, c. 20, Migne PL. 126, 354f. Of course, Hincmar himself referred to Book XVI of the Theodosian Code, "De Episcopis et Ecclesiis," and even to imperial laws concerning the deposition of bishops. See Charles the Bald to Hadrian II, Ep. 8, Migne PL. 124, 890. Cod. Th. XVI, 2, 35 (Br. Th. XVI, 1, 4) and Julian, Constitutiones, CXV, c. 17.

[46] Pro Lib., Migne PL. 125, 1038.

[47] *Ibid.*, col. 1036f, 1055f.

[48] *Ibid.*, col. 1051.

[49] *Ibid.*, col. 1037. Isaiah 14:2.

The views of the elder Hincmar prevailed, and Charles's challenge to the institutional integrity of the episcopacy was put down. But the tension within Frankish political thought was clearly drawn. Although, as the Archbishop strongly reminded him, Charles had given the priesthood solemn oaths to maintain the laws of his predecessors, the Christian Roman emperors and the Frankish kings, and to preserve the force of the canons,[50] and although divine authority maintained that he was "a king established by God, set off from others by a two-edged sword,"[51] Charles was not allowed to vindicate his office against the Bishop of Laon until the Synod of Touzy had formally condemned him. The King acted only as accuser in the trial itself; and even then, although the synod noted the words of Leo I that "the attestation of a Christian prince is sufficient," it took the corroborative testimony of bishops.[52] The King's oaths and even portions of the Roman laws included in the *lex ecclesiastica* warranted his intervention; the civil nature of Hincmar's crimes invited his proceeding against him; but Hincmar, though criminous, was set apart from the commons by "a discrete law" until his self-deposition was acknowledged by synodal act. Charles could not inflict the *castigatio regis* upon him before that formalization.[53] While bishops were subject to Scriptural

[50] Pro Lib., Migne PL. 125, 1040, and Charles the Bald to Hadrian II, Ep. 8, Migne PL. 124, 893, "non est nostri ministerii reum . . . dirigere. . . ."

[51] Ep. cit., col. 889. 1 Peter 2:14.

[52] Leo I, Ep. 135 to Anatolius (Jaffé 509 [287]), Migne PL. 54, 1095, cited Acta Synodi, c. 6, Mansi xvi, 667.

[53] Cf. Hincmar of Rheims to Hincmar of Laon, Migne PL. 126, 506: "omnes episcopi qui in eisdem synodis fuerunt liquido sciunt quoniam

and apostolic admonitions to humble themselves before the civil authority "obedient unto death,"[54] they (and their inferior clergy) were responsible only to the distinct law of their order, to the law of the "one kingdom, one Church," which they composed. Therefore, they belonged to two kingdoms in practice—they were "exalted with temporal as well as spiritual honor"[55]—but their duties and legal commitments were uniformly construed with reference to the law of only one. Though a bishop might enter well-defined juristic relationships with the *potestates exterae,* his violation of those relationships was reviewable only by the members of the episcopal order. The immediate challenge to the prevalent Frankish ecclesiological position had, therefore, been successfully met; but the greater problems of consistency within Frankish political thought had not approached resolution.

---

cum de tuis insolentiis increpabaris timnes regulare judicium vel regis castigationem licentiam eundi Romam petebas." The sequestration of the Bishop from his Church "jussione domni nostri regis" in 869 was clearly a joint action of episcopacy and the royal power. See the letter of Hincmar of Rheims to the clergy of Laon, Migne PL. 126, 532f, and Schrörs, *Hinkmar, Erzbishof von Reims,* p. 329. The legal basis for this action is unclear, but in view of the property disputes in which the Bishop of Laon was involved, it may have been Paulus, Sent., v, 38 int., printed in G. Haenel, *Leges Visigothorum* (Leipzig, 1848), p. 442. Gratian ii, c. ii, qu. vi, c. 26.

[54] Responsa, c. 11, Mansi xvi, 656.
[55] Hincmar of Rheims to Hincmar of Laon, Migne PL. 126, 511.

CHAPTER V · AN ATTEMPTED ENTENTE

1. Covenant and Coronation

A s THE process against Hincmar of Laon indicates, the dualistic position was endangered not only by the external forces of papal and royal monism but also by an internal tension. Frankish political thought contained one primary inconsistency: in dividing the government of the world between two distinct and integral powers, dualistic thought provided no grounds on which those two powers might be coordinated. In the ninth century, the coronation rite expressed liturgically the resolution by contract which that age attempted; for the two principal elements of the coronation order, the profession by the king and his unction and investiture by bishops, constituted the text and the ratification of a covenant between the temporal and the spiritual power. But the rite was not yet considered the incorporation of the secular ruler into the administrative machinery of the Church: it was not termed an "episcopal" ordination,[1] nor was the king ordained "to the government of the Church."[2]

Although much has been written about the Carolingian rite of coronation as a liturgical ceremony, its legal aspects have, on the whole, been neglected. Still, out of these earlier studies have come two general assumptions which

[1] Cf. Wido of Osnabrück, Liber de controversia Hildebrandi et Heinrici, MGH Ldl. 1, p. 467.

[2] Ordo Cencius 11, "ad regendam ecclesiam" (Ordo Romanus x11), c. 49, Migne PL. 78, 1102.

must be modified before we can approach the legal aspects of the ceremony: it is persistently maintained, first, that, in the coronation, churchmen actually bestowed the royal power and/or, second, that the ritual unction in coronation changed the character of the king and made of him a "priest-king." These points contradict both Frankish thought concerning the transmission of royal power and Frankish ecclesiology, which on balance argued toward the institutional separation of the Church from the civil state and toward the exclusively secular character of the king. Reexamination of the evidence indicates that these assumptions are not well founded and that the ceremony did not infer any new powers or change the character of the royal office or the man who held it; the evidence indicates rather that the ceremony of coronation attempted to preserve the principles of dualism by establishing a contractual relationship between the king and the episcopacy as equal parties.

✠

Unlike the tenth, the ninth century was not an age when the king who held the royal office without episcopal benediction could be compared to a hiltless sword;[3] the disposition of the royal title and the symbols of kingly office was not the prerogative of the spiritual power. Before

---

[3] See the Vita Oudalrici, c. 3, MGH SS. IV, pp. 388f, on the refusal of Henry I to be anointed: ". . . et enses duos valde heriles, unum cum capulo et alterum sine capulo, sibi ostendentem, et sic loquentem: 'Dic regi Heinrico, ille ensis qui est sine capulo significat regem qui sine benedictione pontificali regnum tenebit, capulatus autem qui benedictione divina regni tenebit gubernacula.' " See P. E. Schramm, "Die Krönung in Deutschland bis zum Beginn des Salischen Hauses," ZfRG, K. A. 24 (1935), p. 190.

the beginning of the tenth century, indeed, the royal unction is not definitely known at all in East Francia; it is clearly attested only in the West and for the imperial office. In the *Vita Walae*, Lothaire I is described as saying that his imperial consecration merely confirmed the bestowal of office he had already received from his father, and that it added only the quality of personal sanctification to the attributes of power and to the title he had entered into five years earlier.[4] Even Hincmar of Rheims, who once wrote that Charles the Bald had come to the royal office "by episcopal benediction and unction more than by worldly power,"[5] did not question the titles of other rulers who had not been ritually anointed and crowned.

In fact, several grounds of accession far different from sacring and crowning were readily acknowledged. The Emperor Louis II, himself twice anointed, once as King of the Lombards and again as Emperor, wrote that some of his imperial predecessors had assumed their office through the acclamation of senate and people, others through military force, and still others through the favor of women.[6] Hincmar similarly maintained that, while the

[4] Epitaphium Arsenii, 1, 17, MGH SS. ii, p. 564: "ut essem socius et consors non minus sanctificatione quam potestate et nomine." The statement of Pope John VIII that he had anointed Charles the Bald, "ita ut quod ipse [Christ] possidet per naturam, iste [Charles] consequeretur per gratiam" (Bouquet vii, no. 50, p. 695), pertains to the mystical rather than to the administrative qualities of the royal office. Cf. Gelasius I, Tractatus iv, 2 (Thiel, *Epistolae Romanorum Pontificum*, p. 568), as quoted by Hincmar of Rheims, Admonitio Altera, c. 1, Migne PL. 125, col. 1007. See E. H. Kantorowicz, "Deus per Naturam, Deus per Gratiam," *Harvard Theological Review*, 45 (1952), pp. 257ff, and *The King's Two Bodies*, pp. 48ff.

[5] Pro Lib., Migne PL. 125, 1040.

[6] MGH Epp. vii, p. 389.

accession might be accomplished by divine appointment, it could be assured just as well through military force, hereditary succession, or even tyrannical usurpation.[7]

Carolingian political history shows that these means— primarily election and inheritance—and not consecration, were the grounds of effectual succession. Pippin, the first of the dynasty, came to the throne "by the election of the whole kingdom of Francia."[8] After him, election generally yielded to the regular hereditary succession which existed in the East and West Frankish kingdoms and in Lotharingia until the extinction of the line. Louis the Pious was restored "to the throne of his fathers"[9] in 834. Louis the German maintained that his kingdom had been conferred upon him *"divinitus et paterno jure"*;[10] and Charles the Bald,[11] Louis II,[12] and Lothaire II[13] defended their titles

[7] De Divortio, Responsio VI, Migne PL. 125, 758. In his Instructio ad Ludowicum, Hincmar attributes all Carolingian accessions before the time of writing to inheritance and the power of the Frankish nobles. See M. Bloch, *Les rois thaumaturges* (Paris, 1924), pp. 65, 71, 225.

[8] Fredegarii Scholastici Chronicon, Continuatio III, MGH SS. Rer. Mer., II, p. 182, c. 33.

[9] Vita Ludovici, c. 44, MGH SS. II, p. 599. Cf. Annales Bertiniani (a. 835), MGH SS. in usum schol., p. 10: "depositus paterno hereditarioque regno et honore et regio nomine fuerat." See also the letter of Pope Paul I to Charlemagne and Carloman (761/6), MGH Epp. III, no. 35, p. 542: "Unde unam quidem huius divini muneris [i.e., the royal office] gratiam possidetis ex genere et aliam fruimini ex opere." Cf. MGH Cap. I, no. 136, cc. 14, 18, pp. 272f, and MGH Cap. II, no. 194, c. 1, pp. 21f. The Synod of Paris (829) and Jonas of Orléans, however, denied that heredity was in itself a sufficient warrant for succession. MGH Conc. II, no. 50, c. 5, p. 655. *Jonas d'Orléans et son "De institutione regia,"* c. 7, ed. J. Reviron, p. 155.

[10] MGH DL II, no. 26, p. 31.

[11] Charles the Bald to Hadrian II, Ep. 7, Migne PL. 124, 878; Ep. 8, *ibid.*, coll. 881, 886. See also Pope Leo IV's refusal to sanction the establishment of a separate Breton kingdom because it would be "contra fas et patruum statuta quaerere ut regnum Francorum, tam valente

with the same claim. Charles named his son, Louis the Stammerer, King of Aquitaine without any known electoral or sacramental confirmation; later he also ceded his entire kingdom to him by document.[14] Likewise, Charles the Fat granted "the royal dignity" to Louis of Arles, his "adoptive son."[15] However, the elective principle continued to be honored, particularly in the non-Frankish and quite singular instance of imperial accessions. Lothaire I "was created Emperor through the election of the people of the realm of the Romans,"[16] and Charles the Bald acceded by the assent of the Roman clergy, senate, and people.[17] Toward the end of the century, the force of election revived in the Frankish kingdom as well: Louis the Stammerer styled himself "Louis, king by the mercy of the Lord our God and by the election of the people,"[18] and Hincmar of Rheims, casting aside all

---

herede, id est Karolo Calvo, ac nepote Karoli Magni, de potentia sua minueretur." Chronicon Namnetense, c. 11, ed. R. Merlet (Paris, 1896), p. 35.

[12] Hadrian II to the Lotharingian nobles, MGH Epp. VI, no. 19, p. 722, and *passim*.

[13] Hincmar of Rheims, De Divortio Lotharii, Quaestio VI, Migne PL. 125, 756. Lothaire to Nicholas I, MGH Epp. VI, no. 7, p. 218 and passim.

[14] Annales Bertiniani (a. 867), in usum schol., p. 86. See G. Eiten, *Das Unterkönigtum im Reiche der Merovinger und Karolinger* (Heidelberg, 1907), p. 182 n. 5. On the later cession, Synod of Troyes (878), Mansi XVIIA, 356: "praeceptum per quod pater suus Ludovico regnum tradiderat." The Capitulary of Quierzy is clearly meant. See Hincmar of Rheims to Louis the Stammerer, Migne PL. 125, 986, c. 7.

[15] MGH Cap. II, no. 289, p. 377.

[16] Narratio of Adventius of Metz, MGH Epp. VI, no. 5, p. 215.

[17] Bouquet VII, p. 695. Cf. Hadrian II to Charles, MGH Epp. VI, no. 36, p. 745, and the Synod of Ponthion (876), MGH Cap. II, no. 279, p. 348.

[18] Professio Ludovici, MGH Cap. II, no. 283A, p. 364.

thought of accession through "episcopal benediction and unction," reminded Louis III that, "You did not elect me to the prelacy of the Church, but with my fellows and other faithful of God and of your fathers, I elected you to the governance of the kingdom. . . ."[19]

Moreover, Frankish kings and emperors granted the royal title to others and both bestowed and assumed the use of regal insignia without episcopal sanction, a practice approved even by the author of the Donation of Constantine.[20] Charlemagne himself invested Louis the Pious with both the imperial office and the crown, "the sign of Empire";[21] according to one author, he also gave him a sceptre, "as is the custom with emperors."[22] Four years later (817), Louis in turn bestowed the imperial title and

[19] Ep. 20, c. 7, Migne PL. 126, 119. Cf. the address of Charles the Bald to the Lotharingians at his coronation in Metz (869): "vos acclamastis me Dei electione . . . huc advenisse. . . ." MGH Cap. II, no. 276, p. 339. On ep. 20, cf. St. John 15:10.

[20] Hinschius, *Decretales Pseudo-Isidorianae*, p. 253. In describing his transfer of insignia to Pope Sylvester, Ps.-Constantine relates "frigium . . . eius sacratissimo vertici manibus nostris posuimus. . . ."

[21] Annales Bertiniani (a. 835), MGH in usum schol., p. 10: "imperii insigne." See F. Kempf, "Das mittelalterliche Kaisertum." *Vorträge und Forschungen*, III (1956), p. 231. See Appendix B.

[22] S. Abel (B. Simpson ed.), *Jahrbücher des fränkischen Reiches unter Karl dem Grossen*, 2d ed., vol. II (Leipzig, 1883), p. 236 n. Cf. Ermoldus Nigellius, In Honorem Ludovici, II, 11. 68-70, MGH Poet. Lat. II, p. 26: " 'Francis Romuleum nomen habere dedi' / Haec ait [Charlemagne] et capiti gemmis auroque coronam / Inposuit, pignus imperii, sobolis." The apparently similar transmission of royal power by Arnulf to Louis of Arles *per sceptrum* may refer to a ceremony of homage rather than to the transmission of the sceptre as a token of office. MGH Cap. II, no. 289, p. 377. See H. Mitteis, *Lehnrecht und Staatsgewalt* (Weimar, 1933), p. 213. One may compare Charles the Bald's conferral of royal prerogatives on Herespogius "datis manibus." Annales Bertiniani (a. 851), MGH in usum schol., p. 41.

crown upon his son Lothaire; and in 838, elevating Charles the Bald to the kingship, he "girded him with manly arms (that is, with the sword) and imposed the royal crown upon his head."[23] Ermoldus Nigellius reports, in addition, that Louis sent King Harald of Denmark, together with other gifts, a gold-bedecked sword and "a handsome crown" (*corona insignis*).[24] In the fashion of his father, Charles the Bald conferred the use of the royal crown and vesture for his lifetime to Herespogius, the Breton leader.[25] And after his own imperial coronation, he is recorded to have had a crown set on the head of Count Boso of Vienne and to have "ordered that he be called king, so that [Charles] might himself appear to be master of kings in the style of former emperors."[26] Further, Hincmar reports

[23] Astronomus, Vita Ludovici, c. 59, MGH SS. II, p. 643: "Filium suum Karolum armis virilibus, id est ense, cinxit, corona regali caput insignivit." See also Nithard, Historiae, I, 6, MGH in usum schol., p. 10.

[24] Ermoldus Nigellius, In Honorem Ludovici, IV, 376-382, MGH Poet. Lat. II, p. 68.

[25] The Annales Bertiniani (c. 851), MGH in usum schol., p. 47 record only the "regalia indumenta," and the "paternae potestatis ditio"; but the Chronicle of Nantes adds, "coronam regiam Herispogio viventi concessit habere." The author of the chronicle of Nantes records that Salomon "arripiensque coronam capiti suo imposuit," perhaps merely a figure of speech. Chronicon Namnetense, cc. 13, 15, ed. Merlet, pp. 43f, 50. Cf. the Vita S. Corwoionis, c. 11, Mabillon, Acta SS. O.S.B., saec. IV, pt. 2, p. 201: "Salomon rex appellatur, non quod re vera esset sed quia circulo aureo et purpura, concessione Caroli Augusti utebatur. . . ." To this statement, one commentator (*ibid.*) added that Charles granted Salomon, "circulum aureum et purpuram et archiepiscopalem sedem et proprium nomisma et omnia regi convenientia."

[26] Regino of Prüm, Chronicon (a. 877), MGH SS. I, p. 589: At the marriage of Boso, Charles's brother-in-law, and his niece, Irmingard, "Dedit insuper eidem Bosoni Provinciam et corona in vertice capitis imposita, eum regem appellari iussit, ut more priscorum imperatorum regibus videretur dominari." See H. Hirsch, "Das Recht der Königer-

that after Charles's death, the Empress Richildis brought to his successor the royal raiment, a staff of gold and jewels, "and the sword called 'the sword of St. Peter,' through which she was to invest him with the kingdom."[27] Secular coronations (perhaps simple crown-wearings) are attributed to Odo (888) and Rudolf of Burgundy (888).[28] Finally, though none of the East Frankish kings appears to have been anointed before the imperial coronation of

---

hebung durch Kaiser und Papst im hohen Mittelalter," *Festschrift E. Heymann*, v. 1 (Weimar, 1940), p. 215. Regino, however, was by no means partial to Charles; and since none of the sources deriving from Boso's coronation mention this ceremony, the corona which Boso actually received may have been a coronet rather than a royal diadem. Cf. the Chronicon Namnetense, c. 11, ed. Merlet, p. 357. Rejecting Nomenoë's bid for the kingship, Pope Leo IV "Nomenoio concessit ut dux super populum Brittaniae fieret, et circulum aureum, sicut alii duces in festis diebus deferret." In chapter 12 of the same chronicle (p. 40), one reads that Nomenoë had assumed the "coronam regalem" in rebellion against Charles the Bald. The life of St. Corwin (Mabillon, *Acta SS. O.S.B.*, saec. IV, pt. 2, p. 200) maintains that Nomenoë sent a crown to Leo and is silent about the "circulum aureum." One may perhaps compare the symbolic crown wearings which took place when Arnulf sent Odo a crown in 888 (Annales Xantenses, MGH in usum schol., p. 67), and when the Emperor Louis II received a crown (but not a new unction) from Pope Hadrian II (Annales Bertiniani, a. 872, p. 120). On the earlier instance, see Schramm, "Krönung," p. 194, and W. Schlesinger, "Kaiser Arnulf und die Entstehung des deutschen Staates und Volkes," *Hist. Zt.* 163 (1941), p. 466 n. 2.

[27] Annales Bertiniani (a. 877), MGH in usum schol., p. 138.

[28] Regino of Prüm, Chronicon (a. 888), MGH SS. 1, p. 598: "coronam sibi imposuit regemque se appellari iussit." Since Rudolf is also reported to have undergone the royal sacring (Annales Vedastini, MGH in usum schol., a. 888, p. 64), Regino's statement may be more rhetorical than historical. Cf. the address of Hincmar at the coronation of Charles the Bald in 869: "Et quia, ut in historiis sacris legimus, reges, quando regna obtinuerunt, singulorum regnorum sibi diademata imposuerunt. . . ." MGH Cap. 11, no. 276, pp. 340f. Hincmar continues to accept this Scriptural record as a precedent for Charles's coronation by his bishops.

Charles the Fat (881),[29] Louis the German is known to have used the royal *baculus*,[30] and, if one may trust the vision of Audradus Modicus, he also bore the crown and the sceptre.[31]

In the early Carolingian period, anointing did not necessarily attend the purely secular bestowal of the regalia and the royal title. And later, even when the conclusion of a compact with the episcopacy had become requisite for accession to the throne, the episcopal offices did not change their confirmative nature in the coronation ritual for a truly creative one.

The standard of coordination between the kingship and the episcopacy remained the juristic assurances given and received by each, and not the reception of sacramental offices by the temporal power at the hands of the spiritual. One has only to compare Hincmar of Rheims's careful remarks to his kings with those to his rebellious nephew to understand the difference between the consecration of power in the royal coronation and its bestowal in the episcopal ordination. For though the consecrator of kings, the Archbishop never wrote to them, as he did to his suffragan, that he had advanced them to their offices, or that they had acceded through the imposition of his

---

[29] Cf. C. Erdmann, "Der ungesalbte König," *Deutsches Archiv*, 2 (1938), pp. 314ff. On the possibility that Louis the German was "consecrated" in Regensburg, in 826, see Kantorowicz, *Laudes Regiae*, p. 106, n. 135.

[30] Annales Bertiniani (a. 849), MGH in usum schol., p. 37. Cf. Charlemagne's bestowal upon Tassilio of a "baculus in cujus capite similitudo hominis erat sculptum." Mitteis, *Lehnrecht und Staatsgewalt*, p. 202.

[31] Bouquet VII, p. 290.

hands.[32] His well-known admonition to Charles the Bald to remember that he had "followed upon the royal dignity by an episcopal, a spiritual, unction and benediction more than by earthly power," simply prefaces the more fundamental admonition that Charles honor his promises to the episcopacy which had twice anointed him as king, once over Aquitaine and, later, over Lorraine.[33] In his letters to Louis III, Hincmar likewise related the King's oath and his consecration,[34] at the same time leaving no doubt that his very election as well as his coronation depended upon the oath;[35] he did not, however, maintain that the election and the consecration were related. Finally, when Louis III, justifying his intervention in episcopal election, wrote to Hincmar, "We are joined together so that I, a king, and you, a bishop of God, may discharge a worthy ministry in divine and human functions," Hincmar replied by urging him to recall the profession he made on the day of his consecration and to limit his actions to the temporal offices he had then assumed.[36] The Archbishop maintained, not that the king had received or strengthened his title through episcopal benediction, but, rather, that his person had been consecrated to the Lord,[37] on his promise

[32] Migne PL. 126, 337, 437. The very different views of Pope John VIII are shown in his statement, "dignitatem imperialem per impositionem manuum nostrarum adeptus est." Migne PL. 126, 658.

[33] Migne PL. 125, 1040. See A. Wilmart, "Une catéchèse baptismale du IXe siècle," *Revue Bénédictine*, 40 (1928), p. 199, c. 11.

[34] Ep. 19, c. 5, Ep. 20, c. 7. Migne PL. 126, 112f, 119.

[35] Ep. 20, c. 7, *ibid*.

[36] Ep. 19, c. 5, *ibid*., col. 112f.

[37] Hincmar of Rheims at the coronation of Charles the Bald in 869: "Domino consecretur." MGH Cap. II, no. 276, p. 341. Cf. Ps.-Anacletus, Ep. II, c. 23, "Aaron . . . hoc ritu consecrabitur Domino." Hinschius, *Decretales Pseudo-Isidorianae*, p. 78. The words "consecrabitur Domino"

to exercise in an agreed manner the power he already possessed.

The sermon of Pope John VIII on the imperial coronation of Charles the Bald is strongly at variance with these views. Partly because succession to the Roman principate was not bound by inheritance, partly because Charles's position was compromised by his rivalry with Louis the German for the Empire and partly because of his own hierocratic outlook, John confidently affirmed that he had advanced Charles "*ad Imperii Romani sceptra*" by virtue of sacramental unction "through the hands of priests of God and the office of His ministers."[38]

Despite this precedent, the order for the royal coronation of Louis the Stammerer two years after his father's imperial accession held to the more conservative Frankish position. As if to make the nature of their office explicit, Louis' consecrators borrowed the formula said at the imposition of the crown in the 869 coronation of Charles the Bald and interpolated the words "*per officium nostrae beneditionis*" into it. In contrast to the position Pope John had taken in 876, however, this revised version does not say that the crown was bestowed by priestly benediction;

---

do not occur in the Scriptural basis for this passage. See also the letter of Pope Stephen III to Charlemagne and Carloman, MGH Epp. III, no. 45, p. 561: "Recordamini et considerate, quia oleo sancto uncti per manus vicarii beati Petri caelesti benedictione estis sanctificati. . . ."

[38] Bouquet VII, pp. 695f. See A. Kröner, *Wahl und Krönung der deutschen Kaiser und Könige in Italien (Lombardei)* (Freiburg i. B., 1901), pp. 155f, and K. Knauer, *Karls des Kahlen Kaiserkrönung und seine Schenkung an die römischen Kurie* (Coburg, 1909), p. 70. Cf. E. Sperling, *Studien zur Geschichte der Kaiserkrönung und—Weihe* (Stuttgart, 1918), p. 28: "Karl der Kahle lässt sich 869 in der Stephanskirche in Metz von Bischof Hinkmar von Reims zum Kaiser salben und kronen. . . ."

it rather prays that God may crown the King with a crown of glory and justice and with the fruits of steadfastness to the end that he may ultimately come "to the crown of the eternal kingdom . . . through the office of our benediction."[39] In their own eyes, then, Louis' consecrators had merely sanctified his person to the discharge of duties specified in the royal oath.

Thus, neither the royal title nor the use of the royal insignia depended upon the sacramental offices of the Church. Instead, they were bestowed in their fullness by purely secular offices, and they retained the non-sacramental character of their origin.

If the evidence does not support the hypothesis that the royal power was bestowed in the rite of coronation, neither does it sustain the interpretation that the coronation unction imparted a "hierocratic," "quasi-hierocratic," or "theocratic" character to the king. Anointing did not alter the king's personal or official character as a temporal figure or extend his authority to the canonical government of the Church. Without conferring any powers, it merely consecrated the person of the king to perform the precise temporal duties he had assumed by oath.[40] The episcopal rôle in the coronation was, in fact, nothing other

[39] MGH Cap. II, no. 304, p. 461. See also Hincmar, Vita S. Remigii, c. 33, MGH SS. Rer. Mer., v. III, p. 340, "Nam domuit fera corda animo pius [Remigius], ore profusus / Sicambre gentis, *regia sceptra sacrans.*" Cf. Libellus adversus Wenilonem, c. 3, MGH Cap. II, no. 300, p. 451: "sine audientia et iudicio episcoporum quorum ministerio in regem sum consecratus."

[40] MGH Cap. II, no. 276 A, B, pp. 339, 341. See Kern, *Gottesgnadentum und Widerstandrecht,* ed. Buchner, p. 308 and *passim.*

than the ratification of the oath which the king had just rendered, a public sign that the Church received the promise of the king, and, in turn, bestowed upon him its solemn benediction and whatever spiritual benefits and protection derived from it.

This episcopal ratification consisted of two distinct parts, the bestowal of insignia and the royal unction. Of these two acts, the investiture of the king with his insignia by the consecrating prelates is the less critical to the thesis of quasi-hierocratic kingship, and it need only be mentioned that this part of the coronation ritual seems to have been designed to express dramatically the obligation of the king to govern *"pro vice Christi qua fungeris,"*[41] to rule "according to the will of God." In the thought of Pope John VIII, for example, the unction was specifically administered so that, through its sacramental qualities, God might "establish [the Emperor] prince of His people in the likeness [*ad imitationem*] of the true King, Christ, His Son, our Lord";[42] and Frankish bishops maintained that it brought to the king, as *christus Domini*, the special protection of the heavenly King, the *Christus christorum.*[43] The symbols bestowed in the Frankish coronation also appear to have been designedly imitative of the figure of Christ when he was mockingly acclaimed as king before His crucifixion: "And they stripped him," according to the Gospel of St. Matthew, "and put on him a scarlet robe. And when they had platted a crown of thorns, they put it upon his head, and a reed in his right hand: and they

[41] Smaragdus, Via Regia, c. 18, Migne PL. 102, 958.
[42] Bouquet VII, no. 50, p. 695.
[43] Epistola Carisiacensis, c. 15, MGH Cap. II, no. 297, p. 439.

bowed the knee before him and mocked him, saying, 'Hail, the King of the Jews!' " (Matt. 27:28f. Cf. Mark 15:17-19, Luke 19:2f.) Yet, whether they were conferred by bishops in liturgical coronations or assumed in another way, the three principal royal insigna—the crown, "the token of victory," the sceptre, "the rod of virtue," and the purple robe—had their proper symbolic meanings.[44] More critical to the quasi-hierocratic interpretation is the ritual unction which set liturgical coronation apart from purely temporal forms of accession.

The quasi-sacerdotal unction of the king did not extend his powers beyond the purely secular duties assumed in the royal oath; it did not impart any spiritual authority to him. Some scholars have argued to the contrary, claiming as support similarities between the *ordines* for episcopal consecration and royal (or imperial) coronation; and, to be sure, the purpose of the royal benediction and unction, like that of the episcopal, was to consecrate, and the sequence of actions in one ceremony paralleled that in the other. In both imperial and episcopal rituals (perhaps in royal coronations as well),[45] the benedictions were trans-

[44] See Appendix B.

[45] On imperial coronations, see the letter of Louis II, MGH Epp. vii, pp. 387f, "set Dei nutu et ecclesiae judicio summique praesulis impositionem et unctionem manus obtinuit [Charlemagne]. . . ." and Ermoldus Nigellius, In Honorem Ludovici, ii, 439f: "Haec ait [Stephen IV] et celerans sese convertit ad ipsum [Louis the Pious]. Atque manu tangit verticis alta sacra. . . ." The papal benediction follows in Ermoldus, MGH Poet. Lat. ii, pp. 36f. The equation between "impositio-unctio" in the letter of Louis II and "benedictio-unctio" in a letter of Nicholas I, which likewise concerns the imperial coronation (MGH Epp. vi, no. 34, p. 305), suggests the possibility of a similar equation for the royal coronation. This possibility is also allowed by the similarity between the coronation unction and the baptismal unction,

mitted by the imposition of hands; all unctions were performed with the sacred chrism;[46] and in both the royal
and the episcopal *ordines*, consecrators invoked the bestowal of the Spirit of Wisdom, the infusion of "the oil
of the grace of Thy Holy Spirit whence Thou hast anointed priests, kings, prophets, and martyrs."[47]

Neither of the royal *ordines* which survive complete—
those for the coronation of Charles the Bald at Metz (869)
and for that of Louis the Stammerer at Compiègne (877)[48]
—prescribe anointing of the king's hands. In this, they
correspond exactly with the order for episcopal consecration current in ninth-century Gaul, which directed unction

---

where the imposition of hands was a fundamental act. See Ratramnus,
Contra Graecorum opposita, IV, 7, Migne PL. 121, 333: "Quae forma
servatur hodieque in ecclesia, ut baptizentur quidem fideles per pres-
byteros, gratia vero Spiritus sancti per impositionem manuum tribuatur
ab episcopis quod tunc fit, quando frontes baptizatorum chrismate
sancto liniuntur ab episcopis." Cf. Pope John VIII's reference to the
conferral of grace upon Charles the Bald at the latter's imperial consecration through the act of unction, "per sacerdotum Dei manus."
Bouquet VII, pp. 695f. Anglo-Saxon influence may be indicated in Adam-
nan's Vita Columbae III, 5, 2d ed. J. T. Fowler (London, 1895),
pp. 167f, where Columba ordains Aiden "in regem" and "in regnum
. . . imponensque manum super caput eius ordinans benedixit."

[46] For the king, see MGH Cap. II, no. 297, c. 15, p. 439. For the
bishop, *ibid*. Hincmar of Rheims to Adventius of Metz, Ep. 29, Migne
PL. 126, 187; and the Visio Audradi, c. 12; L. Traube, "O Roma nobilis.
Philologische Untersuchungen aus dem Mittelalter," *Abhandlungen der
philos.-philolog. Klasse der kgl. Bayerischen Akademie der Wissenschaften*, 19 (1892), p. 386. See also M. Andrieu, "Le sacre épiscopal
d'après Hincmar de Reims," *Revue d'histoire ecclésiastique*, 48 (1953), pp.
22-73. A. Guinan, "The Christian Concept of Kingship as Manifested
in the Liturgy of the Western Church," *Harvard Theological Review*,
49 (1956), pp. 219-269, does not discuss mediaeval coronation ordines.

[47] MGH Cap. II, nos. 302, 304, pp. 457, 461. See also H. Lietzmann
ed., *Das Sacramentarium Gregorianum* (Münster, 1921), 2, 9, p. 6.

[48] MGH Cap. II, nos. 302, 304, pp. 456ff, 461f.

of the head, without reference to the hands.[49] A ninth-century benedictionary from Freising, however, prescribes unction of the hands in the royal anointing, without reference to the head, a parallel to the consecration of priests. According to the benedictionary, the following prayer was to be said at the moment of anointing: "*Unquantur manus istae de oleo sanctificato, unde uncti fuerunt reges et profetae, sicut unxit Samuhel David in regem, ut sis benedictus et constitutus rex in regno isto, quod dedit tibi dominus deus tuus super populum hunc ad regendum vel gubernandum.*"[50]

Clearly, two different coronation *ordines* are represented —one from the West Frankish kingdom, patterned on the episcopal consecration, and the other from the East Frankish, patterned on the priestly ordination. Yet, the non-priestly character of the ritual, obvious in both *ordines*, is particularly so in the West Frankish *ordo*; for, by not introducing the anointing of hands, the ritual did not bestow upon the king the priestly character with which bishops-elect approached their consecrations. The hands of bishops had been anointed. But the hands of the temporal ruler were not consecrated to making "the body and sacrament of the blood of Christ."[51] His head was

[49] See the discussion by G. Ellard, *Ordination Anointings in the Western Church Before 1000 A.D.* (Cambridge, Mass., 1933), pp. 21, 41ff, 55f. Cf. pp. 30f.

[50] Excerpts from the Freising Benedictionary were published by G. Morin, "Un recueil Gallican inédit de Bénédictiones épiscopales en usage à Freising aux VIIe-IXe siècles," *Revue Bénédictine*, 29 (1912), pp. 168-194. "*Unquantur manus istae*" appears on p. 188. It is probably not earlier than the ninth century. Professor E. H. Kantorowicz kindly directed me to this text.

[51] Epistola Carisiacensis, c. 15, MGH Cap. II, no. 297, p. 439.

anointed to the infusion of divine wisdom; his hands remained excluded from the performance of divine offices. Consequently, he himself remained outside the effectual government of the Church; he was above men but "under God."[52]

The same principles hold for the anointing of hands prescribed by the Freising Benedictionary. Though the formula *"Unquantur manus istae"* was almost surely patterned directly on the prayer which the so-called *Frankish Missal* directs to be said at the ordination of priests, it also occurs with variations in most other ecclesiastical unctions, such as baptism and the anointing of the dying.[53] The non-sacerdotal quality of the royal sacring is indicated quite clearly by comparing the text of *"Unquantur manus istae"* with the corresponding prayers prescribed for priestly ordination. The *Frankish Missal*, for example, reads: *"Consecrentur manus istae et sanctificentur per istam unctionem et nostram benedictionem ut quaecumque benedixerint benedicta sint et quaecumque sanctificaverint sanctificentur per dominum."*[54] Or, in another version: *"Benedic, domine, et sanctifica has manus sacerdotis tui ad consecrandas hostias quae pro delictis atque negligentiis*

[52] *Ibid.*, c. 5, p. 431.

[53] See Ellard, *Ordination Anointings*, p. 21, and the ample discussion by E. H. Kantorowicz, *Laudes Regiae: A Study in Liturgical Acclamations and Mediaeval Ruler Worship* (Berkeley and Los Angeles, 1946), p. 55 n. 142.

[54] Ellard, *Ordination Anointings*, p. 20. As Ellard points out (pp. 20f), the text of *"Unquantur manus istae"* in the *Frankish Missal* is somewhat garbled: "Unguantur manus istae de oleo sanctificato et crismate sanctificationes sicut uncxit samuhel david in regem et prophetam ita unguantur et consummentur in nomine dei patris et filii et spiritus sancti facientes imaginem sanctae crucis salvatoris nostri domini nostri Iheus Christi qui nos a morte redemit et ad regna caelorum perducit."

*populi offeruntur, et ad cetera benedicenda quae ad usus
populi necessaria sunt. Et presta, quaesumus, omnipotens
deus, ut quaecumque benedixerint benedicta sint et quaecumque sanctificaverint sanctificata sint.*"[55]

The simple hope expressed in the royal prayer—"*ut sis
benedictus et constitutus rex in regno isto, quod dedit tibi
dominus deus tuus super populum hunc ad regendum vel
gubernandum*"—contrasts strongly with the explicit transmission of powers implied in the ordination prayers.
Further, as we shall show in considering another coronation prayer, the attribution to the king of government
super populum was a specific rejection of the concept that
the temporal ruler governed *super Ecclesiam.* Therefore,
the Freising Benedictionary cannot be said of itself to
illustrate the monism of "theocratic kingship."[56]

These limitations are clear in the general stages of the
royal *ordines.* As known from the Gregorian Sacramentary
and from a letter by Hincmar of Rheims to Bishop Adventius of Metz, the fundamental steps in the consecration
of a bishop were the following: the imposition of the
Gospels upon the neck of the *electus,* the unction of his
head and hands, the placing of the ring, "the sign of the
Faith," upon his left hand, the bestowal of the "staff of
sacred governance" upon him,[57] and the assumption by

[55] *Ibid.,* pp. 48f.

[56] Cf. W. Ullmann, *Principles of Government and Politics in the
Middle Ages* (London, 1961), p. 129: "It is in fact one of the oldest
prayer texts said on the occasion of the king's anointing—the Bene-
dictional [*sic*] of Freising of the ninth century—which shows us the con-
ceptions underlying theocratic kingship in a most exquisite form."

[57] Hincmar, Ep. 29, Migne PL. 126, 187: "mittat annulum in dextere
manus digito . . . dicens ad quid illi annulus datur. Signum est enim
fidei ut audientibus se ex divinis mysteriis, signet quae et quibus

the new bishop of his seat among the ordainer bishops, after exchanging the kiss of peace with them. The royal consecration, as far as can be determined from fragmentary remains, lacked most of these stages: the Gospels were not placed on the neck of the consecrated, his hands were not anointed (at least in the West Frankish kingdom), he received neither the ring nor the staff, and he was not taken into the episcopal company. To be sure, the ceremonies shared some characteristics: the profession of the bishop-elect rendered before his consecration corresponded to the coronation oath of the king; the ordination of each required the consent of the people; both bishop and king were anointed at the altar and before the action of the Mass; finally, both were elevated onto thrones.[58] But these similarities and, as already noted, the similarity of unction itself by no means approached identity. The duty of preaching and interpreting symbolized by the imposition of the Gospels, the power to seal and to open the divine mysteries represented by the ring,[59] the capacity

---

signanda sunt, et aperiat quae et quibus aperienda sunt. Deinde donet illi baculum sancti regiminis. . . ." Although bishops and kings alike used some insignia (for example, purple robes), the badges of the episcopal office—the ring and the stola—were not shared by kings in the ninth century. Cf. the letter of Nicholas I, MGH Epp. vi, no. 71, p. 399, "sed et dignus paternis complexibus invenitur [Rothad of Soissons] et anulum fidei recipiet et stola circumdatur, per quam quid aliud quam sacerdotii declarantur insignia?" See below, Appendix B.

[58] On royal elevations, see H. Schreuer, *Die rechtliche Grundgedanken der französischen Königskrönung* (Weimar, 1911), pp. 126ff, Ratramnus, Contra Graecorum Opposita, IV, 5, Migne PL. 121, 324. On episcopal elevations, see the *litterae canonicae* for Electramnus of Redon and Gauzebert of Cahors, Mansi XVIII bis, 621, 629f. For a comparison of the episcopal and the royal *ordines* see Schreuer, pp. 14ff.

[59] As Schreuer suggests (p. 121), the royal signet is probably not to

to confer the sacraments and to transmit the gift of the Holy Spirit inferred by the unction of the hands, and the power to exercise discipline in sacred matters betokened by the pastoral stave—in short, the distinctive powers and responsibilities of the episcopal office—were not bestowed upon the anointed king.

In order to emphasize this distinction between the episcopal and the royal *ordines*, one may compare briefly the prayers in each. In the Gregorian Sacramentary, the prayer "*Deus honorum omnium*," prescribed to be said at the unction of the *electus*, contains the petition: "Grant him the episcopal *cathedra* that he may rule Thy *Church* and the whole people. Be Thou his authority [*auctoritas*], be Thou his strength [*firmitas*], be Thou his power [*potestas*]."[60] The same prayer, radically altered, occurs in the coronation *ordo* of Odo (888), where the episcopal imprecation finds a counterpart in the prayer: "Send forth Thy Holy Spirit upon this, Thy servant . . . to teach and govern him that he may rule Thy *people* and in all ways accomplish Thy will."[61] The king was set over the people,

---

be compared with the episcopal ring. However, compare the coronation of Judith, the daughter of Charles the Bald (856), MGH Cap. II, no. 296, p. 426: "Accipe anulum, fidei et dilectionis signum," with the Isidorian statement of Hincmar above n. 57. Cf. also the anonymous Vita S. Rimberti, c. 24, MGH SS. II, p. 775.

[60] H. Lietzmann, *Das Sacramentarium Gregorianum*, 2:7, p. 6: "Tribuas ei cathedram episcopalem ad regendam ecclesiam tuam et plebem universam, sis ei auctoritas, sis ei firmitas, sis ei potestas." This portion of the consecration prayer also occurs in the Gelasian Sacramentary. See H. A. Wilson, *The Gelasian Sacramentary* (Oxford, 1894), 625, pp. 151f. On the spiritual conception of *potestas* and *auctoritas*, see Erich Caspar, *Geschichte des Papsttums*, v. II (Tübingen, 1933), pp. 69f, 753-755.

[61] Schramm, "Krönung," p. 198, III, A: "et emittere digneris super

197

not over the Church. And in the context of the ecclesiastical sanctification which he received, he gained neither *potestas*, nor *firmitas*, nor *auctoritas* for the exercise of his functions. The Gelasian division of the government of the world between the "*auctoritas sacrata pontificum*" and the "*regalis potestas*," however prominent in other ninth-century writings is not present in the consecration *ordines*. Touching the very center of ecclesiastical administration as they did, the *ordines* correspondingly denied the temporal ruler supremacy in the Church and acknowledged only the exercise of spiritual powers—"the power and authority of loosing and binding granted by Christ to bishops, that is to the successors of the Apostles"[62]—and denied those powers to the king.[63] Paralleling the prayer "Be thou his authority, . . ." the following prayer was prescribed for the coronation (but not unction) of Louis the Stammerer in 878: "Be Thou his breastplate against the arrows of enemies, his helmet in adversity, his patience in prosperity, and, as protection, his everlasting shield. . . ."[64] In the coronation ritual, the Church assumed its defender, not

---

hunc famulum tuum ill. Spiritum tuum . . . qui illuminet, doceat et gubernet eum ad regendum poplum tuum et ad perficiendam in omnibus voluntatem tuam." See also the benediction said over Louis III in 878 (*ibid.*, p. 193, c. 3): "ut tua fultus dextera contineat fortiter patriam populumque sibi commissum."

[62] *Jonas d'Orléans et son "De institutione regia,"* c. 2, ed. Reviron, p. 136: "Quod potestas et auctoritas solvendi et ligandi sacerdotibus, id est successoribus apostolorum, a Christo sit adtributa. . . ."

[63] The royal potestas occurs only in the transmission of the sceptre in the coronation of Louis the Stammerer: "Accipe sceptrum, regiae potestatis insigne. . . ." MGH Cap. II, no. 304, p. 461. But even there, the sceptre is dedicated to the defense, not to the governance, of the Church.

[64] Schramm, "Krönung," p. 194, c. 4.

its governor; despite the king's quasi-episcopal unction, he remained outside the canonical government of the priestly order.

✝

If the liturgical coronation did not infer the royal power or alter the temporal nature of kingship by conferring a priestly or quasi-priestly character upon the king, it was critically important in the legal and ecclesiological context of dualism. The coronation was an act which consecrated power without bestowing it. It was the convenanting-place of the two Gelasian powers, where the king promised the support of his legislative and punitive functions to the episcopacy in return for the spiritual sanctions which only that order could bestow.[65] That the establishment of this reciprocity was in fact contractual is apparent in the texts of the royal promises, which made the kings' obligation to defend ecclesiastical laws and privileges conditional upon their continuing to receive aid and counsel from the clergy. In the subsequent act of consecration, the episcopacy, receiving the persons of the kings to the vowed discharge of their office, accepted and ratified the condition of their promise.

This was a ritualizing of the form of agreement made between Charles the Bald and his bishops and magnates at Cologne in 843. There, concerned lest the "royal sub-

[65] Hincmar of Rheims, Admonitio altera, c. 2, Migne PL. 125, 1009; Synodus apud S. Macram, c. 1, *ibid.*, 1071; Ep. 20, c. 7, Migne PL. 126, 119: "pontifices reges consecrare non possunt." See also Jonas of Orléans, De institutione laicali, Migne PL. 101, 133: "Quod vero solius episcopi sit per manus impositionem fidelibus tradere spiritum sanctum"; and Ratramnus of Corbie, Contra Graecorum opposita, IV, 7, Migne PL. 121, 332f.

limity," the "episcopal authority," and the "interest of the vassals" should each act in a different way, Charles and his people entered a *foedus concordiae* so that the diverse parties to it might act "under one head, Christ, truly as one man in the body of one Church—each man being a member one of another." The terms of the covenant were the same as those found in coronations. Charles promised the clergy to guard and to foster ecclesiastical privileges, the vigor of canon law, and the material well-being of the Church. To his other subjects, he made corresponding guarantees of due juridical process and secure property tenure. For their part, the *episcopalis auctoritas et fidelium unanimitas* bound themselves to defend "the kingly honor and the power rightly due to the royal office."[66]

When the act of federation was set into the special context of the coronation (as it was, for example, in the *societatis foedera* which Boso of Vienne concluded with his bishops at his accession),[67] it was conditioned by two principles. For the evidence indicates that, by liturgical sacring and crowning, religious sanction could not be given to temporal government broadly, but only to particular persons who were already seised of office, and that the bestowal of this sanction was conditional upon the establishment of reciprocal obligations between the individual king and the episcopal order. We have already discussed the means by which the kingship was transmitted among the Franks, and we may turn to the second of these principles.

[66] MGH Cap. ii, no. 254, pp. 254f.

[67] Regino of Prüm, Chronicon (a. 879), MGH SS. i, p. 590f. See also the highly instructive allegory of Audradus Modicus on the coronation

Though known from the earliest Carolingian period, the royal oath did not permanently enter the coronation ritual until the later ninth century. Between the imperial accession of Louis the Pious and the coronation of Charles the Bald at Metz (869), there is no unclouded evidence of a coronation oath;[68] but thereafter, such promises were part of all royal and imperial coronations in the fragmented Empire.

Indeed, at the same time that the oath became a regular part of coronation *ordines* it became a positive condition for coronation. This is indicated by a remark made by Bishop Adventius of Metz at the coronation of Charles

---

covenant between the king and God. Bouquet vii, pp. 289f, and Traube, "Philologische Untersuchungen aus dem Mittelalter," p. 387.

[68] Liber Pontificalis, Vita Sergii II, c. 9ff, L. Duchesne ed., v. ii (Paris, 1955), p. 88. To be sure, Pippin and his sons, Charlemagne and Carloman, entered an agreement of mutual defense with Pope Stephen (II) III before he anointed them in 754, but all three were acknowledged as kings before Stephen himself became pope. Aside from possible baptismal professions (themselves unattested by documentary evidence) it is unknown whether Pippin of Italy and Louis the Pious rendered any oaths to Hadrian I at their unction and coronation, or whether, because of their extreme youth, promises were submitted on their behalf. While he had previously given Bishops of Rome assurances of fidelity, promises of defense, and extensive territorial cessions, Charlemagne does not appear to have confirmed or enlarged those assurances at his imperial coronation. Nor is it recorded that his son Charles offered Leo III any profession on the same occasion when he received the royal unction and crown. Of the sons of Louis the Pious, neither Louis the German nor Lothaire is known to have issued such an oath; the same is to be said of Lothaire's sons, the Emperor Louis II and Lothaire II, with the exception of Louis' accession to the Lombard crown, cited above. Even Louis' third son, Charles the Bald, whose promises to his subjects were numerous, does not appear to have declared a guarantee of their rights formally either at his accession in 839 or at his coronation in Orléans in 848.

the Bald in 869. Referring to the act of consecration, he promised "to show with a sure token that we believe God has elected him and given him to us as our prince," only after Charles had rendered his "worthy and necessary" profession.[69] Likewise, Charles's imperial coronation was performed after he had "solemnly performed the *vota regia* at the tomb of St. Peter,"[70] and Louis the Stammerer was required to confirm the declaration of Quierzy (876) and to guarantee legal privileges of the temporal and spiritual orders before his consecration.[71]

After the accession of Louis the Stammerer, this conditional character was still further refined. Then, for the first time, the compact concluded in the coronation ceremony came to be a covenant exclusively between the consecrated king and his episcopal consecrators. At Louis' coronation (877), the coronation oath, already a *sine qua non* for the sacring and crowning of his father in 869, changed from a promise issued broadly to all subjects to one specifically for the clergy. Shortly before his coronation, Louis issued a "spontaneous promise" at the behest

[69] MGH Cap. ii, no. 276, p. 339. Cf. the similar remark of Hincmar of Rheims on the same occasion (*ibid.*, p. 341). On this ceremony, see T. Michels, "La date du couronnement de Charles-le-Chauve (9 Sept. 869) et le culte liturgique de S. Gorgon à Metz," *Revue Bénédictine*, 51 (1939), pp. 288-291, and A. Sprengler, "Die Gebete der Krönungs-ordines Hinkmars von Reims für Karl den Kahlen als König von Lothringen und für Ludwig den Stammler," *ZfKG*, 63 (1950/1), pp. 245-267. I can not agree with Dr. Sprengler (p. 253) that, "In diesem Ordo erscheint der König in geistlicher Stellung. Als Kämpfer gegen böse Mächte kommt er Priestern und Mönchen gleich, nur dass sein Wirkungsbereich noch umfassender ist als der eines einzelnen Mönches, Priesters oder gar Bischofs."

[70] Below, p. 209.

[71] See Hincmar, Instructio ad Ludowicum, cc. 7, 8, Migne PL. 125, 986f.

of his episcopacy in which he stated that, as "king by the mercy of the Lord, our God, and by the election of the people," he would preserve the laws of the Apostles and Fathers for the clergy and that, according to the precedents of earlier rulers, he would preserve the force of "laws and statutes" for his other subjects.[72] The oath required of him on the day of his consecration was significantly different; for in it there is no reference to the source of Louis' title or to the privileges of the temporal order. The oath consists of two parts. The first is an acceptance of the first chapter in the Capitula of Quierzy (876), in which Charles the Bald guaranteed the security of priests in the performance of their ministry.[73] The second and newer part emphasizes the first: Louis must preserve canonical privileges and "due law and justice" for the bishops, and he must render them defense, "as a king in his kingship ought justly to render [it to] every bishop and church committed to him."[74]

This coronation promise, which wholly disregarded the interests of the lay order, was the prototype of later oaths: Louis III and Carloman repeated it at their accession in 879, as did Carloman alone when he assumed the rule of Louis' lands (882), and Odo, in part, six years later (888).[75] Toward the middle of the tenth century, it was incorporated into the so-called Erdmann *Ordo* for royal coronations.[76] Its terms are clear and binding, and they refer exclusively to ecclesiastical interests. Hincmar of Rheims's admonition to Louis III merely illustrates its character as

[72] MGH Cap. ii, no. 283, p. 364.
[73] *Ibid.*, no. 281, pp. 355f.   [74] *Ibid.*, no. 283 C, p. 365.
[75] *Ibid.*, no. 288, p. 376.   [76] Schramm, "Krönung," p. 202.

an agreement between king and episcopacy: "recall your profession which you promised on the day of your consecration . . . subscribed with your own hand and, before all the bishops who were present, offered upon the altar to the Lord."[77]

In this regard, the accession oaths of Charles the Bald generally contrast with those of his successors. At his coronation in Metz, for example, Charles rendered a profession to the laity as well as to the clergy in response to their common acclamation. Certainly, he promised to preserve the honor and worship of God and of the churches, but collateral provisions extended his duties beyond the requirements of the clergy. He also affirmed that he would honor each man according to the dignity of his order and according to his person, and that to each he would preserve "fitting laws, ecclesiastical as well as worldly, law and justice. . . ."[78] Like his father in 813,

[77] See Hincmar of Rheims, Ep. 19, c. 5, Migne PL. 126, 112f. Cf. the petition of the Frankish bishops to Carloman, MGH Cap. II, no. 285, p. 370: "coram altare sancti Petri perdonastis et manu propria una cum fratre vestro confirmastis." Cf. W. Schlesinger, "Die Anfänge der deutschen Königswahl," ZfRG., G. A. 66 (1948), p. 387 n. 30, "von einer Salbung dieser Könige [Louis III and Carloman] verlautet nichts." Charlemagne also placed his oath of 774 upon the altar of St. Peter's. Liber Pontificalis, Vita Hadriani I, c. 43, ed. Duchesne, v. I, p. 478. Cf. Hincmar's statement in regard to the oath Charles the Bald rendered at Beauvais, that "in manibus sacerdotum ad vicem Dei [sacramentum] tradidistis," Migne PL. 125, 1040.

[78] MGH Cap. II, no. 276 B, p. 339. See Flodoard III, 18, MGH SS. XIII, p. 508, "promissione . . . quam verbo ac scripto antequam rex consecraretur, primatibus et episcopis fecerat," probably a reference to the coronation of 869. See Ehrenforth, "Hinkmar von Rheims und Ludwig III von Westfranken," p. 95. On the general development of the oath in the later period, see R. Scheyhing, Eide, Amtsgewalt, und Bannleihe: Eine Untersuchung zur Bannleihe im hohen und späten

Charles acknowledged fifty years later, and twice more, at his election as king of Italy and at the confirmation of that election at Ponthion, that his duty to defend the honor and privileges of his subjects was as immediate toward laymen as it was toward clerics.

Charles himself, however, was largely responsible for the more particular limitation of the oaths indicated above; for, among the numerous assurances which he issued during his reign, several were required by and rendered to the clergy alone.[79] Two of these restricted oaths were considered so important that they were not only opportunely recalled during Charles's own reign[80] but were invoked even after his death. The vow which he rendered at Cologne in 843 (part of his *foedus concordiae*), as repeated in the Synod of Quierzy (876), received the sworn obedience of Louis the Stammerer and of his sons at their respective coronations;[81] and provisions of the promise he submitted to his bishops at Beauvais (845) recur in the accession oath of Odo. Because of their importance in the development of the coronation oath, their content may be mentioned.

In the earlier promise, Charles affirmed that he would maintain the honor and the possessions of the churches under his government as his ancestors had maintained

---

Mittelalter. Forschungen zur deutschen Rechtsgeschichte, vol. ii. Cologne, 1960.

[79] The promise given at Aachen in 842 (below, p. 226), the Oath of Beauvais (845), MGH Cap. ii, no. 292, pp. 387f; the Oath of Cologne (843), *ibid.*, n. 254, p. 255, c. i.

[80] E.g., Migne PL. 125, 1042, 1064ff.

[81] It was also repeated by Hincmar of Rheims in the decree of the Synod of Fismes, Migne PL. 125, 1072f, with some slight changes.

them, and that the cessions which he himself had made to churches would be wholly preserved. "According to venerable authority," bishops and other ecclesiastics would enjoy the force of ecclesiastical government and the privileges due them; and the efforts of the *principalis potestas*, together with those of the members of the civil government (*reipublicae administratores*), were dedicated to enabling the clergy to "fulfill their ministry suitably."[82] The promise of Beauvais, which Charles swore upon his sword[83]—an act without known parallel in his day—elaborates these terms. There, Charles promised to preserve the force of canon law and clerical privileges, to restore property wrongfully taken from the tenure of the Church and to defend ecclesiastical holdings against plunderers.[84]

By these and similar assurances given the clergy during his reign, and by more general oaths to "preserve for each man the law due him"—applicable, of course, to the clergy as well as to the laity[85]—Charles prepared the way for the assurances which his successors rendered the clergy alone at their coronations.

The fullness of this development, however, did not obtain until after the death of Louis the Stammerer, when the conditional nature of the royal oath and the reciprocal bonds, as we have indicated, drew tighter. Then, according to Hincmar of Rheims, not merely the coronation of Louis' son, Louis III, but his very accession depended upon his oath: "Together with my fellows and the other faith-

[82] MGH Cap. II, no. 254, c. I, p. 255.

[83] Hincmar of Rheims, Pro Lib., Migne PL. 125, 1066.

[84] MGH Cap. II, no. 292, cc. 3-7, p. 388.

[85] Migne PL. 125, 1042, 1064ff. See also the consilium of Boneuil (856), MGH Cap. II, no. 295, pp. 424f.

ful of God and your fathers, I elected you to the governance of the kingdom on the condition that you preserve
due laws (*sub conditione debitas leges servandi*)."[86] At
the same time, these very conditions were critical when
Boso of Vienne "tyrannically arrogated to himself the
name of king."[87] The presence of two legitimate and
hereditary heirs, the sons of the late King, militated against
his accession; and, according to Hincmar, he found it
necessary to establish himself as king by bribing the
bishops of Provence with monasteries and *villae* to anoint
and crown him.[88] Hincmar does not mention the profession; but surviving documents show clearly that Boso
secured his election and the subsequent coronation by his
promise as well as by his abbeys and villas.

Three documents derive directly from the election: an
enquiry by the Synod of Mautaille, Boso's response, and
the synod's ratification of the election. In its enquiry, the
synod, "together with the magnates," asked Boso to declare "of what sort you wish to be in the princedom to
which we hope you are to be exalted through divine
mercy." Specifically it asked whether he would seek the
honor and love of God in the orthodox faith, exalt the
Church to the limit of his abilities, preserve the privileges
of individual churches and their bishops and priests, and
guarantee law, justice, and right for all his subjects.[89] In re-

---

[86] Ep. 20, c. 7, Migne PL. 126, 119.

[87] Annales Vedastini (a. 879), MGH in usum schol., p. 45.

[88] Annales Bertiniani (a. 879), MGH in usum schol., p. 150.

[89] MGH Cap. II, no. 284 A, p. 366. On the tentative meaning of the
verb "optamus" in this document, compare the petition of the Parisian
clergy for the consecration of Aeneas as bishop: "Eneam patrem,
Eneam pontificem habere optamus." MGH Epp. VI, no. 98, p. 87.

sponse, Boso professed that he held to the orthodox faith and promised "through your common counsel" to perform the duties required of him.[90] Finally, in the election proclamation, the synod—here the clergy alone—declared that Boso *"obedienter colla promittendo submisit"* to the terms of his electors. The election was complete; on the condition of his affirmation, Boso had acceded to the kingship.[91] The Synod of Mautaille could rightly have applied to its own proceedings the words used by the Synod of Pavia ten years later when it elected Wido King of Italy: "Since the glorious King Wido has seen fit to promise to observe the *capitula* written above . . . it has pleased (*complacuit*) us all to elect him as king, lord, and defender. . . ."[92]

There is one more characteristic of the accession oath which we must consider: namely, that it came progressively to establish an obligation on the part of subjects corresponding to the royal duties and to bind juristically those who received the profession from the king to yield him honor, obedience, and aid.

The juridical affirmation of this reciprocity took two forms. Of them, the simpler was that which established in its own terms that the performance of vowed royal duties was conditional upon the performance of corresponding duties by those who received the oath. This form occurred first used in the affirmation of Charles, Louis the German, and Lothaire I at the second meeting at Meersen (851). After professing that, with the counsel of their subjects, they would maintain law and justice for

[90] MGH Cap. II, 284 B, p. 367.
[91] *Ibid.*, 284 C, p. 368.
[92] *Ibid.*, no. 222, pp. 104f.

them and would in no way work to their detriment, the
three kings qualified their promise: The profession was
made on the condition (*in hoc*) that their people would
not stand against them, but would be faithful, obedient,
and true in their aid and counsel, unfeignedly assisting
them to fulfill their vows.[93] Similar provisions were made
in the coronation oaths of Charles the Bald at Metz
(869),[94] and in those of Carloman (882) and Odo (888).[95]

The second form was the exchange of oaths or guarantees, a usage best and earliest known in dealings between
the Carolingians and contemporary popes. Unfortunately,
the texts of these oaths are not preserved, though they
continued to be cited authoritatively until the end of the
century and though they may have been patterns for the
later royal oaths which concern us. The *vota regia* which
Charles the Bald offered at the tomb of St. Peter in 876[96]
were very likely identical with the "*promissio regum . . .
et sacramenta quae Pippinus et Carolus obtulerunt beato
Petro apostolo*," which Pope John VIII read at the Synod
of Troyes (878) for the edification of Louis the Stammerer.[97] Of these oaths, one knows only that the understanding between Pippin and Pope Stephen was considered "*pacis foedera*,"[98] and that Pippin, for his part, assumed the responsibility of defending militarily the Roman Church and its holdings from its enemies.[99] The

[93] *Ibid.*, no. 205, p. 73.
[94] *Ibid.*, no. 276 B, p. 339.
[95] *Ibid.*, nos. 285, 288, pp. 369, 375.
[96] Confirmation of John VIII to St. Vaast, Migne PL. 126, 658, no. 13.
[97] Synod of Troyes (878), Mansi XVII A, 347, Actio 4.
[98] Liber Pontificalis, Vita Stephani II, c. 26, ed. Duchesne, v. I, p. 447.
[99] Chronicon Moissiacense (a. 741), MGH SS. I, p. 293.

reciprocal element offered Pippin by the Papacy is not known; but one assumes that, like the promise of Charlemagne, it included the obligation to be *"amicus amicis inimicus inimicis."*[100] Quite probably, the verses in which Ermoldus Nigellius recorded the promise Louis the Pious rendered Stephen (IV) V (816) represent their general character:

> Si tua iura manent, Petri qui regmina curas,
> Et vice partita pascis ovile suum;
> Sin aliud, penitus moneo, ut mihi cuncta sacerdos
> Edicas; faciam mox tua verba libens.
> Ut mea progenies Petri servavit honorem,
> Sic ego servabo, praesul, amore dei.
>
> .   .   .   .
>
> Haec est causa, sacer, qua te accersire rogavi:
> Adiutor fortis esto beate mihi![101]

The benedictions which directly followed Pippin's oath in 754 and Louis' in 816 undoubtedly comprised at least partially the papal side of the *foedera.*[102]

This second form occurs first among Frankish records in the Strassburg Oaths (842), where, in an exchange of pledges by kings and subjects, the continued adherence of their subjects to Charles the Bald and Louis the German was made conditional upon continued fidelity between

---

[100] Stephen (III) IV to Charlemagne and Carloman, MGH Epp. III, no. 45, p. 562. See also John VIII to Angilberga, MGH Epp. VI, no. 44, pp. 42f; L. Wallach, "Amicus amicis, inimicus inimicis," *ZfKG*, 52 (1933), pp. 614f.

[101] In Honorem Ludovici, II, vv. 381-388, 403-404, MGH Poet. Lat. II, p. 35. On the confirmation of Louis' "pactum" with the predecessors of Paschal I, see the Annales Einhardi (a. 817), MGH SS. I, pp. 203f.

[102] See the Nota de unctione Pippini Regis, MGH SS. XV, p. 1.

the two kings.[103] It recurred at Quierzy (855), at Gondreville (870), at Rheims (870?),[104] and a second time at
Quierzy (877), when Louis the Stammerer assured his
succession by renewing the earlier vows. During the reign
of Charles the Bald, this exchange of oaths came to be
integrated at coronations with the vows of feudal homage.
At his accession in 839[105] and again at his coronation in
848,[106] Charles received oaths of fealty, but he is not known
to have issued a profession himself on either occasion.
Before he made his coronation vow in 869, he had already
received oaths of fealty from leaders of the Lotharingian
clergy.[107] The oath of homage first assumed a responsive
character at Charles's election as king of Italy and at the
confirmation of that election by the Synod of Ponthion,
where he required his tenants to answer his own profession by swearing that they would not conspire against his
honor and security or against that of the kingdom and
Church committed to him.[108] In the same responsive

[103] Nithard, Historiae, III, 5, MGH in usum schol., p. 36. Annales
Bertiniani, *ibid.* (a. 842), p. 27.

[104] Capitulare Carisiacense (June 14, 877), c. 4, MGH Cap. ii, no.
281, pp. 356f.

[105] Above, p. 134.

[106] See the Libellus Adversus Wenilonem, c. 9, MGH Cap. ii, no.
300, p. 452, and the letter of the Synod of Savonnières to Wenilo,
Mansi xv, 530. On the sacramental importance of the unction, see L.
Levillain, "Le sacre de Charles le Chauve à Orléans," *Bibliothèque de
l'école des chartes*, 64 (1903), pp. 52f.

[107] Annales Bertiniani (a. 869), MGH in usum schol., p. 101; MGH
Cap. ii, no. 276 C, pp. 340f.

[108] On Pavia, MGH Cap. ii, no. 220, p. 100. The text of the oath
rendered at Ponthion appears to have varied slightly. For this variation,
see Hincmar of Rheims's objection to the oath (Migne PL. 125, 1125f),
and his abbreviation of it: "Isti Imperatori secundum meum scire et
posse, iuxta ministerium meum fidelis ero." *Ibid.*, col. 1126.

fashion, his son, Louis the Stammerer, received oaths of fealty and the commendation of lands from his temporal and ecclesiastical subjects at his coronation.[109]

By the end of the ninth century, therefore, the Frankish episcopacy, forced to render unreciprocated oaths of fidelity under Charlemagne and Louis the Pious, had succeeded in establishing juristic guarantees by the king as a condition for the royal consecration and even, in some extreme instances, for the accession. Further, they had set the defense of their own order as the primary object of those oaths, as the first goal of the classic royal duty to defend the law. Still, they did not thereby deliver themselves of juridical responsibility toward their rulers, but, rather, they established a juristic relationship in which their professions of fidelity and assistance were reciprocated by royal guarantees of the legal integrity of the clergy and promises of military defense for ecclesiastical holdings. The bishops themselves were still bound by the canon of the Synod of Aachen (836): "that if any bishop or any of the lower ecclesiastical order through fear, cupidity, or whatever suasion, deserts the Lord and the Orthodox Emperor Louis hereafter, or violates the vow of fidelity promised him . . . let him lose his office [*gradus*] by canonical and synodal sentence."[110] But, at the moment of coronation they had brought their temporal rulers to submit with them to the earlier canon: "He who acts contrary to his profession and subscription deprives himself of office [*honos*]."[111]

[109] Annales Bertiniani (a. 877), MGH in usum schol., p. 138.
[110] MGH Conc. II, no. 56, c. 12, p. 710.
[111] Council of Carthage (390), c. 13, Mansi III, 697, cited by Hincmar

In a real sense, the institution of the coronation contract marked the extent to which the royal authority had decayed by the mid-ninth century; for the same forces which impelled the Carolingian Empire toward its ruin made covenanters of king and episcopacy. Weakened by the alienation of the royal demesne through cession and usurpation, and by the disruption of trade and communication through brigandage and Viking invasions, the monarchy no longer commanded the conventional sources of its strength. The powers and the resources of government fell, despite the best efforts of the Carolingian rulers, into the hands of a local, hereditary nobility. For the political historian, the coronation oaths are important as instruments by which the Carolingian kings attempted to counterbalance this loss to the temporal nobility, winning the support of the lords spiritual by guaranteeing them freedom to enjoy full canonical privileges. An alliance between the clerical hierarchy and the crown might thus have been effected much like the one which the Saxon and Salian rulers established and fostered in the tenth and eleventh centuries; and one could have spoken of the Carolingian imperial Church, describing the administrative incorporation of the Church into the temporal government.

But this institutional fusion did not occur in the ninth century. In fact, the coronation covenant emphasized the division of the two powers and their alliance instead of

---

of Rheims in Pro Lib., Migne PL. 125, 1040, against Charles the Bald and in LV Capitula, Praef., c. 32, Migne PL. 126, 292, 414, against Hincmar of Laon, substituting "honore privabit" for "ab hoc coetu separabit." Cf. Mansi III, 873.

their corporative union; it enacted sacramentally the kind of *foedus* between king and episcopacy also known in purely juristic agreements. In the coronation, just as in those other agreements, the king and clergy entered a compact of common or reciprocal defense. Ecclesiastical privileges and immunities were to be defended by the king through his temporal strength; the royal honor and authority, by the lords spiritual through their material resources and, more immediately, through their spiritual powers in the unction of the king. The offices of king and bishop remained distinct, however, and their respective characters, unchanged. The king did not receive the power to interpret doctrine or to enter into spiritual government; he did not become a "vicar of God in the Church." Conversely, the episcopacy did not assume dominance over the bestowal and exercise of temporal power. The sacramental actions of bishops were by no means requisite to valid assumption of the kingship, for they conferred no powers, spiritual or temporal. Instead, they merely confirmed the king's earlier and complete accession to office and title by consecrating his person to discharge the duties he had promised to perform for the benefit of the Church. At the same time, they ratified the terms of mutual obligation on which the royal oath was made. In the preservation of the integrity of the two powers, however, lay the greatest deficiency of this attempt to resolve the Gelasian tension; for the punishment of breach of contract by the king fell to God, the grantor of royal power, rather than to the episcopacy, its consecrator. The chastening of a perjured king was beyond the competence of the bishops who had crowned him; the attempted entente between the two kingdoms, the world and the Church, ultimately failed through the fineness of its balance.

2. *The Right of Resistance*

In our discussion of Frankish ecclesiology, we indicated that the clergy sought above all to establish its juristic and institutional integrity as distinct from civil government. Without asserting ecclesiastical supremacy over the royal office, authors such as Hincmar of Rheims explicitly denied the legitimate exercise of royal authority in the legal and sacramental functions of the priesthood. We have also seen the effects of this dualistic orientation on the Carolingian concept of the royal office. The kingship was bestowed by God through secular channels, not by the priestly ministry; and its characteristic feature, armed terror, was an instrument alien to the Church. While the clergy strove to establish its independence of this secular office in law, it sought to reconcile, or to correlate, episcopacy and kingship by establishing "contractual" responsibilities between the individual kings and the episcopal corps. In this context, the liturgical sacring and crowning of the king was the ratification by the clergy of the obligations the king specified in his coronation oath; it was the visible sanctification of the person, but not of the office. The rigid duality of power was preserved. The basic flaw of the coronation covenant lay in its character as a legal, or theological, fiction: the parties to the compact were—occasionally explicitly, but always implicitly—the king and God, not the king and the clergy. In law, therefore, God alone could punish breach of the royal contract.

Liturgical coronation did not establish the king as head

of the Church; conversely, it did not subordinate his office to the Church. The ratification of the coronation contract by the submission of the people to their king indicates the fundamental weakness of the alliance between royal and episcopal powers. Whether expressed in oaths or in liturgical formulae of the coronation order, the act of submission was final and irretractable. For neither the machinery of the compact itself nor the general background of contemporary political thought offered any basis for its enforcement; the subjection of the royal power to the episcopal, like that of the episcopal to the royal (a subjection necessary to exacting implementation of the contract) was alien to the ninth century. Threats against the king who violated his "professions and subscriptions" remained incapable of realization.

The coronation *ordines* themselves implicitly deny the subordination of the royal power to the episcopal authority. Among the accession oaths in the period under review, only those rendered by Charles the Bald in Pavia (876)[1] and by Boso[2] provide correctives for royal negligence; both prescribe voluntary emendation by the king himself, rather than his subjection to juristic constraint. Further, the prayer "*Clerum et populum*," which occurs in the coronation *ordines* of Charles the Bald (869) and Louis the Stammerer, tacitly rejects the right of resistance with the petition that clergy and people, obedient to divine admonitions, would gain eternal rewards by submitting to their king.[3] And Pope John VIII bound with the anath-

---

[1] MGH Cap. II, no. 220, p. 100.   [2] *Ibid.*, no. 284 B, p. 367.

[3] *Ibid.*, nos. 302, 304, pp. 457, 462. Cf. the profession of obedience at the coronation of Boso, MGH, Cap. II, no. 222, p. 105.

ema anyone who, as "an enemy of God, . . . and a foe of the Church of God" attempted to overturn Charles's imperial accession.[4]

On this point, the vision of Audradus illustrates the principle of Frankish thought that the authority to withdraw the royal power belonged to the bestower of the kingship: Audradus mentions with approval the deposition of Lothaire by Louis the Pious, who had earlier brought him to the throne.[5] The same principle appears in the actual petition of bishops to Louis for Lothaire's removal from imperial power,[6] in the *Ordinatio Imperii* (817), which reserves the judgment of delinquent kings to the emperor and to the community of the realm,[7] and finally in the apparent acknowledgment by the East Franks that their deposition of Charles the Fat was valid only in their lands and not in the West or in the empire.[8] Naturally, this principle was applicable to the coronation only when it was maintained that power was actually transferred through the act of consecration. But one such instance is known in Frankish sources from the ninth century. In 859, when Wenilo of Sens, who had consecrated Charles

[4] Bouquet VII, no. 50, p. 697.

[5] Cf. Agobard to Louis the Pious, MGH Epp. v. no. 15, c. 4, p. 225: "Et ecce sine ulla ratione et consilio quem [Lothaire] cum Deo elegistis sine Deo repudiastis." See also Annales Bertiniani (a. 855), MGH in usum schol., p. 45, where Charles the Bald is reported as sending his son, Charles, to Aquitaine as "rex designatus," and *ibid.* (a. 865), p. 75, "filium suum Karolum necdum bene spassatum in Aquitaniam cum regio nomine ac potestate redire permittit."

[6] Charles the Bald to Nicholas I, Migne PL. 124, 872: "Lotharium vero ab imperiali potestate secedere hortati sunt."

[7] MGH Cap. I, no. 136, p. 272, c. 10.

[8] P. Kehr, "Aus den letzten Tagen Karls III," *Deutsches Archiv*, I (1937), pp. 145f.

the Bald at Orléans eleven years earlier, deserted him and joined Louis the German, then invading Charles's lands, Charles declared that he should not in any event be deprived of his consecrated character or of the royal office without legal hearing and judgment by "the bishops through whose ministry I was consecrated king and who are called 'thrones of God,' in whom God sits and through whom He decrees His judgments."[9]

This statement, however, is unique; and its variance with the more common standpoint, which required submission to the ruler whether he were good or evil, is to be explained by the unusual political circumstances which prompted it and by the peculiar relationship established between Wenilo and Charles in the act of consecration. Charles himself, fully aware that he had been king for nine years before his first sacring, on another occasion discarded the claim to accession through unction in favor of that to accession through the grace of God and inheritance. At the same time, he denied the validity of a process instituted against him before the papal court by Hincmar of Laon, one of his consecrators.[10] Charles, therefore, would scarcely have disputed the common position that

---

[9] MGH Cap. II, no. 300, c. 3, p. 451. A similar position is stated in the related letter of Charles's bishops to Louis the German, *ibid.*, no. 297, c. 15, p. 439: "Maxime autem nobis necesse est loqui cum illis archiepiscopis et episcopis, qui consensu et voluntate populi regni istius domnum nostrum fratrem vestrum unxerunt in regem. . . ." In his letters to Pope Hadrian II, Charles also appears to acknowledge that, through his own confession, he could be brought to trial and even convicted for misconduct (Epp. 7, 8, Migne PL. 124, col. 876, 881, 883f), a concept also suggested by the Frankish bishops during the trial of Hincmar of Laon (Concilium Duziacense, Responsa 7, Mansi XVI, 651f).

[10] MGH Cap. II, no. 302, p. 456.

the king was the elect of God and that the royal power was held by God's grace, a position which discredited all grounds for resistance to established authority.[11] In fact his own coronation in Metz and in Rome—and even the professed subjection to episcopal judgment cited above— had as their fundamental premise this principle of divine election and religious submission;[12] the king held his power of God and could be deposed only by the judgment of God. In this, the coronation *ordines* represented accurately the tenor of ninth-century thought.

That is not to discount the importance of the right of resistance in Carolingian thought. Certainly, there were authors who advocated the most vigorous resistance to wicked kings, who revered "all the saints and prophets who manfully resisted kings and fought to the death for justice."[13] It must be observed, however, that such opinions were expressed more often by the bishops of Rome, who were suitably remote from the "avenging sword" of the Frankish kings to be able to stand firmly against them;

[11] See Rhabanus Maurus, MGH Epp. v, no. 16, pp. 417f. Jonas of Orléans, however, represents the reverse of this principle. De institutione laicali, ii, 20, Migne PL. 106, 211, "Imitentur ergo in venerandis et obtemperandis sacerdotibus potentia, et copiosissimis honoribus sublimatum Theodosium orthodoxum imperatorem, quam humiliter reverenterque beati Ambrosii memorabilis viri monitis et increpationibus, atque excommunicationibus paruerit. Sciebat nempe potestatem imperialem, qua insignitus erat, ab illius pendere potestate, cujus famulus et minister Ambrosius erat."

[12] E.g., MGH Cap. ii, no. 276, p. 339. Cf. the threat of the Synod of Thionville (844) to the sons of Louis the Pious, MGH Cap. ii, no. 227, p. 115, c. 4: "ne . . . praesens regnum, quod absit, vobis patrum labore adquisitum et hereditate relictum a vobis ipse Christus dividat. . . ." See also the image of God as the king's *senior* in Hincmar's Instructio ad Ludowicum, c. 9, Migne PL. 125, 988f.

[13] Epitaphium Arsenii, ii, 14, MGH SS. ii, p. 561.

the geographical as well as the hierarchical position of Pope Nicholas I was far different from that of Adventius of Metz, whom he urged to take care that the rulers to whom he subjected himself were "truly king and princes. ... See whether they govern by law; for if they do not, they are to be considered tyrants rather than to be held as kings, and we ought to resist them and to rise up against them rather than to be subject to them."[14] Significantly, the attempt of Pope John VIII to remove Carloman of Italy from the royal office because of his physical incapacity failed when the bishops he had called to consider the case in synod did not obey his summons.[15] By no means rejecting the right of resistance, Frankish sources still affirmed it in a far more subdued manner than did the papal writers. For example, clerical authors commonly adopted the apostolic maxim that one should "obey God rather than man" (Acts 5:29); but they generally used it to sanction tacit rather than active resistance to wicked rulers, even to the point of willing submission to martyrdom.[16] A similar position also obtained in actual political

[14] MGH Epp. vi, no. 31, p. 299. Cf. *Ibid.*, no. 24, p. 288: "Si unanimes fueritis, quis est, qui vobis resistat? Patres nostri etiam regibus restiterunt." See also the letter of John VIII to the East Frankish bishops (876), Epp. vii, no. 7, p. 322: "Et ubi est, quaesumus, quod vice Christi in ecclesia fungimur, si pro Christo contra insolentiam principum non luctamur. . . ."

[15] See John VIII to Anspert of Milan, MGH Epp. vii, no. 163, p. 133. On the other hand, the deposition of Pippin of Aquitaine in 848 by his magnates on the grounds of incapacity (Annales Bertiniani, a. 848, MGH in usum schol., p. 36) succeeded, as did that of Charles the Fat in 887 by his on the same grounds (Annales Vedastini, a. 887, *ibid.*, p. 64; Regino, Chronicon, a. 887, MGH SS. i, p. 597); neither deposition was effected entirely by ecclesiastics, or on religious grounds.

[16] E.g., Haimo of Halberstadt, Expositio in Rom. 13:1-4, Migne PL.

affairs. The subjects of Charles the Bald and Louis the German affirmed at Strassburg (842) that if either king violated his oath to the other and joined forces with Lothaire I, they, as subjects, would withdraw their support from their own kings.[17] And at Quierzy (856), Charles's clergy and nobles declared that if, "according to human frailty," Charles should act contrary to his agreement (*pactum*) to preserve the privileges and legal processes due each of his subjects, his subjects would "admonish him—with reverence, suitable to a *senior*—to correct and amend this act himself, and to preserve due law for each man in his order." Thereafter, if Charles should prove unwilling to honor his obligations, the whole body of his subjects, lay and clerical, would take counsel "to the end that, even if he should wish to act contrary to the law, to right reason, and to the just judgment of anyone (which Heaven forbid), our King should not be able to do it."[18]

The prevalent position, however, denied the right of resistance and left the punishment of evil rulers to God; the bishops who rebelled against Louis the Pious as a perverter of the royal ministry were deposed by their

---

117, 478ff; Walafrid Strabo, Glossa Ordinaria, to Rom. 13:1-4, Migne PL. 114, 512f; *Sedulii Scotti Liber de Rectoribus Christianis*, c. 6, ed. S. Hellmann (Munich, 1906), p. 38.

[17] MGH Cap. II, no. 247, pp. 171f.

[18] *Ibid.*, no. 262, c. 10, p. 281. Cf. Annales Bertiniani (a. 851), MGH in usum schol., p. 40, c. 8. One may also cite, as representative of the literature of resistance, Hincmar of Rheims's De ordine palatii, c. 31, MGH Cap. II, p. 527: The king is to appoint counsellors "qui . . . talem fidem haberent, ut *excepta vita aeterna* nihil regi et regno praeponerent." Cf. *Sedulii Scotti Liber de Rectoribus Christianis*, c. 6, ed. S. Hellmann, p. 38: "ut divina consilia praeponantur humanis, cum oboedire magis oporteat Deo quam hominibus."

episcopal colleagues. This standpoint was most clearly expressed by the Synod of Pavia (850), which warned Lothaire I and his son Louis II to avoid bestowing monasteries upon persons not canonically qualified to receive them, so that "they who are to be judged now by no one for their action may avoid being judged quite severely by God the Omnipotent in the judgment to come."[19] The Synod of Thionville, six years earlier, while complaining vigorously against the personal delinquencies and the official abuses of the sons of Louis the Pious, held before them only the threat of the Last Judgment, when "you must render account to the King of kings for the royal ministry."[20] According to this position, the errant king, of whom Saul and Pharaoh were favorite examples,[21] was to be left to the judgment of an angry God.[22] The sacred character of the royal office, as set forth in "divine admonitions" made obedience to the king, good or evil,

[19] MGH Cap. II, no. 228, p. 121, c. 16.

[20] *Ibid.*, no. 227, p. 113, c. 1.

[21] Cf. *Jonas d'Orléans et son "De institutione regia,"* c. 10, ed. J. Reviron (Paris, 1930), p. 163, and Sedulius Scottus, c. 8, ed. Hellmann, p. 43.

[22] The apocryphal literature of the ninth century is especially forceful on this point. See the punishments inflicted upon Charlemagne and members of Louis the Pious' family in the Visio cuiusdam pauperculae mulieris (ca. 822) in W. Wattenbach-H. Löwe, *Deutschlands Geschichtsquellen im Mittelalter* (Weimar, 1957), pp. 317f n. 85. One may add the punishment of Charles Martel which the West Frankish bishops recalled for the edification of Louis the German Epistola Carisiacensis, MGH Cap. II, no. 297, p. 432, and Ademar of Chabannes's Chronicon, III, 19, ed. J. Chavanen (Paris, 1897), p. 136. Cf. also Hincmar of Rheims, Vita S. Remigii, c. 14, MGH SS. Rer. Mer., v. III, p. 296: "[Romani] . . . viam veritatis reliquerint et diversos vitiorum fuerint secuti anfractus, quibus . . . Deus offenditur ac per hoc regna solent subverti atque de gente in gentem transferri."

a sacred duty:[23] for the kingship "is the Lord's, and He gives it to whomever He may wish."[24] Further, as the bishops of Lothaire II once indicated on a more worldly level, the oaths of fidelity which they had sworn to their King were strong arguments against taking up arms against him.[25] And finally, law, as expressed in synodal decrees and in edicts of popes and emperors, prohibited conspiracy against the royal office and rebellion against one's lord.[26]

The prevalence of this second position in clerical thought is clearly indicated by the sparing use of excommunication

[23] See the prayer "Clerum et populum" in the coronation *ordines* of Charles the Bald and Louis the Stammerer. MGH Cap. II, nos. 302, 304, pp. 457, 462.

[24] John VIII to the counts of Louis the German, MGH Epp. VII, no. 8, p. 325.

[25] MGH Epp. VI, no. 13, p. 229. Cf. Lupus of Ferrières, Vita Maximini, MGH SS. Rer. Mer., V. III, p. 76, c. 5: "Sed o nostri temporis mores degeneres! . . . Quis iam imperatoribus divinorum praeceptorum reserare salutarem non reformidet severitatem? Quis eis sua pericula zelo divini timoris accensus, absque fuco adulationis aperiat?"

[26] See the decrees of the Synod of Lorch as they appear in the Synod of Meaux-Paris (845/6), MGH Cap. II, no. 293, cc. 14, 15, p. 402: "Si quis contra regiam dignitatem dolose ac callide ac perniciose satagere comprobatus fuerit, nisi dignissime satisfecerit, anathematizetur, c. 15. Si quis potestati regiae . . . contradicere praesumperit . . . anathematizetur." See also the letter of Nicholas I in response to enquiries by the Bulgarians, MGH Epp. VI, no. 99, c. 19, p. 578; the Capitulatio de partibus Saxoniae (775-90), c. 10, MGH Cap. I, no. 26, p. 69; the decree of the Synod of 786, c. 12, MGH Epp. IV, p. 24: "In necem regis nemo communicare audeat, quia christus Domini est, et si quis tali sceleri adhaeserit, si episcopus est aut ullus ex sacerdotali gradu, ex ipso detrudatur et a sancta hereditate deiciatur. . . ." See also the confirmation of Charles the Fat to Doge John of Venice (883) MGH DK III, no. 77, p. 127, and the pastoral letter of Wulfhad of Bourges (ca. 870), MGH Epp. VI, no. 27, p. 190. See E. Perels, "Ein Berufsschreiben Papst Nikolaus' I zur frankischen Reichssynode in Rom," *Neues Archiv*, 32 (1907), p. 144.

against Carolingian rulers and by circumstances surrounding the depositions of Louis the Pious and Lothaire I. Certainly, the Carolingians were frequently threatened with ecclesiastical censure by popes. Charlemagne and his brother Carloman, Louis the Pious, Charles the Bald, Louis the German, and Lothaire II all stood in danger of papal excommunication at least once during their respective reigns. Frankish bishops were more cautious than the Roman. Indeed, the bishops of Lothaire II maintained that a king could not be excommunicated at all. We know only three instances in which they regarded their kings as tainted by excommunication. Hincmar of Rheims, who later threatened Louis III with "ecclesiastical censures in this world and the next," actually excommunicated Lothaire I, Charles the Bald, and their families. Hincmar of Laon bound Charles the Bald in the terms of a general interdict. And Louis the German was considered excommunicated by Charles's bishops (859), although no formal ban was issued against him.

Only Louis the Pious and Lothaire I were rejected as kings by a united episcopacy, and only in the case of Louis was excommunication added to the rejection of his sovereignty. Excommunication against a Christian king in its strictest construction assumes the character of suspension from office or of effectual deposition from government over orthodox Christians: the open threat of Nicholas I to "loose vengeance" against Lothaire I with bloodshed and war should he incur the papal anathema strongly underscores that premise.[27] Even in the case of Louis the

[27] MGH Epp. vi, no. 38, p. 311. Cf. the letters of John VIII to the East Franks on the wrongdoing of Louis the German, where he parallels

Pious, however, it is by no means clear that the episcopacy adopted that extreme weapon of resistance against a ruling emperor. Indeed, the records of the process against Louis suggests that his "excommunication" was imposed after his deposition as part of his penance, rather than that the sequence excommunication-deposition-penance was followed. Prudentius of Troyes recorded that as part of his penance, Louis was cast beyond the limits of the Church "in such circumstances that no one dared speak with him except those who were delegated to that purpose."[28] And the Synod of Troyes (867) stated: "So as to make it believable for the people that he had been cast out of the kingship rightly, certain criminal charges were fabricated against him on the basis of which, by the judgment of some bishops and under the pretext of public penance, they succeeded in excluding him from the limits of the Church. . . ."[29] Unfortunately, the records deriving immediately from the process are ambiguous. But the *Narratio Episcoporum*, which describes Louis' penance in St. Médard, appears to support Prudentius and the Synod of Troyes by stating that "by divine and just judgment, the imperial power was suddenly withdrawn from him" and that he was *later* admonished "since he had been deprived of earthly power, [that] he should endeavour with all his might—set as he was in desperate circumstances—to work according to divine counsel and ecclesiastical authority, so as not to lose his soul."[30]

"si tamen filius dici debet," and "si rex dici debet." MGH Epp. vii, no. 8, pp. 325f.

[28] Annales Bertiniani (a. 833), MGH in usum schol., p. 7.

[29] Concilium Tricassinum (867), Mansi xv, 792.

[30] MGH Cap. ii, no. 197, p. 53: "Quia potestate privatus erat terrena

While lacking the element of excommunication, the action against Lothaire (842) is quite similar to that against Louis, and may serve to elucidate the earlier process. Louis the German and Charles the Bald, in heavy military action against Lothaire, learned that he had fled from his kingdom. They then took counsel with their bishops in Aachen, so as to consider the circumstances *veluti numine divino*. The synod declared that since Lothaire had cast his father from the royal office, led his people into perjury through his acquisitiveness, attempted to deprive his brothers of their inheritance and to destroy them, and committed diverse wicked acts, and, moreover, since he lacked "the knowledge of governing a state [*respublica*]," "that his flight—first from battle and second from his own kingdom

---

juxta divinum consilium et ecclesiasticam auctoritatem, ne suam animam perderet, elaborare in extremis positus totis viribus studeret." See L. Halphen, "La pénitence de Louis le Pieux a Saint-Médard de Soissons," Université de Paris, *Bibliothèque de la Faculté des lettres*, 18 (1904), p. 185. See also Astronomus, Vita Ludovici, c. 54, MGH SS. II, p. 640: "Septem archiepiscopi septem reconciliationis ecclesiasticae orationes super eum cecinerunt. . . ." Louis' own thought is represented in a portion of one of his charters interpolated in a cession of Charles the Bald to St. Denis (where the restoration occurred), DC II, no. 246, p. 55, "Sed et octavo decimo kalendas februarii, quando me Rex regum, fugatis atque contritis ante faciem divinae potentiae nobiscum agente, in regnum restituit. . . ." Annales Bertiniani (a. 834), MGH in usum schol., pp. 8f, "Domnum imperatorem reconciliaverunt," Hincmar of Rheims, De Divortio, Responsio VI, Migne PL. 125, 757: "episcopalis unanimitas . . . ecclesiae et regno restitui." Cf. Hincmar's statement, "Si quis publicam poenitentiam pro culpis criminalibus egit," one might not become a bishop. Ep. 39, Migne PL. 126, 260. Cf. M. David, *La souveraineté et les limites juridiques du pouvoir monarchique du IXe au XVe siècle* (Paris, 1954), p. 115: "Si cette interprétation était la bonne, la pénitence de Saint Médard n'aurait, pas plus que celle d'Attigny, de portée juridique. Se présentait elle aussi, objectivement tout au moins, comme une auto-limitation. . . ."

—took place by a just judgment of Omnipotent God."
"The chastisement of God had cast him out because of
his wickedness, and had justly transferred his kingdom
to be ruled by his more worthy brothers."[31] Lothaire was
able to invalidate this pronouncement by force of arms;
and, supported by his own bishops, he did not fall under
the censure of his brothers' clergy. Indeed, no censure
was offered. But in this instance, just as in the process
which Lothaire had instituted against his father, the episcopal action was technically acquiescent, not initiative.
Louis the Pious stripped himself of the symbols of his
military office, an act of abdication; only thereafter, his
clergy invested him with the robes of a penitent.[32] Similarly, the synod at Aachen declared, not Lothaire's deposition, but the fact that "by divine judgment" he had already
been deposed. Ecclesiastics of the ninth century were accustomed to the voluntary alienation of sovereignty by
their temporal rulers;[33] but active resistance against the
"elect of God" was foreign to them.

This position is explicitly represented in the political

[31] Nithard, Historiae IV, 1, MGH in usum schol., p. 40.

[32] Relatio Episcoporum, MGH Cap. II, no. 197, p. 53. Agobardi
Cartula, ibid., no. 198, p. 57.

[33] Among the Carolingians themselves, the example of Carloman,
the brother of Pippin, was quite familiar (Annales Larissenses, aa.
745, 746, MGH SS. I, pp. 135f; Chronicon Moissiacense, a. 741, MGH
SS. I, pp. 292f). There were also fears in 819 that Louis the Pious
would "wish to relinquish the helm of kingship" (Astronomus, Vita
Ludovici, c. 32, MGH SS. II, p. 624); and Lothaire I did, in fact, abdi-
cate (Annales Bertiniani, a. 855, MGH in usum schol., p. 45; Regino,
Chronicon, a. 855, MGH SS. I, p. 569; Adrevaldus, De Miraculis S.
Benedicti, Migne PL. 124, 946, c. 41). More exotic instances among the
Bulgars were also known. Annales Einhardi (a. 813), MGH SS. I, p.
200; Regino, Chronicon (a. 868), MGH SS. I, p. 580.

thought of Hincmar of Rheims, the supposed author of two extant coronation *ordines* for Frankish kings and an outspoken champion of the oath as a binding juristic restraint upon temporal rulers.[34] Certainly, Hincmar did not reject excommunication as an instrument against temporal rulers. Two fragmentary letters of Pope Leo IV[35] and Flodoard's record of an absolution of the Emperor[36] leave no doubt that shortly after Hincmar's accession to Rheims he set Lothaire I under the ban; Leo stated that Charles the Bald and the families of the two rulers were also suspended from the communion in the same act. When Hincmar contested Charles's handling of church property twenty years later, he sinisterly referred to separation "from the body of the Church," to "penance and the reconciliation of priestly indulgence."[37] And again, when Charles's grandson, Louis III, attempted to establish his

[34] See his Pro Lib., Migne PL. 125, 1042, 1064ff. In view of Hincmar's actions, David's opinion is perhaps overstated (*La Souveraineté*, p. 127): "A vrai dire, ce n'est pas sur les rapports de l'*auctoritas* et de la *potestas* que la doctrine d'Hincmar est in plus nette de contours. Le véritable merite de l'archevêque de Reims, parvenu au faîte de l'influence politique, est ailleurs. Il sent la fragilité d'une doctrine juridique, reposant somme toute exclusivement sur des axiomes théologiques et sur des précédents historiques. Le plus sûr moyen pour renforcer l'efficacité des sanctions prises contre un monarque ne serait-il pas de les fair découler d'une infraction juridique caractérisée, comme la violation d'une promesse solennelle par exemple?" Consequently, David continues, Hincmar inserted the royal profession into the coronation *ordines*.

[35] MGH Epp. v, nos. 36, 37, p. 605. Kern, *Gottesgnadentum und Widerstandsrecht*, pp. 348f. Schrörs, *Hinkmar, Erzbischof von Reims*, pp. 58f, and W. Sickel, "Zum karolingischen Thronrecht," *Festschrift A. S. Schutz* (Leipzig, 1903), pp. 129f.

[36] Historia Remensis Ecclesiae, iii, 10, MGH SS. xiii, p. 483.

[37] Pro Lib., Migne PL. 125, 1058f. Cf. his warning to Charles against implication in the excommunication of Carloman's followers, Ep. 15, Migne PL. 126, 97.

favorite Odacre in the see of Beauvais contrary to Hincmar's judgment, the Archbishop warned the young King, "See to it that you do not suffer canonical sentences in this world and in the next for this illicit act."[38]

Neither of these last two threats was implemented; and Hincmar's fundamental position appears to have remained that kings were to be left to divine chastisement whenever possible: "Kings and bishops correct the wrongful acts of their subjects, but they ought not to forget that their evils will be judged by the Lord himself."[39] By wrongdoing, kings might deprive themselves of the royal name and office in the eyes of God, he wrote, although they might continue to enjoy the royal title in the eyes of men "by worldly, transient power."[40] And since God either brought good kings to government or allowed evil ones to rule, subjects were not to resist the iniquitous commands of the evil and therein to strive against the ordination of God.[41]

On four occasions, Hincmar explicitly rejected resistance to the royal authority: at the invasion of Louis the German (858), at the excommunication of Charles the Bald by Hincmar of Laon, at the second major invasion of West Francia by Louis the German (876), and at the command by Hadrian II that Hincmar withdraw from

[38] Ep. 20, c. 8, Migne PL. 126, 119f. Cf. Ep. 19, c. 10, cols. 116f; Ep. 33, c. 6, cols. 250f.

[39] De Divortio Lotharii, Responsio xii, Migne PL. 125, 701: "Reges enim et sacerdotes subditorum prava acta corrigunt sed oblivisci non debent, quia illorum mala per ipsum Dominum judicabuntur. . . ."

[40] Ibid., cols. 699f.

[41] Letter to Charles the Bald, Ep. 15, Migne PL. 126, 98. See also the Capitula Pistensia (862), MGH Cap. ii, no. 272, p. 305.

communion with Charles (870). In 858, denouncing
Louis' invitation to institute a general uprising against
Charles the Bald, the bishops of the provinces of Rheims
and Rouen, through Hincmar's pen, condemned such
rebellion against "the Lord's anointed" as both contu-
macious and perfidious. Even after he had been rejected
by the Lord, Saul was regarded with great reverence by
Samuel, "whose place in the Church we hold"; and David,
though elected and anointed to succeed Saul did not
"stretch forth his hand against the anointed of the Lord."
The bishops, therefore, could not rise against Charles without the counsel of the archbishops[42] and bishops who had
anointed him as king with the approval of his people,[43]
an act subsequently confirmed by the Apostolic See. If
God should unite their kingdom and Church in Louis'
hand, the bishops could then transfer their loyalty to their
new king; but while Charles remained king, they could
undertake no action against him.[44]

Eighteen years later, on different grounds, Hincmar
refused to excommunicate Louis the German when Louis
again invaded his brother's lands. To be sure, his attitude
then derived from quite practical considerations. He and
his fellow bishops were, as he wrote, "between the mallet
and the anvil"; if they welcomed the invader, they would
surely incur the wrath of Charles when he returned from
the Italian campaign, but if they strongly opposed Louis,

[42] Chief among them was Wenilo of Sens, who had joined forces
with Louis.

[43] MGH Cap. II, no. 300, c. 3, p. 451.

[44] *Ibid.*, no. 297, c. 15, p. 439. See Hincmar's remark that this strongly
worded letter was meant for Charles more than for Louis. Migne PL.
125, 955.

he would treat them harshly.[45] The refusal, however, is none the less distinct. Hincmar invoked the precedent of St. Ambrose, who did not excommunicate the Emperor Theodosius, and his colleague St. Martin, who, like Ambrose, retained the tyrants Maximus and Eugenius in communion and even broke bread with them.[46] In accordance with these holy precedents, the Frankish bishops could not rightly excommunicate the invading King, especially as he came professing that he wished to restore what had been destroyed, to defend peace and justice, and to render due honor to the Church and to the priesthood.[47] Without suggesting future actions, he concluded that so long as the liberties of the churches, or at least the performance of the Divine Office, remained undisturbed, the bishops were to make no resistance to Louis; at the same time, they must not join Louis against Charles.[48]

Of the two excommunications against Charles, the one threatened by Hadrian II is both the more important, and, happily, the better documented. The excommunication by Hincmar of Laon was issued, according to his uncle, to deter Charles from interfering in the administration—particularly in the territorial administration—of the diocese of Laon.[49] Nothing is known of its specific terms. But it was condemned by Hincmar of Rheims as "a scandal to the Church, as well as to the King and the kingdom";[50] it was considered of no effect, and it appears to have been a major cause for the deposition of the younger Hincmar.

---

[45] Ad Episcopos et Proceres, cc. 8, 9, Migne PL. 125, 965f.
[46] *Ibid.*, cc. 25-27, cols. 975f.
[47] *Ibid.*, c. 8, col. 965.   [48] *Ibid.*, cc. 4, 5, cols. 963f.
[49] Schedula adversus Hincmarum, c. 31, Migne PL. 126, 623.
[50] Letter to Hincmar of Laon, Migne PL. 126, 500.

By contrast, the letters Hincmar wrote to Hadrian II
in his own name and in the name of Charles when
Hadrian threatened Charles with excommunication are
full and informative. Both in the episcopal letter and in
the royal letters, two arguments are most prominent. The
first was the procedural objection that Hadrian had
threatened to excommunicate Charles on insufficient
grounds. For the King's royal title was based on incon-
testable hereditary succession; his devotion to the orthodox
faith was firm, since he had been schooled in sacred learn-
ing and in ecclesiastical and secular laws from early youth;
and he had never been regularly accused or convicted
either publicly in episcopal audience or by his own confession.[51] The second objection was one of privilege:
Hadrian had not "preserved its honor for the royal power."[52] While prosecuting vigorously the "open adultery"
of Lothaire II, Nicholas I had retained due honor for the
royal office; he had neither cast the epithets of "tyrant,"
"perjurer," and "violator of the Faith" upon Lothaire, as
Hadrian had cast them upon Charles, nor had he excommunicated him as, without authority or legal cause (*ratio*),
Hadrian threatened to excommunicate Charles.[53] Constantius the Arian, Julian the Apostate, the tyrant Maximus,
and all "other heretical schismatic and tyrannical emperors
and kings" had continued, despite their faults, to enjoy
the company and conversation of "pontiffs of the Apostolic
See and other bishops of great authority and sanctity."
Moreover, the just duties of a subject toward his ruler—
especially those of one who ruled a principal city—made
it impossible for an archbishop to withdraw from associa-

[51] Ep. 8, Migne PL. 124, 881. [52] Ep. 7, *ibid.*, 876. [53] *Ibid.*

tion with his king, as Hadrian had commanded Hincmar to do.[54] Unlike his predecessors, therefore, Hadrian had dishonored himself by commanding wrongful and impossible things;[55] and, since his sentence violated both secular and temporal laws, it was *ipso facto* void.[56]

Three less explicit rejections of royal excommunication will illustrate Hincmar's position further. The first is an *argumentum ex silentio*. In a well-known passage in his *De Divortio Lotharii*, Hincmar took issue with the assertion that, as a king established in his office by God, Lothaire II was subject to the laws and judgment of God alone and that he might not be excommunicated by his own nor judged by other bishops. Hincmar's argument discreetly avoids the point of excommunication. In his historical precedents of rulers who fell under ecclesiastical censure, he explicitly avoids mentioning the ban. St. Ambrose, he wrote, "separated" Theodosius from the Church and "recalled him through penance," and Louis the Pious, "deposed from the royal office," was "restored to Church and kingship after rendering satisfaction."[57] Although he maintained that "Holy Scripture and the sacred canons show that in judgment the person is not to be respected, but the quality of the case determined,"[58] and by inference suggested that a king might be brought before a synodal court to answer for his misdeeds, he did not explicitly affirm that a king might be excommunicated.

His actions toward Louis the German in 858/9 and Louis III in 880 indicate that this silence derived from

[54] Hincmar of Rheims to Hadrian II, Ep. 27, Migne PL. 126, 179, 183.
[55] Ep. 8, Migne PL. 124, 883.   [56] *Ibid.*, col. 894.
[57] Responsio VI, Migne PL. 125, 757.   [58] *Ibid.*, col. 759.

at least partial agreement with the Lotharingian bishops. When Louis the German invaded his lands, Charles the Bald convened a synod at Brienne-le-Château to excommunicate his brother and Louis' followers.[59] The records of that synod are not preserved; but the process of the Synod of Metz (859), which dealt with the same matter, indicates that the ban was not issued at Brienne and suggests further that no formal ban was to be issued. To be sure, the synod, of which Hincmar was president, declared that Louis had perverted his office. Rather than defending ecclesiastical properties from theft and violence and preserving the established privileges of bishops and their churches as a "minister of God,"[60] he joined those who preyed upon church lands; since they were excommunicate, he also fell under the ban by implication, but not directly.[61] Furthermore, rejecting the counsel of bishops, "who function as legates of Christ,"[62] he fell under censure as a schismatic.[63] The synod declared that Louis himself must be admonished to render a full confession of his wrongdoing and to undertake a fitting penance.[64] If he refused to render ecclesiastical satisfaction, his bishops were urged to withdraw themselves from his communion.[65] Charles's bishops, however, neither pronounced Louis excommunicate, nor pressed the East Frankish bishops to issue the ban against him.

[59] Hincmar of Rheims, Pro Lib., Migne PL. 125, 1067.

[60] Synodus Mettensis (859), MGH Cap. II, no. 298 A, c. 9, p. 444.

[61] Cf. Epistola Synodi Carisiacensis, *ibid.*, no. 297, cc. 12, 15, pp. 436, 439.

[62] Synodus Mettensis, c. 1, p. 442.   [63] *Ibid.*, c. 7, p. 443.

[64] *Ibid.*, cc. 4, 5, pp. 442f.   [65] *Ibid.*

The vitiating effects of Hincmar's doctrine of nonresistance upon the binding power of the coronation compact became apparent toward the end of his life in dealings with Louis III. After acceding "on the condition that you preserve due laws," the canons among them, Louis attempted to dispose of the bishopric of Beauvais in a manner which Hincmar thought contrary to canon law. On the premise that he could give the see of Beauvais to whomever he chose,[66] Louis named his "vassal,"[67] Odacre, bishop, and ordered his consecration by Hincmar and his suffragans. Hincmar considered Odacre canonically unqualified for the episcopacy and refused consecration. In the vigorous conflict which ensued, the Archbishop fulminated against the King, excommunicated Odacre, and, as already noted, hinted that Louis himself might incur "canonical sentences in this world and the next."[68] Significantly, however, in his letters to persons other than the King, Hincmar never censured Louis by name but always referred to him obliquely as the *potestas saecularis* or the *personae non ignotae* responsible for the uncanonical elevation.[69] Even in his letters to Louis himself, Hincmar made no specific threats of ecclesiastical punishment. To the contrary, his tone is uniformly that of submission, however unwilling. "It is just," he wrote, "as the Scripture shows, that 'one is punished through one's sins.' For since I gave my assent to your election against the will, threats, and voices of many, I hope and rejoice that, if I have sinned therein, by God's permission I may receive punishment here at your

[66] Hincmar of Rheims, Ep. 19, cc. 3, 4, Migne PL. 126, 111f.
[67] *Ibid.*, c. 8, col. 115.
[68] *Ibid.*, Ep. 20, c. 8, col. 120.
[69] E.g., Ep. 33, cc. 4, 5, Migne PL. 126, 248, 250.

hands and not in the future at the hands of the Lord...."[70]
Before Louis' eyes, Hincmar held only punishment by
God Himself, to whom he had directly given his corona-
tion oath.[71] "The Emperor Louis did not live as many years

[70] Ep. 20, c. 10, *ibid.*, 121. Cf. Paschasius Ratbertus, Vita Adalhardi,
c. 37, MGH SS. II, p. 528. Supra, Chapter I, note 15.

[71] Hincmar to Louis III, Ep. 19, c. 5, Migne PL. 126, 112: "Recordamini,
quaeso, professionis vestrae, quam in die consecrationis vestrae promisistis, sicut ab illis qui interfuerunt accepimus, quamque manu propria
subscripsistis, et super altare coram episcopis omnibus qui adfuerunt
Domino obtulistis. . . ." Though this manner of presentation was
singular among the royal oaths of the ninth century, it had a precedent
in the imperial coronation of Charles the Bald. For Pope John VIII
records that Charles presented his "vota," not to the Pope, but "Domino
Deo" (MGH Epp. VII, no. 6, p. 318), and that the presentation occurred
"at the tomb of St. Peter" (Migne PL. 126, 658). John's later emphasis
on the "promissio regum . . . et sacramenta quae Pippinus et Carolus
obtulerunt beato Petro apostolo" (Mansi XVII A, 347, Actio 4), recalls
also the donation of Charlemagne (774) "Quam prius super altare
beati Petri et postmodum intus . . . sancta eius confessione ponentes
tam ipse Francorum rex quamque eius iudices . . . beato Petro et eius
vicario sanctissimo Adrianae papae . . . tradiderunt." Liber pontificalis,
Vita Hadriani I, c. 43, ed. Duchesne cit., v. II, pp. 49f. Cf. Hincmar
to Charles the Bald, Migne PL. 125, 1065, "Deo et nobis promisistis,"
and the letter of Charlemagne to Michael I (MGH Epp. IV, no. 37),
p. 556, ". . . ita et memorati legati nostri foederis conscriptionem tuam
et sacerdotum patriciorumque ac procerum tuorum subscriptionibus
roboratam, a sacrosancto altari tuae manus porrectione suscipiant. . . ."
As the coronation of Louis III occurred in a Benedictine monastery
(Ferrières), some influence of the Rule of St. Benedict upon his manner
of presentation is possible. See Regula S. Benedicti, c. 58, 20 (*CSEL* 75,
p. 136). In contrast to his action, episcopal oaths among the Franks
appear not to have been presented on the altar, but to have been given
directly to the examining or consecrating bishops. See the Professio of
Adalbert of Thérouanne (Mansi XVIII bis, 616-618), the Examinatio of
Willebert of Châlons-sur-Marne (Mansi XV, 861-866), and Hincmar of
Rheims, LV Capitula, Praefatio (Migne PL. 126, 292). In Rome, however,
episcopal oaths were laid on the tomb of St. Peter, as Charles's *vota*
appear to have been. See MGH Epp. V, no. 3, p. 586, "Sacramentum . . .
quod consecrationis tuae tempore supra corpus beati Petri promi-
sisti. . . ."

as his father Charles, nor did your grandfather Charles [the Bald] live as many years as his father, nor did your father [Louis the Stammerer] live as many as his. When you stand in the place where your grandfather and your father are buried at Compiègne, turn your eyes toward your father's tomb. If you do not know yourself, ask when he died and when your grandfather was laid to rest . . . and be certain that you know not the day nor the hour when you will die. . . . Therefore, let not your heart be lifted up against Him in whose hand our life and days are kept. You will die soon, but the Holy Church with her rectors will abide under Christ, her Rector, according to His promise, 'as the full moon forever.' "[72]

Hincmar's words and actions illustrate in practical terms the limitations of the contractual view of Church-State relations. He rejected human resistance to the king as to the elect of God and "the anointed of the Lord"—even resistance by the Church itself. Breach of contract by the king could be punished by divine chastisement, just as Louis the Pious and Lothaire I were declared to have lost their kingdoms by the judgment of God, and as Louis III was offered the prospect of premature death; but it could not be punished by ecclesiastical constraint or opposition. Ninth-century Franks, like the authors of the *Libri Carolini* at the end of the eighth century, held that, "As long as [the king] remains in his office, he is to be honored, if not for his own qualities, at least for his rank. Wherefore the Apostle says: 'Be ye subject to all higher powers:

[72] Ep. 20, c. 9, Migne PL. 126, 120.

for there is no power save of God,' and in another place:
'Fear God; honor the king.' "[73]

[73] III, 29, MGH Conc., Suppl., p. 166. The authors refer to the
honor shown Saul by David even after God had withdrawn His favor
from Saul, and continue: "Quamdiu ergo in ea dignitate est, honorandus
est, si non propter se, vel propter ordinem. Unde Apostolus: 'Omnibus,
inquit, potestatibus sublimioribus subditi estote. Non est enim potestas
nisi a Deo'; et in alio loco: 'Deum timete; regem honorificate.' " Cf.
Gregory IV to the Frankish bishops (833): "In tantum autem honoranda est cathedra pontificalis et propter cathedram sedens in illa...."
MGH Epp. v, n. 17, p. 230. See also the frequent distinction made
between the bishop and the episcopal order. E.g., Charles the Bald
to John VIII, Ep. 32, c. 6, Migne PL. 126, 233, "quia si nos sacrum
ordinem in personis eorum [episcoporum] vilipendimus . . . a districto
judice . . . dijudicabimur. . . ."

CHAPTER VI · CONCLUSIONS

ONE metaphorical figure, the ship of the Church, may illustrate the change in Frankish thought about Church-State relations which occurred between the early and the later ninth century.[1] In the *Libri Carolini*, which he ordered composed in answer to Byzantine iconodulism, Charlemagne describes the Church as a ship containing the souls of all the redeemed, a ship set *"in sinu regni."* Christ himself was the chief steersman, but He had delegated to Charlemagne the responsibility of guiding the ship to safety, of ruling, defending, and exalting her.[2] This metaphor in which the king acts as the helmsman of the Church is, however, singular in Frankish writings. Significantly, though Byzantine and Roman authors in the later ninth century acknowledged the bipartite government of Christendom by the pontifical authority and the royal power by describing the temporal ruler as the helmsman[3]—and consequently as the

[1] For a general discussion of the history of this figure, see H. Rahner, "Navicula Petri," *Zeitschrift für katholische Theologie*, 69 (1947), especially pp. 1, 9, 22f. Rahner neglected to mention the liturgical sanction for the figure. See Wilson, *The Gelasian Sacramentary*, 511, p. 20. For a summary of general interpretations applied to it, see Rhabanus Maurus, Allegoriae in S. Scripturam, Migne PL. 112, 1004f.

[2] MGH Conc. Suppl., pp. 1f, praefatio. The metaphor appears twice more in the records of the Synod of Frankfurt, once with the Holy Spirit as *gubernator* (Charlemagne to Elipandius, MGH Conc. 1, no. 19 F, p. 158), and once with Christ as helmsman (*ibid.*, no. 19 D, pp. 131f).

[3] Curiously, Pope John VIII once acknowledged Louis III as the helmsman. MGH Epp. VII, no. 205, p. 165, "studeatis quatenus sanctam Dei ecclesiam in magna nunc fluctuatione positam ad portam salutis et tranquillitatis efficaciter perducatis et terram perditam per vos Deo

239

effective representative of Christ, "the supreme *guberna-tor*"[4]—no Frankish author followed their example. Rather, the Franks uniformly attributed supreme responsibility for the management of the spiritual ship, not to a layman nor to one preeminent ecclesiastic,[5] but to the episcopal order.[6] Through the ministry of all bishops, the *navis* was to be defended from "the peril of the wave, the temptations of the devil";[7] all others on board were to obey their directions. Pseudo-Isidore offers by far the most elegant example of the *navis* figure. In a rigid hierarchical structure, he took Christ as his *gubernator*, the bishop as his pilot, priests as seamen, deacons as quartermasters, catechiz-

---

propitio ad pristinam revocetis incolumitatem. . . ." Cf. *ibid.*, no. 268, p. 237. In the fourth Council of Constantinople (869), the Emperor Basil I affirmed: "Cum divina et benignissima providentia nobis gubernacula universalis navis commisset, omne studium arripuimus et ante publicas curas, ecclesiasticas contentiones dissolvendi et procellas, quae per multos annos ex invidia odientis bonum satanae expansae sunt, in stabilem tranquillitatem per meliorem quamdam provisionem transferendi. . . ." Actio I, Mansi XVI, 18. One may add the related figure employed early in the tenth century by John XII of Ravenna: "Portus vero per metafforam rex intelligi potest ecclesia vero navis in mari, quae undique nigris tunditur fluctibus. . . ." S. Löwenfeld, "Acht Briefe aus der Zeit König Berengars," *Neues Archiv*, 9 (1884), pp. 521f.

[4] Epistola Synodi Carisiacensis, MGH Cap. II, no. 297, c. 15, pp. 440f.

[5] The words of Walafrid Strabo, "in quo Petro est typus totius ecclesiae" which Rahner cites as admitting Roman supremacy to the *navis*, refer neither to the *navis* nor to Matthew 5:6 as cited. The reference is rather to St. Peter's work in the draught of fishes described in Luke 5: 10. Strabo, Glossa Ordinaria, Migne PL. 114, 256.

[6] The figure was often applied to local churches and prelates. See, for example, the letter of the Church of Cologne to Pope Hadrian II, MGH Epp. VI, no. 4, p. 244, Hincmar's Vita S. Remigii, c. 30, MGH SS Rer. Mer., v. III, pp. 326f, and MGH DL II, no. 133, p. 185, "rector et gubernator abbas Prumiae ac sui fratres."

[7] Walafrid Strabo, Expositio in Mattaeum, Migne PL. 119, 872. Cf. *ibid.*, coll. 878, 881.

ers as *nautologae*, and laymen as *epibatae*.[8] While the ship was buffeted by storms of heresy and tribulation, the clerical crewmen were to go about their duties and at last to bring the ship safely "into the port of the desired city." The laymen, on the other hand, were merely "to sit each one in his place," so as not to endanger the entire ship by distracting the crewmen from their duties.[9] Pseudo-Isidore employed this figure merely to illustrate the relationships he sought between the clergy, as the guardians and teachers of doctrine, and laymen as their disciples. His contemporaries, however, transposed the same figure to the area of administrative relationships with striking effect. The Synod of Thionville (844), for example, affirmed that Christ, the *gubernator*, roused by the prayers of the Faithful, would never allow His ship to sink. And it praised the three sons of Louis the Pious, since "according to the precept of the Lord, where it is said, 'Ask the priests my law,' and 'Ask your fathers and they will declare unto you,' you deign to seek divine counsel from us, the vicars of Christ, however unworthy, and with benign devotion to await it as though it truly came from the mouth of God Himself."[10] Fifteen years later, the bishops of the

---

[8] Pseudo-Isidore appears to have confused his figure, for before he compared laymen to *epibatae* (light-armed infantrymen), he wrote "epibatis autem totius fraternitatis [i.e., the clergy] multitudo sit similis." The definition of Rhabanus Maurus, however, leaves no doubt that the comparison was specifically meant for the laymen: "Epibata Graeco nomine appellatur, qui Latine dicitur superveniens: hic [in the *navis*] nihil habet negotii, sed naulo dato in alias terras transire disponit." De Universo xx, 39, Migne PL. iii, 554.

[9] Ps.-Clement, Ep. i, cc. 14, 16, Hinschius, *Decretales Pseudo-Isidorianae*, pp. 34f. Cf. the related figure in the letter of Ps.-Alexander, Ep. ii, c. 15, p. 103, where the bishops are also clearly *gubernatores*.

[10] MGH Cap. ii, no. 227, p. 113. Cf. *ibid.*, no. 254, pp. 253f.

dioceses of Rouen and Rheims more resolutely divided the earthly kingdom from the kingdom of Christ, the Church, which Christ had commended to the Apostles and to their episcopal successors. Moreover, they declared that they would pray to the "Supreme *Gubernator*" on behalf of Louis the German—a "son of the Church," although a king—and they affirmed at the same time that God had given Louis bishops as the immediate governors of the tempest-tossed Church "to rule and to teach" him.[11] The reversal of the image of Charlemagne was complete; the direction of the Church had devolved from the king upon the entire episcopal order. The king no longer guided the Church; rather, as a Christian, he was guided by it. We have been concerned to define the legal thought which attended and, indeed, motivated this ecclesiological revolution, this assertion of the freedom of the Church in the face of an aggressive temporal government.

In any system of political thought, there are two universal questions: "What is the character of human society?" and "How is society properly governed?" The ninth century had three major answers. Papal monism held that human society was primarily spiritual and that

[11] *Ibid.*, no. 297, c. 15, p. 441. Cf. Florus of Lyon, where the personified Ecclesia says, "Legibus antiquis edicta recentia junxit [princeps] / / Et bona prisca novis auxit ubique bonis: / / Ne me per pelagus mundi, per turbida saxa / / Obrueret subito nox fera naufragio." MGH Poet. Lat. ii, p. 558. vv. 105-108. See the pessimistic usage of Agobard of Lyon, MGH Epp. v, no. 16, c. 6, p. 228. Compare the rarer image of the *navis reipublicae* in *Sedulii Scotti Liber de Rectoribus Christianis*, c. 6, ed. S. Hellmann (Munich, 1906), p. 38: "Si quis ergo navim rei publicae tamquam bonus gubernator regere feliciter disponit et exoptat, optima Domini consilia, quae in sacris eloquiis sunt propalata, non negligenter custodiat." See also c. 16, p. 74.

its rightful government was an ecclesiastical monarchy. Its counterpart, royal monism, maintained that society was temporal and that temporal monarchy should rule it. Finally, dualism, to which we have devoted our primary attention, argued that society was spiritual and temporal in equal measure and that supremacy in those domains was held respectively by the episcopal and the royal offices. We have described the antagonism between the two monistic schools and the dualistic, and the tensions within dualistic thought itself which vitiated dualism and, in a later age, led to theoretical resolution in a higher unity.

Carolingian thinkers, however, did not know the legal principles which led to that resolution. *Plenitudo potestatis* was a concept foreign to them either in the temporal or in the ecclesiastical context, as were all other principles of Roman and canon law which later mediaeval writers used in formulating their doctrines of sovereignty. For the Franks, sovereignty—and thus the resolution of dualistic tensions—was inconceivable: the burden of their thought was that there was no sovereignty except the direct government of God. If, therefore, they lacked the knowledge of jurisprudence necessary to frame a doctrine of unitary, sovereign government, they also lacked the inclination to do so. The whole structure of the juristic doctrine maintained by the Frankish dualists centered rather upon their effort to make a theological reality a legal fiction. That theological reality was the Kingdom of the Church, transcending the bounds of all earthly realms and governing itself independently of temporal rule by its own laws and its own institutional apparatus. Legal fictions, even those grounded in theology, are real facts, and the major effort of the Carolingian clergy was bent toward gaining from their kings the recognition of the *Regnum Ecclesiae* that would establish the independence and the integrity of canonical government.

For later Frankish authors who thought of Church and State as juristic entities, the episcopacy and the kingship, the offices governing those institutions respectively, were discrete and independent one from the other. The origins of the two offices were different, as were their proper duties. The episcopacy (or the priesthood) was instituted directly by God for the performance of sacramental functions, and the kingship derived from human practice for the maintenance of civil law and security. Further, the laws by which those offices were discharged were distinct in competence and legislative origins. While binding on laymen in some matters, such as marriage, the canons were more specifically the peculiar law of the priesthood. They had been ordained by the Holy Spirit through the assent of the whole clergy and supplemented by papal decretals and by privileges which temporal rulers issued in favor of the priesthood. On the other hand, civil laws were generally binding on all laymen and on priests and bishops as well where the canons did not take precedence (i.e., in civil matters outside the competence of ecclesiastical jurisdiction). They had been established, not as common enactments of one collective body, but either as imperial or royal edicts, or as joint declarations framed by the consensus of the people and promulgated by royal authority. Finally, and most important, the authority exercised in each office was of a peculiar species: The bishops exercised a spiritual supremacy which resided in the corps of the episcopacy itself, while royal jurisdiction, supreme in temporal matters, centered in the office of the king.

As we have seen, this dualistic position was subject to external and internal tensions: it was jeopardized by the theological monism of contemporary popes, by the royal monism present under Charlemagne and continued in some measure by his successors, and by the fineness of its own intellectual balance between temporal and spiritual jurisdictions. The weakness of the contract between king and clergy, epitomized in the coronation ritual, suggests this internal tension which obscured the limits of the jurisdiction of royal and episcopal courts and which could, as a consequence, lead to *de facto* royal monism or to a doctrine of ecclesiastical supremacy, either of which would destroy the dualistic structure.

Though great, the challenge offered by papal monism was not so critical or immediate as were the difficulties created by royal monism and by the fundamental inadequacy of dualism itself. The border between the spiritual and the temporal could be drawn in theory, but it could not always be established beyond question in actual problems of jurisdiction. For example, it was not clear whether cases of land tenure—such as that of Hincmar of Laon—which involved temporal interests of spiritual rulers, should be settled by secular judges according to civil law or by ecclesiastics according to the canons. There was no arbiter to decide whether a given case fell within the competence of the spiritual or of the temporal power; for the dualism in Frankish thought established no superior authority to resolve such questions definitively. Ninth-century dualists, therefore, did not frame a consistent solution for the problem of Church-State relations. But in striving toward a solution, they formulated juristic doctrines of conciliarism and of constitutional limits upon the royal power which deeply influenced political thought in later generations and marked the beginning of a new era in the unending struggle for ecclesiastical liberty.

APPENDIX A: THE COMPARATIVE USE
OF ROMAN AND FRANKISH LAW BY
HINCMAR OF RHEIMS

HINCMAR cites both the *capitula* of Frankish kings and the edicts of Roman emperors as authoritative legal sources. Once, he referred to some Frankish statutes as "*capitula* which the Church approves as regular,"[1] and again he mentioned them as "constitutions of sacred laws."[2] Such terms were rarely applied to Frankish law, however, and, though he was well acquainted with the compilations of Ansegisus and Benedictus Levita and with the whole texts of some of the edicts excerpted in them, he consulted Roman law far more often that he did Frankish. For example, in his indictments of his nephew (the *Opusculum LV Capitulorum* and the *Schedula adversus Hincmarum Laud.*), there are liberal citations of Roman law, but not one reference to Frankish; and in all the records of the Synod of Touzy itself—though Charles the Bald specifically asked that the trial be conducted according to secular as well as canon law[3]—Frankish law is represented only by a general reference by Charles himself to the practices of his predecessors,[4] and by one citation from the collection of Ansegisus.[5] There

[1] Ep. 52, Migne PL. 126, 274f.

[2] Ad Episcopos Admonitio Altera, c. 17, Migne PL. 125, 1016f. Since there are no citations of Roman Law in the declaration of the Synod of Fismes, the term "*constitutiones legum sacrarum*" can only refer to the copious quotations from the Frankish capitularies in it. There can be no question that Hincmar regarded the written capitularies as law. Cf. De Divortio, Responsio v, Migne PL. 125, 754, "capitula sunt legalia imperatorum et regum" and De Ordine Palatii, c. 8, MGH Cap. II, p. 520, where the admonition of St. Augustine to judge according to the laws, not of them, which Hincmar customarily applied to Roman law, was applied to the *capitula*.

[3] Proclamatio Regis, c. 6, Mansi xvi, 581.

[4] *Ibid.*   [5] Responsa, c. 5, col. 650.

are at least two possible explanations for this preference. First, Hincmar conceived of Roman law as being applicable throughout the world and saw a general relationship between its universality and that of the Church.[6] Second, numerous titles of the Roman law were issued at the petition of the clergy,[7] while such instances were rare in Frankish law. Furthermore, Frankish laws lacked the approval of popes and councils which had judged Roman laws "ecclesiastical"[8] and "canonical" and had consequently "received and reverently approved" them.[9] This general preference for Roman law over Frankish may be seen also in the character of the works in which Hincmar inserted excerpts from the two laws. In writings to the Frankish clergy or especially to the Frankish kings on matters of civil order,[10] ecclesiastical discipline,[11] or clerical privileges,[12] he found Frankish law applicable and even employed it liberally. However, Roman law, as "the law by which the Church is governed together with the canons," was cited in those same works and also in letters to popes, in works on the nature of the Faith,[13] and in comments on episcopal maladministration; that is, in any consideration of matters concerning the general government of the clergy, the legal relevance of Roman law was patent, while that of Frankish law was not.

The matters which Hincmar treated by citing one law or

[6] Cf. Ad Regem de Coercendo Raptu Viduarum, c. 5, Migne PL. 125, 1020f. Pro Lib., *ibid.*, cols. 1056f. De Divortio, Responsio v, *ibid.*, col. 653.

[7] See De Divortio, Responsio v, Migne PL. 125, 652f. MGH Epp. VIII, fasc. I, no. 160 b, c. 9, p. 138 and *passim*.

[8] Cf. the exception of the edict issued by Louis the Pious in 829 mentioned in "De ecclesiis et capellis," ed. Gundlach, pp. 107ff, and De Divortio, Responsio v, Migne PL. 125, 652.

[9] LV Capitula, c. 51, Migne PL. 126, 489.

[10] Ep. 24, Migne PL. 126, 161; and the Synod of Fismes, Migne PL. 125, 1077-1081.

[11] De Presbyteris criminosis, cc. I-IV, Migne PL. 125, 1093-1095.

[12] De Officiis, *ibid.*, 1088; Pro Lib., *ibid.*, cols. 1040, 1048, 1060, 1064, 1065.

[13] De Praedestinatione, Diss. Post., c. 37, Migne PL. 125, 401f.

the other also illustrate this difference. Both laws were cited as guaranteeing the Church in the tranquil possession of its property and the clergy in the right to canonical trial before an ecclesiastical court.[14] Frankish law was particularly cited on those relatively few matters treated in it, but not in Roman law: for example, on the admission of serfs to the priesthood,[15] on feudal tenure,[16] on rendering tithes to the Church,[17] and on the supervision of ecclesiastical order by *missi dominici* (Synod of Fismes). Most often, however, as in the *Pro Libertatum Ecclesiae Defensione*, it was cited as law corroborating the establishments of Roman law.[18] On the other hand, the variety of matters to which Roman law was applied testifies that it held the position of primary importance. The manumission of slaves,[19] the character of marriage,[20] clerical celibacy,[21] the punishment of heretics,[22] the force of conciliar decrees,[23] and the nature of legal documents,[24] together with the matters already mentioned, all fell within its competence. In addition, the general character of episcopal administration was prescribed in it, and questions of episcopal abuse were adjudicable with reference to it. The bulk of Hincmar's citations from Roman law, indeed, pertain to the criminal process: to laws excluding intervention in trials by powers not directly concerned in them and governing the competence of ecclesiastical courts, the

[14] E.g., Pro Lib., *ibid., passim.*

[15] De Divortio, Responsio x, Migne PL. 125, 683.

[16] Mansi xvi, 647f.

[17] "De ecclesiis et capellis," ed. Gundlach, p. 96.

[18] Migne PL. 125, 1039.

[19] Migne PL. 126, 562.

[20] Ad Regem de Coercendo Raptu Viduarum, c. 19, Migne PL. 125, 1032. De Divortio, Responsio xii, *ibid.*, 690.

[21] Capitula Presbyteris Data, c. 21, *ibid.*, 781. De Presbyteris Criminosis, cc. 9, 10, *ibid.*, col. 1097.

[22] De Praedestinatione, Diss. Post., c. 37, *ibid.*, cols. 401ff.

[23] lv Capitula, c. 26, Migne PL. 126, 391.

[24] *Ibid.*, c. 36, col. 429. De Divortio, Responsio xii, Migne, PL. 125, 703f.

qualification of witnesses and accusers, the place of adjudication, the delegation and conduct of judges, the character of the sentence, the punishment of calumniators and informers, and the conditions of conviction.

APPENDIX B: ROYAL SYMBOLS IN THE
CORONATION SERVICE

THE EXCLUSIVELY temporal nature of the royal office is illustrated by the kingly symbols, particularly by those bestowed in the coronation ritual. Perhaps because the Scriptures attribute no sword to Christ when they describe the Roman soldiers' mocking acclamation of Him as King, the sword is curiously absent from all Frankish coronations except the secular investiture of Charles the Bald by Louis the Pious in 838.[1] Firmly established by St. Paul's words as emblematic of the royal office,[2] the sword appears frequently in ninth-century writings as a major sign of kingship. Charles the Bald swore upon his sword that he would honor the promises rendered his bishops at Beauvais (845);[3] and, like his father before him,[4] he sent a sword from his death-bed to his successor, "the sword called 'the Sword of St. Peter,'" with which Louis the Stammerer was to be invested with the royal office.[5] Yet, the sword occurs only in the imperial coronation of Lothaire I (823),[6] in the coronation of Louis II as king of the Lombards (844)[7] —both of them non-Frankish ceremonies—and in the procla-

[1] Astronomus, Vita Ludovici, c. 59, MGH SS. II, p. 643, and Nithard, Historiae, I, 6, MGH in usum schol., pp. 9f. See Cl. Frhr. v. Schwerin, "Zur Herkunft des Schwertsymbols," *Festschrift Paul Koschaker*, v. III (Weimar, 1939), p. 347.

[2] See the Visio Caroli Magni in P. Jaffé ed., *Bibliotheca Rerum Germanicarum*, v. IV, pp. 701-704.

[3] Hincmar of Rheims, Pro Lib., Migne PL. 125, 1066.

[4] Astronomus, Vita Ludovici, c. 63, MGH SS. II, p. 647. See Schwerin, "Zur Herkunft des Schwertsymbols," p. 335.

[5] Cf. Annales Fuldenses (a. 840), MGH in usum schol., p. 31: "missis ei insigniis regalibus, hoc est sceptro imperii et corona."

[6] Epitaphium Arsenii, II, 17, MGH SS. II, p. 564.

[7] Annales Bertiniani (a. 844), MGH in usum schol., p. 30. Also see the letter of Nicholas I to Charles the Bald, MGH Epp. VI, no. 34, p. 305.

mation of Charles the Bald (838). Again, the *"arma"* with which Louis the Pious was reinvested in 834 almost certainly included the sword;[8] Louis himself alluded to the military buckler.[9] One must observe, however, that the sword in Charles's accession ceremony is mentioned as *"arma virilia,"* not as *"arma regalia,"* perhaps a telling distinction in view of the particular description of the crown as a *"corona regalis."* Furthermore, the arming of Louis the Pious in 834 had the peculiar character of a ceremony in which those to whom Louis had surrendered his weapons returned them to him, but did not exercise the function of original bestowal or reenact the coronation ceremony. Since the coronations of Lothaire I and his son occurred in Rome, then, investiture with the sword as a canonical part of the royal coronation appears first among the Franks in the Erdmann *Ordo*, toward the middle of the tenth century.[10]

Admittedly, the scarlet or purple robe also does not appear in contemporary descriptions of coronations, but its connection with the ceremony seems more probable than that of the sword. Like the sword, it was an acknowledged symbol of kingship, an ancient symbol among the Carolingians, for Pippin, the father of Charlemagne, is said to have soaked the royal purple with his tears at the translation of the relics of St. Stemonius.[11] The Monk of St. Gall also mentions the *"imperatoria purpura"*

[8] Cf. Annales Bertiniani (a. 839), MGH in usum schol., p. 8: "et regalibus vestibus armisque induerunt."

[9] MGH Epp. v, no. 19, p. 327. Relatio Episcoporum, MGH Cap. ii, no. 197, pp. 51ff. Cf. Agobardi Cartula, *ibid.*, no. 198, p. 56, and Thegan, Vita Ludovici, c. 44, MGH SS. ii, p. 599: "Abstulerunt ei gladium a femore suo, iudicio servorum suorum induentes eum cilicio." For the formula "deposito militiae cingulo," see canon xviii, Council of Nicea, Migne PL. 56, 396; and for the formula of public penance among the Franks, apparently used in Louis' deposition, see Jonas of Orléans, De Institutione Laicali, i, 10, Migne PL. 106, 138f.

[10] Schramm, "Kronung," pp. 201f.

[11] Translatio S. Stremonii, c. 4, Mabillon, *Acta SS. O.S.B.,* v. iii, pt. ii, p. 174.

together with the sceptre as emblematic of the royal office;[12] and Smaragdus joins the royal *stola*, the *"regalis purpura,"* and the royal diadem with similar meaning.[13] Further, its connection with the accession is illustrated by a late source which maintains that Charlemagne was robed in purple at his imperial coronation;[14] and by a contemporary account which relates that Louis the Pious was revested with royal robes at his restoration.[15] In addition, Richildis took "royal vesture" to Louis the Stammerer, together with a golden staff and the Sword of St. Peter, the means of investiture with the kingship, and Charles the Bald had earlier conferred upon Breton leaders the right to wear *"vestes regales"* at the same time he granted them the royal title.[16] Finally, since revesting

[12] I, 18, MGH SS. II, p. 738: "Sedebat autem ipse [episcopus] mollissimis plumis praeciosissimo serico vestitis exstructus, imperatoria purpura indutus, ita ut nihil illi nisi sceptrum illud et nomen regium deesset. . . ." On the episcopal use of the purple, see also Thegan, Vita Ludovici, c. 44, MGH SS. II, p. 599; Donation of Constantine, Hinschius, *Decretales Pseudo-Isidorianae*, p. 253. Cf. MGH Epp. Gregorii I Regestrum v. I, pt. I, p. 31, IX, I, 24. In passing, one may mention the figure of Charles the Bald in Hincmar of Rheims's Visio Bernoldi, Migne PL. 125, 1117, where the spirit of Charles the Bald appears "sanum corpore et indutum regiis vestibus." Charles's preference for splendid raiment, however, was not always approved by Hincmar. See the Annales Bertiniani (a. 876), MGH in usum schol., pp. 128ff, and by way of comparison, the Annales Fuldenses (a. 876), *ibid.*, p. 86.

[13] Via Regia, c. 11, Migne PL. 102, 952. See also cc. 6, 9, cols. 946, 950. On the comparable *stola* of the bishop, see Hincmar of Rheims, Vita Remigii, c. 16, MGH SS. Rer. Mer. III, p. 302. See also *Sedulii Scotti Liber de Rectoribus Christianis*, c. 11, ed. S. Hellmann (Munich, 1906), p. 52: "ut regias purpuras, sceptra, quoque et apicem imperatoriae dignitatis divinis praeceptis et canonicis institutis Domino inspirante subderent."

[14] Annales Nordhumbrenses: "A domino Leone papa purpura regaliter induitur, cui corona aurea capiti imponitur et regale sceptrum in manibus datur." See S. Abel, *Jahrbücher des fränkischen Reiches unter Karl dem Grossen*, 2d ed., II (Leipzig, 1883), p. 236n.

[15] Annales Bertiniani (a. 834), MGH in usum schol., p. 8. Cf. Nithard, Historiae I, 4, *ibid.*, p. 6: "coronam et arma regi suo imposuerunt."

[16] Annales Bertiniani (a. 851), *ibid.*, p. 41.

was a part of the baptismal service[17] and of the episcopal ordination,[18] one may suppose that it also occurred in the royal consecration to which they are comparable in form.

The two other symbols in the Scriptural account of the acclamation of Christ, the crown and the rod, which appear regularly in descriptions of coronations, became strongly representative of the king's promised duty to govern according to the will of God, to stand as the guarantor of law and as the defender of civil order.

The crown assumed a particularly mystical import in the coronation orders. Significantly, in the coronation of Charles the Bald at Metz, the same words began the benedictions and the prayer at the imposition of the crown itself: "The Lord crown you with a crown of glory...."[19] It came, therefore, to represent the infusion of divine grace, symbolized by the unction, the infusion of the divinely given "*scire et posse*" according to which the king promised to discharge his duties. Thus it did "signify victory"[20] over visible and invisible enemies, the final triumph of anointed "priests, kings, prophets, and martyrs who overcame kingdoms through faith and did justice";[21] and Alcuin, congratulating Charles, the son of Charlemagne, on receiving the "crown of the royal dignity," urged him to discharge the office it represented by performing "acts of justice and mercy amongst the Christian people."[22]

[17] Wilmart, "Une catéchèse baptismale du IXe siècle," *Revue Bénédictine*, p. 199, c. 14.

[18] Hincmar of Rheims, Ep. 29, Migne PL. 126, 187.

[19] MGH Cap. II, no. 302, p. 457.

[20] Hincmar of Rheims, De ordine palatii, c. 5, MGH Cap. II, p. 519.

[21] *Ibid.*, no. 302, p. 457.

[22] Alcuin to Charles, the son of Charlemagne, MGH Epp. IV, no. 217, p. 360. Charles had been king since 788. See the Annales S. Amandi Brevis (a. 788), MGH SS. II, p. 184: "Carolus rex factus est." The priesthood shared this mystical symbolism of the crown. See Ratramnus of Corbie, Contra Graecorum Opposita, IV, 5, Migne PL. 121, 323f; Synod of Aachen (816), MGH Conc. I, no. 39, p. 318. See also the Donation of Constantine for the papal claim to a material crown. Hinschius, *Decretales Pseudo-Isidorianae*, p. 253.

The sceptre was the secular counterpart of the "stave of sacred government," the "sign of the pastoral office,"[23] with which bishops governed and corrected their churches and strengthened "the infirmities of the infirm";[24] it not only held the punitive symbolism of the sword[25] but it also betokened the rule of justice and law. One sees these concepts blended in the formula prescribed at the bestowal of the sceptre in the

[23] Concilium Constantinopolitanense IV (869), Actio 7, Mansi XVI, 97. Marinus, the Roman legate, orders the deposition of Photius, saying, "Tollite baculum de manu eius, signum est enim dignitatis pastoralis, quod hic habere nullatenus debet; quia lupus est, et non pastor."

[24] Isidore of Seville, De ecclesiasticis officiis II, 5, 12, Migne PL. 83, 783f.

[25] Cf. the Monk of St. Gall, I, 17, MGH SS. II, p. 738: "Qui cum familiaritate illius animari coepisset, in tantam progressus est proterviam, ut virgam auream incomparabilis Karoli quam ad statum suum fieri iussit, diebus feriatis vice baculi ferendam pro episcopali ferula improbus [episcopus] ambiret." See also I, 34, p. 747. C. v. Amira, Der Stab in der germanischen Rechtssymbolik, Abh. d. kgl. Bay. Ak. d. Wiss., philos.-philol. u. hist. Kl., Bd. 25, Abh. 1 (Munich, 1909), p. 124. On the "status" which Charlemagne intended his staff to represent, one should observe the punitive significance of the royal stave. In his war against the pagans, for example, Louis the Pious appeared "sceptra manu gestans," Ermoldus Nigellius, In Honorem Ludovici, I, 386, MGH Poet. Lat. II, p. 17. Cf. the construction Lothaire II put on the palm and staff given him by Pope Hadrian II: "per palmam victoria se in his quae coeperat demonstraret, per ferulam episcopos suae voluntati resistentes obsistendo distingeret." Annales Bertiniani (a. 869), MGH in usum schol., p. 100. On the similar episcopal usage, see the Gesta Aldrici, c. 44, MGH SS. XV, pt. 1, p. 323: "Misit [Gregory IV] etiam ei [Aldricus] bacculum pastorale, qui ferula nuncupatur." As the Monk of St. Gall suggests, the sceptre and the episcopal staff were easily, though not suitably, interchangeable. Regino of Prüm affords one instance in which the episcopal baculus served the royal office of vengeance. Chronicon (a. 862), MGH SS. I, p. 571. Though the royal staff (baculus) does not appear in royal coronations before that of Otto I, or before the Erdmann Ordo, it was firmly established as a royal symbol in the ninth century. See the Annales Bertiniani (a. 849), MGH in usum schol., p. 37, for the exchange of baculi by Charles the Bald and Louis the German, and (a. 876), p. 130, for the presentation of a "sceptrum et baculus aureus" to Charles as gifts from Pope John VIII.

coronation order of Louis the Stammerer. "Receive the sceptre," said the consecrators, "the token of royal power, the straight staff of kingship, the rod of virtue. With it, rule yourself well, defend the Holy Church (that is, the Christian people committed to you by God) from wicked men by your power, correct the iniquitous, and by your assistance, direct the righteous that they may hold to the way of righteousness. . . ."[26] In the legalistic mind of Hincmar of Rheims, this symbolism paralleled that of the book of law set in the hands of Old Testament kings at their anointing "so that they might know how they ought to rule themselves, correct the iniquitous, and direct the good to the way of righteousness. . . ."[27] The sceptre represented, therefore, the fullness of the royal office as set forth in the accession oaths: to defend the Church, to preserve law and justice, and therein to rule *"secundum Dei voluntatem."* As the consecrators prayed when they transmitted the sceptre and palm to Charles the Bald in Metz: "The Lord give you the desire and capacity [*velle et posse*] for what he

[26] "Accipe sceptrum, regiae potestatis insigne, virgam scilicet rectam regni, virgam virtutis, qua te ipsum bene regas, sanctam ecclesiam, populum videlicet christianum tibi a Deo commissum, regia virtute ab improbis defendas, pravos corrigas, rectos, ut viam rectam tenere possint, tuo iuvamine dirigas. . . ." MGH Cap. II, no. 304, p. 461. The palm conferred upon Charles the Bald in 869 does not recur in any subsequent coronation, undoubtedly because it represented his coming into Lotharingia as a triumphant king. One may compare the letter of John VIII to Charles (MGH Epp. VII, no. 32, p. 31), and that of Stephen V to Charles the Fat (MGH Epp. VII, no. 13, p. 340), which elucidate the symbolism of the palm. Cf. the prayer "Victoriosum te atque triumphatorem" in the coronation of Louis the Stammerer (MGH Cap. II, no. 304, p. 462), repeated from the 869 ordo of his father, but with the phrase "et pace in diebus tuis concessa cum corona victoriae" substituted for "et pace in diebus tuis concessa cum palma victoriae" (cf. *ibid.*, no. 302, p. 457). Cf. the Vita Hadriani I, c. 36, Liber Pontificalis, ed. Duchesne, I, p. 497, and the Apologetici Ebonis forma posterior, MGH Conc. II, no. 61, p. 801.

[27] De ordine palatii, c. 5, MGH Cap. II, p. 519. Cf. Synod of Fismes, c. 1, Migne PL. 125, 1071. See Schramm, "Krönung," pp. 130f.

commands so that serving well [*proficiens*] in the rule of kingship according to His will, you may come with the victorious palm of him who perseveres, to the palm of eternal glory. . . ."[28]

As bishops did not bear any of these royal symbols, except the purple which was theirs through ancient liturgical usage, nor did kings yet receive the episcopal symbols, the ring and the staff, at their coronations, one may conclude that the interpenetration of symbols which obtained later between the two offices was not present in the mid-ninth century.

[28] MGH Cap. II, no. 302, p. 457.

APPENDIX C: OUTLINES OF
PAPAL MONISM

AMONG papal theorists, a new monistic doctrine arose after the time of Charlemagne in opposition to royal monism. The clear formulation of papal monism did not occur before the pontificate of Nicholas I. To be sure, its doctrinal principles were present and were applied to papal relationships with temporal rulers very early in Carolingian history. But the temper of that early usage was far different from that of the later. Its theological basis, the Petrine commission, only supported assertions of Rome's spiritual hegemony in the Church, without vindicating her direction of political affairs. Early popes asked royal defense of the Roman Church on the ground that St. Peter, through his vicar, had commended that Church to the Frankish kings for protection; later popes required it as the due and obligatory service of the king to a higher power.[1]

The ground of earlier papal dealings with the Carolingians was, in fact, more the functional division of ecclesiastical and secular powers than their union in a theologically construed relationship. During the reign of Charlemagne, the theoretical correlation of papal and royal duties remained largely as the King himself described it in his well-known statement to Leo III. He wrote that he wished to enter a compact with Leo like the one he had entered with Hadrian I, specifying that he, on the one hand, would defend the Church everywhere from external attacks and fortify it internally by knowledge of the orthodox faith, and that the Pope, on the other, would

[1] See especially the letter of Stephen II in the name of St. Peter to Pippin, Charlemagne, and Carloman, MGH Epp. III, no. 10, pp. 501ff. On the earlier relations between the Papacy and the Franks, see W. Sickel, "Kirchenstaat und Karolinger," *Hist. Zt.*, 84 (1900), pp. 385-409, who concludes that the early Carolingians did not exercise any considerable power in Rome itself.

assist the royal forces to victory through his intercessory prayers.[2] The letters of Hadrian and those of Leo indicate that these pontiffs did indeed consider their relations with the Frankish King an alliance between their sacramental and the King's temporal office. For example, Hadrian frequently wrote to Charlemagne that the victories of the Frankish armies were due to papal prayers and St. Peter's intercession, and he praised that coordination between Charlemagne's *regalis potentia* and "the head of the entire world, the Holy Roman Church," which was responsible for the military successes.[3]

With some modifications, the same concept persisted under Leo III. As the tenant of imperial power, Charlemagne remained the "guardian of the Holy Church."[4] The personal dangers which beset Leo brought him to enhance the office of his defender with spiritual honor somewhat more than his predecessor had done. He referred trials of priests to Charlemagne's attention,[5] sent pronouncements on matters of faith for his perusal,[6] and affirmed that the episcopal order "all hope to remain safe in your service."[7] But he did not thereby alter the terms of Charlemagne's former pact with Hadrian: the areas of competence proper to their offices remained divided according to their respective functions.[8]

The earliest significant statements deviating from this position occur in the letters of Gregory IV, who maintained that spiritual government was superior to temporal even in earthly affairs and gave emphasis to his thought both by threatening Louis the Pious with excommunication and by joining the forces which deposed him.[9] Subsequent papal writers tended

[2] MGH Epp. iv, no. 93, p. 137.

[3] MGH Epp. iii, no. 72, pp. 602f; no. 61, p. 588, and *passim*.

[4] MGH Epp. v, no. 9, pp. 100f. Cf. Hadrian I, MGH Epp. iii, no. 59, p. 585.

[5] MGH Epp. v, no. 2, p. 91.   [6] *Ibid.*, no. 8, pp. 66f.

[7] *Ibid.*, no. 2, p. 91.

[8] *Ibid.*, no. 6, p. 97; no. 1, p. 87, and *passim*.

[9] *Ibid.*, no. 17, pp. 228f.

to refine this argument even more carefully and to place it within the waiting framework of Petrine primacy. Toward the middle of the century, Leo IV maintained in a letter to the Emperor
Louis II that, by virtue of his supreme pontifical office, he had
the charge "of all who are in the world";[10] and he defended
the Emperor Lothaire I from excommunication by Hincmar
of Rheims on the ground that the Apostolic See had conferred
a sacred unction upon Lothaire and had taken him as its
"heir."[11] Leo's successor, Benedict III, affirmed even more
strongly that through Christ's commission to St. Peter, the
bishop of Rome became the overseer "of all who believe in
Christ,"[12] the mediator of peace among earthly princes,[13] and
the monitor of their laws.[14]

[10] *Ibid.*, no. 10, p. 589.

[11] *Ibid.*, no. 37, p. 605. Cf. the Judicatum Leonis IV et Ludovici II,
Migne PL. 115, 658ff. Leo allowed the emperors considerable power
in the disposition of episcopal sees (see MGH Epp. v, no. 19, p. 597;
no. 21, p. 598), and on one occasion he even invited Louis II to judge
his actions, *ibid.*, no. 40, p. 607.

[12] Migne PL. 115, 693.

[13] *Ibid.*, cols. 692f. In the following remarks on the development of
papal thought, I am in fundamental agreement with Dr. Ullmann
(*Growth of Papal Government*). Some aspects of his argument, however, require modification along the lines suggested in the text above.
For example, he tends to overstate Nicholas I's views of papal supremacy
over temporal authorities by citing a remark of Pope John VIII, whose
position was far more hierocratic than Nicholas's, to illustrate Nicholas's
judgment toward the papal role in imperial elections (*ibid.*, pp. 202f);
in discussing Nicholas's assertion of papal jurisdiction in the divorce
case of Lothaire II, he neglects to mention that Lothaire himself had
appealed to papal judgment (pp. 204f); in describing Nicholas's position on the supremacy of ecclesiastical laws over temporal, he does not
observe, as Nicholas did, that the supremacy existed only in ecclesiastical
cases; and finally, in sketching Nicholas's doctrine of resistance, he
does not make it clear that Nicholas did not claim that a wicked king
might be deposed by his clergy, but merely that the clergy ought to
withdraw its loyalty from such a ruler (p. 207). Similarly, in his discussion of Hadrian II, Dr. Ullmann does not mention Hadrian's
acknowledgment that the imperial office might be conferred by temporal
authority and only confirmed by the sacramental action of the popes.

These tendencies first approached broad formulation in the letters of Nicholas I. Defining relations between the royal and the papal offices, Nicholas joined three conventional premises: that as a man and a member of the Church, the temporal ruler was subject to ecclesiastical discipline; that the royal office derived from the Church; and that it was instituted to serve spiritual ends.[15] In the particular relations of kings to the Roman See, the head of Christendom, these premises had three corollaries: that the royal (or imperial) office was effectually bestowed through the sacramental actions of the pope;[16] that under some circumstances a king who proved himself unable to discharge his office to the benefit of the Christian community was liable to excommunication and might be tried by a synod or by the papal curia; and that the pope might enlist armed forces sufficient to depose an incorrigible ruler.[17]

Nor does he observe the peculiar circumstances—namely, the failure of hereditary succession—which made it possible for Hadrian to claim the power of imperial nomination, or the fact that Hadrian exercised that claim, not merely as the Bishop of Rome, but as the spokesman of the Roman Senate, clergy, and people (pp. 212ff). He does not mention that in the imperial accession of Charles the Bald, John VIII acted, like Hadrian, in the name of the Roman people, admittedly at the same time emphasizing the constitutive force of his sacramental functions more than his predecessors. Further, in the remarks on John, there is some confusion between that Pope's regular use of the word *respublica*, as meaning the Roman commonwealth, and the much rarer phrase *respublica christiana* (pp. 220ff).

[14] Migne PL. 115, 693f.

[15] MGH Epp. VI, no. 90, p. 508, "matrem vestram ex qua imperandi fastigium vos et patres vestri ordine caelitus disposito percepistis, . . ." repeated, no. 91, p. 530. See also *ibid.*, no. 99, c. 18, p. 578, and the letter of Louis II, MGH Epp. VII, pp. 388f. See F. Schneider, *Rom und Romgedanke im Mittelalter* (Munich, 1926), pp. 53f, and F. A. Norwood, "The Political Pretensions of Pope Nicholas I," *Church History*, 15 (1946), esp. p. 281.

[16] MGH Epp. VI, no. 34, p. 305.

[17] See E. Perels, "Ein Berufsschreiben Papst Nikolaus' I. zur fränkischen Reichssynode in Rom," *Neues Archiv*, 32 (1907), p. 144.

In attempting to implement this doctrine, Nicholas acted "as though he were lord of the earth."[18] He accepted the services of Louis II as his equerry;[19] he received weapons and trophies from the victorious King of the Bulgars;[20] he intervened in the temporal affairs of the Carolingian kingdoms.[21] Both Eastern and Western emperors were censured by him, and learned what broad powers he claimed when he attributed both the material and the spiritual swords to St. Peter.[22]

Nicholas intended primarily, not to erect the papacy as the directive power over temporal rulers, but rather to exclude civil authorities from clerical affairs and to impose uniform canonical government upon all the clergy. He left the systematization of his concept of Church-State relations to his successors. For this reason, the monism which Nicholas advanced preserves some marks of the earlier functional dualism.[23]

His actions in the divorce of Lothaire II illustrate the still rather tentative nature of his monism. Certainly, he maintained that the divorce of a king, like that of any other layman, should be reviewed by ecclesiastical judges and that the king could fall under spiritual censure like any of his subjects. Further, when Lothaire rejected the papal sentence, Nicholas threatened him with excommunication and anathema and

[18] Regino, Chronicon (a. 868), MGH SS. I, p. 579.

[19] Liber Pontificalis, Vita Nicolai I, c. 9, ed. Duchesne, v, II, p. 152.

[20] Annales Bertiniani (a. 866), MGH in usum schol., p. 86.

[21] E.g., MGH Epp. vi, no. 44, pp. 318f.

[22] *Ibid.*, no. 123, p. 641. For Nicholas's Byzantine relations, see H. Laemmer, *Papst Nikolaus der Erste und die byzantinische Staats-Kirche seiner Zeit* (Berlin, 1857).

[23] *Ibid.*, no. 57, p. 357; no. 88, p. 469, and *passim*. Haller's argument that Nicholas's actions did not tend toward papal monism, however, ignores that Pope's well-attested claim to be numbered among the Apostles and his coordinate assertions of directive power over temporal princes. J. Haller, *Nikolaus I. und Pseudoisidor* (Stuttgart, 1936), pp. 140ff. A more comprehensive study could lead only to Perels's conclusion, that "den erfolgreichsten Päpsten des hohen Mittelalters hat keiner der Vorgänger den Boden besser bereitet als er." E. Perels, *Papst Nikolaus' I. und Anastasius Bibliothecarius* (Berlin, 1920), p. 180 and pp. 17ff.

mustered the forces of Charles the Bald and Louis the German for his deposition. But he did not fulfill his threats; even if Lothaire had been deposed, Nicholas' own part in executing the sentence would have been indirect; for ultimately, Nicholas left the punishment of kings to their royal peers.[24]

More important, the assertions Nicholas made in the intermittent course of the trial were not spontaneous. To the contrary, his intervention in the process and the threats he subsequently issued against Lothaire derived entirely from the fact that Lothaire himself had appealed the case to Rome and had refused to observe the judgment Rome delivered.[25] Lothaire wrote that he had voluntarily put aside the privileges of his royal office and set himself under Nicholas' jurisdiction as an ordinary layman.[26] Nicholas' actions, consequently, were wholly in accord with the terms Lothaire had proposed. The Pope's threats of excommunication and mustering of military force to punish an incorrigible sinner—in this instance, to depose a king—were conventional not only in papal but even in episcopal procedure against the recalcitrant. Though Nicholas must have known the implications of these actions within the context of Church-State relations, he left their explicit statement to Hadrian II and John VIII.

The whole thought of Hadrian in his political as well as in his hierarchical relationships was guided by the classic concept of Petrine primacy. Christ had committed to St. Peter and his vicars, he said, the task of governing all the redeemed[27] and had given them ultimate and comprehensive power to bind and to loose.[28] Supreme jurisdictional power and authority resided in the Roman see; and, through the prescience of

[24] See above note 17. Cf. MGH Epp. vi, no. 2, p. 268.

[25] *Ibid.*, no. 53, p. 342; no. 14, p. 231; no. 17, p. 237; no. 11, pp. 276f.

[26] See above p. 57, n. 70.

[27] Liber Pontificalis, Vita Adriani II, c. 17, ed. Duchesne, v. ii, p. 176: "qui commissit beato Petro apostolo cunctos regere quos redemit. . . ."

[28] MGH Epp. vi, no. 36, p. 743; no. 4, p. 701.

Christ, no pontiff who judged unrighteously would ever sit
in the chair of St. Peter. The kingship was not, primarily, a
juridical office, but a ministry for the defense and exaltation
of the Roman Church.[29] The vicar of St. Peter had assumed
the duty of guaranteeing due law to every man, formerly a
characteristically royal function;[30] kings must heed his words,
for they were "the voice of God transmitted through the
office of the Apostolic See,"[31] to which Christ had charged
the care of the whole Church with the words, "Feed my
sheep; feed my lambs."[32]

The fulfillment of these tendencies obtained in the writings
of John VIII, where the classic Petrine primacy was clearly
joined to the even more ancient concept of Rome as the
capital of a universal temporal state. For John, the head of
the Church, the vicar of St. Peter, was also through the exercise of indirect powers the head of the temporal government
of Rome. While he acknowledged that kings held some
peculiar powers,[33] he still applied to them as well as to the
clergy the principle that there should be "one flock, one
pastor."[34] By virtue of divine cession and imperial grants, the
government of Rome, the head of the Empire,[35] the head of
all nations and kingdoms,[36] had been transmitted to St. Peter

[29] Mansi xv, 890ff.

[30] MGH Epp. vi, no. 18, p. 720, "unicuique ius proprium reservandum
competenter admonens. . . ."

[31] *Ibid.*, no. 37, p. 747.   [32] *Ibid.*, no. 1, p. 695.

[33] Notably in the disposition of bishoprics. See MGH Epp. vii, no.
179, p. 143; no. 247, pp. 215f; no. 248, p. 217.

[34] *Ibid.*, no. 210, p. 187. Cf. *ibid.*, no. 8, p. 323, "Ministerii nostri
est . . . quid in qualibet mundi parte congruat sive non congruat
censoria gravitate depromere. . . ." See also *ibid.*, no. 208, p. 177; no.
203, p. 163.

[35] *Ibid.*, no. 33, p. 33.

[36] *Ibid.*, no. 205, p. 165, "Si Deo favente Romanum sumpseritis imperium, omnia vobis regna subiecta existent." Cf. no. 198, p. 159,
"Romanam ecclesiam . . . quae omnium gentium retinet principatum et
ad quam totius mundi quasi ad unam matrem et unum caput conveni-
unt nationes."

and his successors.[37] Rome was the "head of the world," the "priestly and royal city,"[38] "the mistress of the world,"[39] of whom it was said, "Lo, I have set thee this day over nations and over kingdoms, to root out and to pull down, to destroy and to throw down, to build and to plant."[40]

Although John once affirmed that he sought, not to gain civil dominion through his actions, but only to vindicate his hierarchical headship of the clergy,[41] his deeds and the bulk of his writings lead one to suppose only that his chief principle was that of universal papal omnicompetence. For he tended to expound in its widest construction the view that his ministry was, "according to the sentence of St. Paul, to bear the superintendence of the whole Church of God and to draw out with weighty censure the suitable and the unsuitable in every part of the world. . . ."[42] He himself claimed temporal power[43] and attempted to direct the exercise of temporal power by inferior princes of the clergy and of the laity in Gaul.[44] And his letters to the Frankish kings, to Sventapulc of Moravia, to Michael of Bulgaria, and to the Eastern and Western emperors repeatedly command their obedience to the vicar of St. Peter.[45]

---

[37] *Ibid.*, no. 74, p. 70. See F. Kampers, "Roma aeterna und sancta Dei ecclesia rei publicae Romanorum," *Hist. Jb.* 44 (1924), pp. 242ff, and W. Gundlach, *Die Entstehung des Kirchenstaates und der curiale Begriff Res publica Romanorum* (Breslau, 1889), pp. 100ff, n. 320. Cf. the illuminating reply the Monk of St. Gall attributes to the Emperor Michael when Leo III asked him for aid: "Ille papa regnum habet per se, et nostro praestantius, ipse se per se ipsum vindicet de adversariis suis." Gesta Caroli, I, 26, MGH SS. II, pp. 743.

[38] MGH Epp. VII, no. 78, p. 74.

[39] *Ibid.*, no. 67, p. 61.

[40] *Ibid.*, no. 69, p. 64. Jeremiah 1:10.

[41] *Ibid.*, no. 66, p. 59, "Nam non patriae regimen et rei publicae moderamen adipisci cupimus, sed dioeceseos eiusdem regionis curam et dispositionem more prisco resumere volumus. . . ."

[42] *Ibid.*, no. 8, p. 323.   [43] *Ibid.*, no. 82, pp. 77f.

[44] *Ibid.*, no. 219, pp. 195f.

[45] See *ibid.*, no. 111, p. 103; no. 88, p. 84; no. 200, p. 160, and *passim*. His words to Michael of Bulgaria are especially noteworthy (*ibid.*, no.

He went further. Of his own judgment he added to the body of secular law when it was thought insufficient,[46] and he consolidated his assumption of royal prerogative by declaring his power to delegate the kingship, to correct its administration, and, if necessary, to withdraw it. Certainly, the power of the pope to depose temporal rulers is not treated extensively in John's extant letters, but it is explicitly claimed. When, for example, John wrote to Charles the Bald threatening to continue the process Hadrian II had instituted against Charles, he certainly refers to excommunication, and his tone is so vigorous that it suggests even more serious punishment.[47] Somewhat later, when Carloman of Italy proved physically unable to discharge his office, John proposed to depose him in his metropolitan synod and, at the same time, to elect Carloman's successor.[48] John held the conventional view that the defense of the Church was the primary responsibility of the

---

182, p. 146): "Cui vos in primordio Christianitatis vestrae ad regendum commisistis eiusque successoribus ad obediendum. . . ."

[46] Mansi XVII A, 351. Nicholas I had established a precedent in his dealings with the Bulgars, MGH Epp. VI, no. 99, c. 13, p. 575.

[47] MGH Epp. VII, no. 6, pp. 276f. See the letter of Hadrian II to Louis the German on his process against Charles for his invasion of Lotharingia (MGH Epp. VI, no. 25, p. 731): "Iam vero si idem rex ab invasione illa cessaverit et suae tyrannidi cesserit, ecce bene; sin autem, scitote, quia per nos illuc iter veniendi accelerabimus et utpote periurum ac invasorem eum sinodice iudicabimus et velut in contemptorem Dei ac apostolicarum monitionum ultionem debitam inferemus. . . ."

[48] *Ibid.*, no. 163, p. 133, to Anspert of Milan. "Et quia Karolusmannus corporis, sicut audimus, incommoditate gravatus regnum retinere iam nequit, ut de novi regis. . . . [lacuna] omnes pariter consideremus, vos predicto adesse tempore valde oportet. Et ideo antea nullum absque nostro consensu regem debetis recipere, nam ipse, qui a nobis est ordinandus in imperium, a nobis primum atque potissimum debet esse vocatus atque electus, quoniam et nos una cum vestra fraternitate cupimus pertractare et de hoc et quo tenore vel ordine communes causas et utilitates ecclesiarum Dei nobis commissarum ordinemus et iure canonico statuamus. . . ."

royal, or imperial, office. For him, however, this duty did not consist primarily of general warfare against barbarian invaders, as popes had thought in the time of Charlemagne, but much more of the protection of Rome itself and of service directly to the bishop of Rome. He advanced Charles the Bald to the imperial dignity, he wrote, so that Charles might defend him from the assaults of pagans and unbelievers;[49] and he acclaimed Charles as the "saviour of the world" for his defense of the Roman see.[50] The same thought predominates in his relations with Louis the Stammerer and Charles the Fat.[51]

John's attitude toward the imperial accession shows the same sharply focused particularism. During his pontificate for the first time since the translation of the Empire from East to West under Leo III, the imperial succession by inheritance failed, and the election of a suitable candidate devolved upon "the Roman senate, clergy and people."[52] As the supreme head of the "priestly and royal city," John completed the structure of his hierocratic thought by applying the theological basis for Rome's spiritual primacy to Church-State relations. After considering other candidates with his suffragans and with the Roman Senate,[53] the vicar of St. Peter and St. Paul, the vicar of God, called Charles the Bald to the imperial office.[54] The

[49] *Ibid.*, no. 36, pp. 35f. Cf. *ibid.*, no. 110, p. 102: "Bosonem . . . per adoptionis gratiam filium meum effeci ut ille in mundanis discursibus, nos libere in his, quae ad Deum pertinent, vacare valeamus."

[50] Bouquet VII, p. 695. Cf. MGH Epp. VII, no. 32, p. 31.

[51] Mansi XVII A, 354f, c. 12; MGH Epp. VII, no. 224, p. 199. See M. Pacaut, *La théocratie* (Paris, 1957), pp. 58f.

[52] Bouquet VII, p. 695. Cf. Hadrian II, MGH Epp. VI, no. 19, p. 722; referring to Louis II: "Quoniam ipsi et paterno et hereditario jure secundum legem et rationem hoc regnum debetur et per paternae hereditatis successionem summopere pertinet, quippe cum *eum* praefatus *genitor illius* quondam imperator *constituerit imperatorem* regnique totius heredem prae ceteris sublimaverit natis." The papal coronation, Hadrian continued, merely confirmed this nomination.

[53] Cf. his offer to Charles the Fat, MGH Epp. VII, no. 59, p. 311.

[54] See the election of Charles the Bald as King of Italy (MGH Cap. II, no. 220, p. 99): "Iam quia divina pietas vos beatorum principum

source of Charles's government as well as that of his religious belief, John later maintained, was the Roman Church.[55]

In John's comments upon his part in the imperial accession of 876, two thoughts predominate: namely, that Charles's election had been divine, but had been made known through the Pope's mediacy, and that Charles had entered upon imperial government by his consecration at John's hands. Charles did not owe his office to human bestowal, the Pope wrote, although he had received it through the ministry of the Pope; it was due rather to divine dispensation.[56] Offering his coronation oath to God, and depositing his *vota* at the tomb of St. Peter, Charles "received the imperial office through the imposition of [John's] hands";[57] God Himself had consecrated Charles, but He had acted through the papal ministry.[58] The year after Charles's coronation, John asked a synod at Ravenna to confirm what he had done "in the Roman Church, which is the mistress, the mother, and the head of churches." The synod accepted John's election and consecration of Charles without reserve; for "As St. Boniface, the Pope, teaches, no one may ever raise his hand against the apostolic office unless he wishes to be condemned." Election, benediction, unction, and corona-

---

apostolorum Petri et Pauli interventione per vicarium ipsorum, domnum videlicet Iohannem . . . ad profectum sanctae Dei ecclesiae nostrorumque omnium incitavit et ad imperiale culmen sancti Spiritus iudicio provexit. . . ."

[55] MGH Epp. VII, no. 22, p. 20: "huic ecclesiae matri vestrae, a qua non solum regnandi, sed et in Deum unum et verum credendi exordium percepistis. . . ." *Ibid.*, no. 87, p. 82, "in defensionem matri vestrae, a qua et potum predicationis in proavis et infulam imperii accepistis. . . ." comments to Louis the Stammerer who was not crowned by a pope.

[56] *Ibid.*, no. 7, p. 321, "imperium quod ei constat non humano collatum beneficio, licet per nostrae mediocritatis ministerium, sed divino pertingere potuisset. . . ." Cf. *ibid.*, no. 304, p. 263, "post augustale sceptrum per humilitatis nostrae ministerium vobis divinitus adtributum. . . ."

[57] Migne PL. 126, 658. Cf. the related grant of Charles the Bald to St. Vaast, DC II, no. 408, p. 413. See also MGH Epp. VII, no. 6, p. 318.

[58] Bouquet VII, p. 695.

tion were all confirmed: *"Placet et valde placet in omnibus vestra serenissima sectari vestigia, neque fas est ut a culmine apostolatus vestri in aliquo dissentiamus, quem videlicet ipse Christus Dominus noster omnium nostrum ad vicem suam in terris esse voluit caput."*[59]

By the end of John's pontificate, therefore, the theological basis of the hierarchical monarchy conventional in ecclesiastical thought had been vigorously applied to papal relations with temporal rulers as well. The vicar of St. Peter, become also the vicar of God, was no longer the supreme arbiter of ecclesiastical matters alone, but also of the highest temporal affairs. He might establish ecclesiastical law and add to the body of secular law; through his consecration, both bishops and kings acceded to their offices; through his judgment, both might be deposed. The functional dualism which popes had maintained in the time of Charlemagne had disappeared, and a Petrine monism had entered into its place.

[59] *Ibid.*, pp. 696f.

BIBLIOGRAPHY OF WORKS CONSULTED

Abel, S. (B. Simson contin.), *Jahrbücher des fränkischen Reiches unter Karl dem Grossen*. 2d ed., 2 vols. Leipzig, 1883, 1888.

Amann, E., *L'époque carolingienne*. Paris, 1936.

Amira, C. v., *Der Stab in der germanischen Rechtssymbolik, Abhandlungen der königlichen Bayerischen Akademie der Wissenschaften*, philos.-philol. und hist. Kl. Bd. 25, Abh. 1. Munich, 1909.

Andrieu, M., "Le sacre épiscopal d'après Hincmar de Reims," *Revue d'histoire ecclésiastique*, 48 (1953), pp. 22-73.

Arnold, F. X., *Das Diözesanrecht nach den Schriften Hinkmars von Reims*. Vienna, 1935.

Arquillière, H. X., *L'Augustinisme politique*, 2d ed. Paris, 1955.

Baix, F., "Les sources liturgiques de la *Vita Remigii* de Hincmar," *Miscellanea historica in honorem Alberti de Meyer* v. 1. Louvain, 1946, pp. 211-227.

Barion, H., *Das fränkisch-deutsche Synodalrecht im Frühmittelalter*. Bonn, 1931.

Beck, H. G. J., "Canonical Election to Suffragan Bishoprics According to Hincmar of Rheims," *Catholic Historical Review*, 43 (1957), pp. 137-159.

Bernheim, E., *Mittelalterliche Zeitanschauungen in ihrem Einfluss auf Politik und Geschichtschreibung*. Teil 1. Tübingen, 1918.

Beumann, H., "Nomen Imperatoris. Studien zur Kaiseridee Karls d. Gr." *Historische Zeitschrift*, 185 (1958), pp. 515-549.

Bloch, M., *Les rois thaumaturges*. Strasbourg and Paris, 1924.

Bonnaud-Delamare, R., *L'idée de paix à l'époque carolingienne*. Paris, 1939.

Born, L., "The *Specula Principis* of the Carolingian Renaissance," *Revue Belge de philologie et d'histoire*, 12 (1933), pp. 583-612.

Boudriot, W., *Die altgermanische Religion in der amtlichen kirchlichen Literatur des Abendlandes vom 5. bis 11. Jahrhundert*. Bonn, 1928.

Bourgeois, E., *Le capitulaire de Kiersy-sur-Oise (877): Etude sur l'état et le régime politique de la société carolingienne à la fin du IXe siècle, d'après la législation de Charles le Chauve*. Paris, 1885.

Bressoles, A., *Saint Agobard, évêque de Lyon, 769-840*. Paris, 1949.

Buchner, M., "Grundlagen der Beziehungen zwischen Landeskirche und Thronfolge im Mittelalter," *Festschrift Georg von Hertling*. Kempten, 1913, pp. 234-252.

———, "Pseudoisidor und die Hofkapelle Karls des Kahlen," *Historisches Jahrbuch*, 57 (1937), pp. 180-208.

———, "Rom oder Reims die Heimat des Constitutum Constantini?" *Historisches Jahrbuch*, 53 (1933), pp. 137-168.

Cabaniss, J. A. *Agobard of Lyons, Churchman and Critic*. Syracuse, 1953.

———, *Amalarius of Metz*. Amsterdam, 1954.

Calmette, J., *La Diplomatie carolingienne (843-877)*. Paris, 1901.

Carlyle, A. J. and R. W., *A History of Mediaeval Political Theory in the West*, v. 1. London, 1930.

Caspar, E., "Das Papsttum unter fränkischer Herrschaft," *Zeitschrift für Kirchengeschicte*, 54 (1935), pp. 132-264.

———, *Geschichte des Papsttums*, v. 11. Tübingen, 1933.

Clercq, C. de, *La législation réligieuse franque de Clovis à Charlemagne*. Louvain, 1936.

———, "La législation religieuse franque depuis l'avènement de Louis le Pieux jusqu'aux Fausses Décrétales," *Revue du droit canonique*, 4 (1954), pp. 371-404; 6 (1956), pp. 144-162, 263-289, 340-372; 7 (1957), pp. 15-48.

Cochet, M. A., *Essai sur l'emploi du sentiment religieux comme base d'autorité politique du IIIe au XXe siècle*. Paris, 1925.

Conrat (Cohn), M., *Geschichte der Quellen und Literatur des römischen Rechts im früheren Mittelalter*, v. i. Leipzig, 1891.

———, "Der Novellenauszug *De ordine ecclesiastico*, eine Quelle des Benedikt Levita," *Neues Archiv*, 24 (1899), pp. 341-348.

———, "Über eine Quelle der römischrechtlichen Texte bei Hinkmar v. Rheims," *Neues Archiv*, 24 (1899), pp. 349-357.

Davenport, E. H., *The False Decretals*. Oxford, 1916.

David, M., *La souveraineté et les limites juridiques du pouvoir monarchique du IXe au XVe siècle*. Paris, 1954.

Dekkers, E. and E. Gaar, *Clavis Patrum Latinorum*. Sacris Eruditi III, Bruges, 1951.

Doizé, J., "Le gouvernement confraternel des fils de Louis le Pieux et l'unité de l'Empire (843-855)," *Le moyen âge*, 2 (1898), pp. 253-285.

Dümmler, E., "Ermahnungsschreibung an einen Karolinger," *Neues Archiv*, 13 (1887), pp. 191-196.

———, *Geschichte des Ostfränkischen Reichs*. 2d ed., 2 vols. Leipzig, 1887, 1888.

———, "Karolingische Miscellen," *Forschungen zur deutschen Geschichte*, 6 (1866), pp. 113-129.

———, "Radberts Epitaphium Arsenii," *Abhandlungen der königlichen Akademie zu Berlin*, phil.-hist. Kl. 1900, Abh. 2, pp. 1-98.

Ehrenforth, G., "Hinkmar von Rheims und Ludwig III von Westfranken," *Zeitschrift für Kirchengeschicte*, 44 (1925), pp. 65-98.

Ehrhardt, A., "Das Corpus Christi und die Korporationen im spät-römischen Recht," *Zeitschrift für Rechtsgeschichte*, R. A. 70 (1953), pp. 299-347, 71 (1954), pp. 25-40.

Eichmann, E., "Die Adoption des deutschen Königs durch den Papst," *Zeitschrift für Rechtsgeschichte*, G. A., 37 (1916), pp. 291-312.

Eichmann, E., "Das Exkommunikationsprivileg des deutschen Kaisers im Mittelalter," *Zeitschrift für Rechtsgeschichte,* K. A., 1 (1911), pp. 160-194.

——, *Die Kaiserkrönung im Abendland.* 2 vols. Würzburg, 1943.

——, "Die rechtliche und kirchenpolitische Bedeutung der Kaisersalbung im Mittelalter, "*Festschrift Georg von Hertling.* Kempten, 1913, pp. 263-271.

Eiten, G., *Das Unterkönigtum im Reiche der Merovinger und Karolinger.* Heidelberg, 1907.

Ellard, G., *Ordination Anointings in the Western Church Before 1000 A.D.* Cambridge, Mass., 1933.

Elze, R., "Die Herrscherlaudes im Mittelalter," *Zeitschrift für Rechtsgeschichte,* K. A., 71 (1954), pp. 201-223.

Ensslin, W., "Auctoritas und Potestas," *Historisches Jahrbuch,* 74 (1955), pp. 661-668.

——, "Das Gottesgnadentum des autokratischen Kaisertums der frühbyzantinischen Zeit," *Studi bisantini e neoellenici,* 5 (1939), pp. 154-166.

Erdmann, C., "Der ungesalbte König," *Deutsches Archiv,* 2 (1938), pp. 311-340.

Esmein, A., *Les ordinales dans l'église gallicane au IXe siècle: Hincmar de Reims et ses contemporains.* Paris, 1898.

Ewig, E., "Zum christlichen Königsgedanken im Frühmittelalter," *Vorträge und Forschungen,* III (1954), pp. 7-73.

Faulhaber, R., *Der Reichseinheitsgedanke in der Literatur der Karolingerzeit bis zum Vertrag von Verdun.* Berlin, 1931.

Feine, H. E., "Vom Fortleben des römischen Rechts in der Kirche," *Zeitschrift für Rechtsgeschichte,* K. A., 42 (1956), pp. 1-24.

Fichtenau, H., *Das karolingische Imperium.* Zürich, 1949.

Finsterwalder, P. W., "Die sogenannte Homilia Leonis IV. und ihre Bedeutung für Hinkmars Capitula und Reginos Inquisitio," *Zeitschrift für Rechtsgeschichte,* K. A. 27 (1938), pp. 639-664.

Fischer, Jürgen, *Oriens—Occidens—Europa: Begriff und Gedanke 'Europa' in der späten Antike und im frühen Mittelalter.* Wiesbaden, 1957.

Folz, R., *L'idée d'empire en Occident du Ve au XVIe siècle.* Paris, 1953.

——, *Le Souvenir et la légende de Charlemagne dans l'Empire germanique médiéval.* Paris, 1950.

Föste, C. H., *Die Reception Pseudo-Isidors unter Nikolaus I. und Hadrian II.* Leipzig, 1881.

Fournier, P. and G. LeBras, *Histoire des collections canoniques en Occident depuis les Fausses Décrétales jusqu'au Décret de Gratien.* v. I. Paris, 1931.

Fuhrmann, H. "Pseudoisidor und die Abbreviatio Ansegisi et Benedicti Levitae," *Zeitschrift für Kirchengeschichte*, 69 (1958), pp. 309-311.

Funk, P., "Pseudo-Isidor gegen Heinrichs III Kirchenhoheit," *Historisches Jahrbuch*, 56 (1936), pp. 305-330.

Ganshof, F. L., "Zur Entstehungsgeschichte und Bedeutung des Vertrags von Verdun," *Deutsches Archiv*, 12 (1956), pp. 313-330.

——, "La fin du règne de Charlemagne, une décomposition," *Zeitschrift für Schweizerische Geschichte*, 28 (1948), pp. 433-452.

——, "L'immunité dans la monarchie franque," *Recueil de la société Jean Bodin*, v. 12 (Brussels, 1958), pp. 171-216.

——, *The Imperial Coronation of Charlemagne: Theories and Facts.* Glasgow, 1949.

——, "Louis the Pious Reconsidered," *History*, 42 (1957), pp. 171-180.

——, "Observations sur le Synode de Francfort de 794," *Miscellanea historica in honorem Alberti de Meyer*, v. I. Louvain, 1946, pp. 306-318.

——, *Recherches sur les capitulaires.* Paris, 1958.

Gaudemet, J., "Survivances romaines dans le droit de la monarchie franque du Ve au Xe siècle," *Tijdschrift voor Rechtsgeschiedenis*, 23 (1955), pp. 149-206.

Gericke, W., "Das Constitutum Constantini und die Silvester-
legende," *Zeitschrift für Rechtsgeschichte*, K. A., 44
(1958), pp. 343-350.

———, "Wann entstand die Konstantinische Schenkung?"
Zeitschrift für Rechtsgeschichte, K. A., 43 (1957), pp. 1-88.

Gierke, O., F. W. Maitland trans., *Political Theories of the
Middle Age*. Cambridge, 1900.

Gietl, A. M., "Hincmars collectio de ecclesiis et capellis," *Historisches Jahrbuch*, 15 (1894), pp. 556-573.

Gladiss, D. v., "Fidelis Regis," *Zeitschrift für Rechtsgeschichte*,
G. A., 57 (1937), pp. 442-451.

Gmelin, O., *Auctoritas, römische Princeps, und päpstliche
Primat. Forschungen zur Kirche und Geitesgeschichte*,
v. 11. Stuttgart, 1937. Another edition was published simultaneously under the title, *Römische Herrscheridee und
päpstliche Autorität*.

Gottlob, T., *Der kirchliche Amtseid der Bischöfe*. Bonn, 1936.

Greinacher, A., *Die Anschauungen des Papstes Nikolaus I.
über das Verhältnis von Staat und Kirche*. Berlin, 1909.

Grundmann, H., ed., *Gebhardts Handbuch der deutschen
Geschichte*, v. 1, 8th ed. Stuttgart, 1956.

Guinan, A., "The Christian Concept of Kingship as Manifested in the Liturgy of the Western Church," *Harvard
Theological Review*, 49 (1956), pp. 219-269.

Gundlach, W., *Die Entstehung des Kirchenstaates und der
curiale Begriff Res publica Romanorum*. Breslau, 1899.

———, "Hincmars von Reims De ecclesiis et capellis," *Zeitschrift für Kirchengeschichte*, 10 (1889), pp. 92-145, 258-310.

Haller, J., *Nikolaus I. und Pseudoisidor*. Stuttgart, 1936.

Halphen, L., *Charlemagne et l'empire carolingien*. Paris, 1947.

———, "L'idée d'état sous les Carolingiens," *Revue historique*,
185 (1939), pp. 59-70.

———, "La pénitence de Louis le Pieux à S.-Médard de
Soissons," Université de Paris, *Bibliothèque de la Faculté
des Lettres*, 18 (1904), pp. 177-185.

Hampe, K., "Zum Streite Hincmars von Reims mit seinem Vorgänger Ebo und dessen Anhängern," *Neues Archiv*, 23 (1898), pp. 180-195.

Hartmann, G., *Der Primat des römischen Bischofs bei Pseudo-Isidor*. Diss. Tübingen. Stuttgart, 1930.

Hashagen, J., "Spätkarolingische Staats-und Soziallehren," *Deutsche Vierteljahrsschrift für Literaturwissenschaft und Geistesgeschichte*, 17 (1939), pp. 301-311.

Hauck, A., *Kirchengeschichte Deutschlands*. 5 vols. Leipzig, 1904-1911.

Hefele, K. J. v.—H. Leclercq, *Histoire des conciles*, 5 vols. Paris, 1907-1913.

Heintschel, D. E., *The Mediaeval Concept of an Ecclesiastical Office*. Washington, D.C., 1956.

Helbig, H., "Fideles Dei et Regis," *Archiv für Kulturgeschichte*, 33 (1951), pp. 275-306.

Heldmann, K., "Kommendation und Königsschutz im Vertrage von Ponthion (754)," *Mitteilungen des Instituts für Oesterreichische Geschichtsforschungen*, 38 (1920), pp. 541-570.

———, *Das Kaisertum Karls des Grossen*. Weimar, 1928.

Hellmann, S., ed., *Sedulii Scotti Liber de Rectoribus Christianis*. Munich, 1906.

Henggeler, A., *Die Salbungen und Krönungen des Königs und Kaisers Ludwigs II (844-850-872)*. Freiburg (Schweiz) 1934.

Henze, W., "Über den Brief Kaiser Ludwigs II an den Kaiser Basilius I.," *Neues Archiv*, 35 (1910), pp. 663-676.

Hinschius, P., ed., *Decretales Pseudo-Isidorianae*. Berlin, 1863.

Hirsch, H., "Das Recht der Königserhebung durch Kaiser und Papst im hohen Mittelalter," *Festschrift Ernst Heymann*, v. 1. Weimar, 1940.

Hoechstetter, M. *Karl der Grosse, König, Patrizius und Kaiser als Rector Ecclesiae*. Diss. Munich, 1931. Augsburg, 1943.

Höfler, O., "Der Sakralcharakter des germanischen Königtums," *Vorträge und Forschungen*, III (1954), pp. 75-104.

Holder-Egger, O., "Zum Texte von Hincmars Schrift de villa Novilliaco," *Neues Archiv*, 23 (1898), pp. 196-198.

Holtzmann, R., "Der Weltherrschaftsgedanke des mittelalterlichen Kaisertums," *Historische Zeitschrift,* 159 (1939), pp. 251-264.

Imbart de la Tour, P., *Les élections épiscopales dans l'Eglise de France du IXe au XIIe siècle.* Paris, 1891.

Imbert, J., "Le droit romain dans les textes juridiques carolingiens," *Studi in onore di Pietro De Francisci*, v. III (Milan, 1956), pp. 61-67.

Jaeger, H., *Das kirchenrechtssystem Pseudoisidors.* Munich, 1908.

Jäkel, K., "Libertas: Der Begriff der Freiheit in den Germanenrechten," *Geschichtliche Landeskunde und Universalgeschichte: Festgabe für Hermann Aubin.* Hamburg, 1950.

Kampers, F., "Rex et Sacerdos," *Historisches Jahrbuch*, 45 (1925), pp. 495-515.

———, "Roma Aeterna und Sancta Dei Ecclesia Rei Publicae Romanorum," *Historisches Jahrbuch*, 44 (1924), pp. 240-249.

Kantorowicz, E. H., "Deus per Naturam, Deus per Gratiam," *Harvard Theological Review*, 45 (1952), pp. 253-277.

———, *The King's Two Bodies.* Princeton, 1957.

———, *Laudes Regiae: A Study in Liturgical Acclamations and Mediaeval Ruler Worship.* Berkeley, 1946.

Kaufmann, E., *Aequitas Iudicium: Königsgericht und Billigkeit in der Rechtsordnung des frühen Mittelalters.* Frankfurter Wissenschaftliche Beiträge, Rechts-und Wirtschaftswissenschaftliche Reihe, Bd. 18. Frankfurt a. M., 1959.

Kehr, P., "Aus den letzten Tagen Karls III," *Deutsches Archiv*, 1 (1937), pp. 138-146.

Kempf, F., "Das mittelalterliche Kaisertum," *Vorträge und Forschungen,* III (1954), pp. 224-242.

Kern, F., *Gottesgnadentum und Widerstandsrecht im früheren Mittelalter*, 2d ed. by R. Buchner. Münster, 1954.

Kirn, P., "Aequitatis judicium von Leo dem Grossen bis auf Hinkmar von Reims," *Zeitschrift für Rechtsgeschichte*, G. A. 52 (1932), pp. 53-64.

Klauser, T., "Die liturgischen Austauschbezeihungen zwischen der römischen und fränkisch-deutschen Kirche vom achten bis zum elften Jahrhundert," *Historisches Jahrbuch*, 53 (1933), pp. 169-189.

Kleinclausz, A., *Alcuin*. Paris, 1948.

———, *Charlemagne*. Paris, 1934.

Knauer, K., *Karls des Kahlen Kaiserkrönung und seine Schenkung an die römischen Kurie*. Coburg, 1909.

Koschaker, P., *Europa und das römische Recht*. 2d ed. Munich, 1953.

Krause, V., "Hincmar von Reims der Verfasser der sogenannten Collectio de raptoribus im Capitular von Quierzy, 857," *Neues Archiv*, 18 (1893), pp. 303-308.

Kröner, A., *Wahl und Krönung der deutschen Kaiser und Könige in Italien (Lombardei)*. Freiburg i. B., 1901.

Krusch, B., "Reimser Remigius-Fälschungen," *Neues Archiv*, 20 (1895), pp. 509-568.

Laehr, G., *Die Konstantinische Schenkung in der abendländlischen Literatur des Mittelalters bis zur Mitte des 14. Jahrhunderts*. Historische Studien, v. 166. Berlin, 1926.

———, "Die Konstantinische Schenkung in der abendländischen Literatur des ausgehenden Mittelalters," *Quellen und Forschungen aus Italienischen Archiven und Bibliotheken*, 23 (1931/2), pp. 120-181.

——— (C. Erdmann, ed.), "Ein karolingischer Konzilsbrief und der Fürstenspiegel Hincmars von Reims," *Neues Archiv*, 50 (1935), pp. 106-134.

Laemmer, H., *Papst Nikolaus der Erste und die byzantinische Staats-Kirche seiner Zeit*. Berlin, 1857.

Laistner, M. L. W., "The Date and the Recipient of Smaragdus' *Via Regia*," *Speculum*, 3 (1928), pp. 392-397.

———, *Thought and Letters in Western Europe (A.D. 500-900)*, 2d ed. Cornell, 1957.

Lambot, C., "L'homélie du Pseudo-Jérôme sur l'assomption et l'évangile de la Nativité de Marie d'après une lettre inédite d'Hincmar," *Revue Bénédictine*, 46 (1934), pp. 265-282.

Lardone, F. G., "Il diritto romano e i concilii," *Acta Congressus Iuridici Internationalis*, v. ii. Rome, 1935, pp. 101-122.

Lee, G. C., "Hincmar: An Introduction to the Study of the Revolution in the Organization of the Church in the Ninth Century," *Papers of the American Society of Church History*, 8 (1897), pp. 231-260.

Lesne, E., *La hiérarchie épiscopale. Provinces, métropolitains, primats en Gaul et Germanie depuis la réforme de Saint Boniface jusqu'à la mort d'Hincmar. (742-882).* Paris, 1905.

——, "Hincmar et l'Empereur Lothaire," *Revue des questions historiques*, 78 (1905), pp. 5-58.

——, *Histoire de la propriété ecclésiastique en France.* 6 vols. Lille and Paris, 1905-1943.

Levillain, L., "Le sacre de Charles le Chauve à Orléans," *Bibliothèque de l'Ecole des Chartes*, 64 (1903), pp. 31-53.

——, "Le couronnement impérial de Charlemagne," *Revue d'histoire de l'Eglise de France*, 18 (1932), pp. 5-19.

Levison, W., *Aus rheinischer und fränkischer Frühzeit.* Düsseldorf, 1948.

——, *England and the Continent in the Eighth Century.* Oxford, 1946.

Levy-Bruhl, H., *Etude sur les élections abbatiales en France jusqu'à la fin du règne de Charles le Chauve.* Paris, 1913.

Lietzmann, H., ed., *Das Sacramentarium Gregorianum.* Münster, 1921.

Lilienfein, H., *Die Anschauungen von Staat und Kirche im Reich der Karolinger.* Heidelberg, 1902.

Lintzel, M., "Das abendländische Kaisertum im 9. und 10. Jahrhundert," *Die Welt als Geschichte*, 4 (1938), pp. 421-447.

Lot, F., *Fidèles ou vassaux?* Paris, 1904.

——, "Le serment de fidélité à l'époque franque," *Revue Belge de philologie et d'histoire*, 12 (1933), pp. 569-582.

—— and L. Halphen, *Le règne de Charles le Chauve*, v. 1 (840-851). Paris, 1909.

Löwe, H., "Von den Grenzen des Kaisergedankens in der Karolingerzeit," *Deutsches Archiv*, 14 (1958), pp. 345-374.

——, *Die Karolingische Reichsgrundung und der Südosten*. Stuttgart, 1937.

Löwenfeld, S., "Acht Briefe aus der Zeit König Berengars," *Neues Archiv*, 9 (1884), pp. 513-540.

Lubac, H. de, *Corpus Mysticum: L'Eucharistie et l'Eglise au moyen âge*. Paris, 1948, 2d ed., 1949.

Maassen, F., "Ein Commentar des Florus von Lyon," zu einigen der sogenanten Sirmond'schen Constitutionen," *Sitzungsberichte der Akademie der Wissenschaften zu Wien*, phil.-hist. Kl. 92 (1878), pp. 301-324.

——, "Eine Rede des Papstes Hadrian II. vom Jahre 869," *Sitzungsberichte der Akademie der Wissenschaften zu Wien*, phil.-hist. Kl. 92 (1878), pp. 301-324.

——, *Geschichte der Quellen und der Literatur des canonischen Rechts im Abendlande bis zum Ausgange des Mittelalters*, v. 1. Gratz, 1870.

Maccarrone, M., *Il Papa "Vicarius Christi."* Rome, 1948.

Mayer, T., "Staatsauffassung in der Karolingerzeit," *Historische Zeitschrift*, 173 (1952), pp. 467-484, and *Vorträge und Forschungen*, III (1954), pp. 169-183.

Meyer, O., "Zum Rechte der Besetzung der bischöflichen Stühle im Karolingerreich," *Zeitschrift für Rechtsgeschichte*, K. A. 24 (1935), pp. 333-337.

Meyer, W., "Über Hincmars von Laon Auslese aus Pseudo-Isidor, Ingilram, und aus Schreiben des Pabstes Nicolaus I," *Nachrichten von der kgl. Gesellschaft der Wissenschaften zu Göttingen*, philol.-hist. Kl., 1912, pp. 219-227.

Michels, T., "La date du couronnement de Charles-le-Chauve (9. Sept. 869) et le culte liturgique de S. Gorgon à Metz," *Revue Bénédictine*, 51 (1939), pp. 288-291.

Mitteis, H., *Lehnrecht und Staatsgewalt*. Weimar, 1933.

Mohr, W. *Die karolingische Reichsidee*. Münster, 1962.

Mor, C. G., "La recezione del diritto romano nelle collezioni canoniche dei secoli IX-XI in Italia e oltr' Alpe," *Acta Congressus Iuridici Internationalis*, v. ii, Rome, 1935, pp. 281-302.

Morghen, R., "La concezione dell' imperio romano-germanico e la tradizione di Roma da Carolomagno a Frederico II," *Reale accademia nazionale dei Lincei*—Scienze morali—Classe di Rendiconti. Ser. 6, vol. 14 (1938), pp. 293-346.

Müller, E., "Die Anfänge der Königssalbung im Mittelalter," *Historisches Jahrbuch*, 58 (1938), pp. 317-360.

Munding, E., ed., *Texte und Arbeiten herausgegeben durch die Erzabtei Beuron*, I. Abt., Heft 6. Beuron, 1920.

Munier, C., *Les sources patristiques du droit de l'Eglise du VIIIe au XIIe siècle*. Mulhausen, 1957.

Noorden, C. F. J. v., "Ebo, Hinkmar und Pseudo-Isidor," *Historische Zeitschrift*, 7 (1862), pp. 311-350.

——, *Hinkmar Erzbischof von Rheims*. Bonn, 1863.

Norwood, F. A., "The Political Pretensions of Pope Nicholas I," *Church History*, 15 (1946), pp. 271-285.

Odegaard, C. E., "The Concept of Royal Power in the Carolingian Oaths," *Speculum*, 29 (1945), pp. 279-289.

——, *Vassi and Fideles in the Carolingian Empire*. Harvard, 1945.

Ohnsorge, W., "Byzanz und das Abendland im 9. und 10. Jahrhundert," *Saeculum*, 5 (1954), pp. 194-220.

——, *Das Zweikaiserproblem im früheren Mittelalter*. Hildesheim, 1947.

Pacaut, M., *La Théocratie: l'Église et le pouvoir au moyen âge*. Paris, 1957.

Perels, E., "Ein Berufsschreiben Papst Nikolaus' I. zur fränkischen Reichssynode in Rom," *Neues Archiv*, 32 (1907), pp. 133-149.

——, "Eine Denkschrift Hinkmars von Reims im Prozess Rothads von Soissons," *Neues Archiv*, 44 (1922), pp. 43-100.

———, "Hinkmar von Reims und die Bonifatiusbriefe," *Neues Archiv*, 48 (1930), pp. 156-160.

———, *Papst Nikolaus I. und Anastasius Bibliothecarius.* Berlin, 1920.

Pfeil, E., *Die fränkische und deutsche Romidee des frühen Mittelalters.* Munich, 1929.

Posse, B. O., *Die Siegel der deutschen Kaiser und Könige*, 4 vols. 1909-1913.

Prichard, J. C., *The Life and Times of Hincmar, Archbishop of Rheims.* Oxford, 1849.

Pringsheim, F., "Römische *aequitas* der christlichen Kaiser," *Acta Congressus Iuridici Internationalis*, v. 1. Rome, 1935, pp. 119-152.

Rahner, H., "Navicula Petri," *Zeitschrift für katholische Theologie*, 69 (1947), pp. 1-35.

Reviron, J., *Les idées politico-religieuses d'un évêque du IXe siècle: Jonas d'Orléans et son "De institutione regia."* Paris, 1930.

Roberti, M., "Il corpus mysticum di S. Paolo nella storia della persona giuridica," *Studi di storia e diritto in onore di Enrico Besta*, v. IV. Milan, 1937.

Rota, E., "La consecrazione imperiale di Carlo Magno e l'orientamentazione anti-romana della monarchia carolingia," *Studi di storia e diritto in onore di Enrico Besta*, v. IV. Milan, 1937.

Sägmüller, L., "Die Idee von der Kirche als Imperium Romanum im kanonischen Recht," *Theologische Quartalschrift*, 80 (1898), pp. 50-80.

Scharf, J., "Studien zu Smaragdus und Jonas," *Deutsches Archiv*, 17 (1961), pp. 333-384.

Scheyhing, R., *Eide, Amtsgewalt, und Bannleihe: Eine Untersuchung zur Bannleihe im hohen und späten Mittelalter.* Forschungen zur deutschen Rechtsgeschichte, vol. II. Cologne, 1960.

Schieffer, T., "Die Krise des karolingischen Imperiums," *Aus Mittelalter und Neuzeit, Festschrift G. Kallen*. Bonn, 1957, pp. 1-15.

Schlesinger, W., "Die Anfänge der deutschen Königswahl," *Zeitschrift für Rechtsgeschichte*, G. A. 66 (1948), pp. 381-440.

——, "Kaiser Arnulf und die Entstehung des deutschen Staates und Volkes," *Historische Zeitschrift*, 163 (1941), pp. 457-470.

Schneider, F., *Rom und Romgedanke im Mittelalter*. Munich, 1926.

Schramm, P. E., "Die Anerkennung Karls des Grossen als Kaiser," *Historische Zeitschrift*, 172 (1951), pp. 449-515. (Reprinted as a separate volume, Munich, 1952.)

——, *Die deutschen Kaiser und Könige in Bildern ihrer Zeit*, 2 vols. Leipzig and Berlin, 1928.

——, *Herrschaftszeichen und Staatssymbolik*, 3 vols. Stuttgart, 1954-1956.

——, *Kaiser, Rom und Renovatio*, 2d ed. Leipzig, 1957.

——, *Der König von Frankreich*, v. 1. Weimar, 1939.

——, "Die Krönung in Deutschland bis zum Beginn des Salischen Hauses," *Zeitschrift für Rechtsgeschichte*, K. A. 24 (1935), pp. 184-332.

——, "Das Versprechen Pippins und Karls des Grossen für die Römische Kirche," *Zeitschrift für Rechtsgeschichte*, K.A. 27 (1938), pp. 180-217.

Schreuer, H., *Die rechtliche Grundgedanken der französischen Königskrönung*. Weimar, 1911.

Schrörs, H., *Hinkmar, Erzbischof von Reims*. Freiburg i. B., 1884.

Schwerin, Cl. Frhr. von, "Zur Herkunft des Schwertsymbols," *Festschrift Paul Koschaker*, v. III. Weimar, 1939, pp. 324-349.

Schubert, H. v., *Geschichte der christlichen Kirche im Frühmittelalter*. Tübingen, 1921.

Schubert, H. v., *Der Kampf des geistlichen und weltlichen Rechts*. Heidelberg, 1927.

Schulte, A., *Die Kaiser-und Königskrönungen zu Aachen: 813-1531*. Bonn, 1924.

Schulze, A., *Kaiserpolitik und Einheitsgedanke in den karolingischen Nachfolgestaaten (876-962)*. Berlin, 1926.

Sdralek, M., *Hinkmars von Rheims kanonistisches Gutachten über die Ehescheidung des Königs Lothar II*. Freiburg i. B., 1881.

Seckel, E., "Studien zu Benedictus Levita," *Neues Archiv*, 1900, 1904, 1905, 1909 (2), 1910, 1914, 1915, 1916. Continued by J. Juncker in *Zeitschrift für Rechtsgeschichte*, K. A. 1934, 1935.

Semmler, J., "Reichsidee und kirchliche Gesetzbung," *Zeitschrift für Kirchengeschichte*, 71 (1960), pp. 37-65.

Sickel, W., "Zum karolingischen Thronrecht," *Festschrift zu A. S. Schultzes 70. Geburtstag*. Leipzig, 1903.

——, "Kirchenstaat und Karolinger," *Historische Zeitschrift*, 84 (1900), pp. 385-409.

Simson, B., *Jahrbücher des fränkischen Reichs unter Ludwig dem Frommen*. 2 vols., Leipzig, 1874, 1876.

Sperling, E., *Studien zur Geschichte der Kaiserkrönung und—Weihe*. Stuttgart, 1918.

Sprengler, A., "Die Gebete der Krönungsordines Hinkmars von Reims für Karl den Kahlen als König von Lothringen und für Ludwig den Stammler," *Zeitschrift für Kirchengeschichte*, 63 (1950/1), pp. 245-267.

Stein, Simon, "Lex Salica," *Speculum*, 22 (1947), pp. 113-134, 395-418.

Stengel, E. E., "Kaisertitel und Souveränitätsidee," *Deutsches Archiv*, 3 (1939), pp. 1-56.

Tellenbach, G., *Römischer und christlicher Reichsgedanke in der Liturgie des frühen Mittelalters*. Heidelberg, 1934.

——, R. F. Bennett trans., *Church, State, and Christian Society at the Time of the Investiture Contest*. Oxford, 1948.

Thaner, F., "Hinkmar von Rheims und Bernald," *Neues Archiv*, 30 (1905), pp. 694-701.

Thiel, A., *Epistolae Romanorum Pontificum*. Braunschweig, 1868.

Tiralla, H., *Das augustinianische Idealbild der christlichen Obrigkeit als Quelle der Fürstenspiegel des Sedulius Scottus und Hinkmar von Reims*. Diss. Greifswald, 1916.

Traube, L., "*O Roma nobilis*. Philologische Untersuchungen aus dem Mittelalter," *Abhandlungen der philos.-philolog. Klasse der kgl. Bayerischen Akademie der Wissenschaften*, 19 (1892), pp. 299-395.

Ullmann, W., *The Growth of Papal Government in the Middle Ages*. London, 1955.

———, *Principles of Government and Politics in the Middle Ages*. London, 1961.

Voigt, K., *Staat und Kirche von Konstantin dem Grossen bis zum Ende der Karolingerzeit*. Stuttgart, 1936.

Waitz, G., *Deutsche Verfassungsgeschichte*, vv. II-IV, 2d ed. Kiel, 1883-1885.

Wallace-Hadrill, J. W., "Archbishop Hincmar and the Authorship of Lex Salica," *Tijdschrift voor Rechtsgeschiedenis*, 21 (1953), pp. 1-29.

Wallach, L., *Alcuin and Charlemagne*. Cornell, 1959.

———, "Amicus amicis, inimicus inimicis," *Zeitschrift für Kirchengeschichte*, 52 (1933), pp. 614-615.

———, "The Roman Synod of December 800 and the Alleged Trial of Leo III," *Harvard Theological Review*, 49 (1956), pp. 123-142.

Wattenbach, W., W. Levison, H. Löwe, and R. Buchner (Beiheft: Die Rechtsquellen), *Deutschlands Geschichtsquellen im Mittelalter*, fasc. I-III. Weimar, 1952-1957.

Weckwerth, A., "Das altchristliche und das frühmittelalterliche Kirchengebäude—ein Bild des 'Gottesreiches,'" *Zeitschrift für Kirchengeschichte*, 59 (1958), pp. 26-78.

Weinzierl, K., "Erzbischof Hinkmar von Reims als Verfechter des geltenden Rechts," *Episcopus, Festschrift Kardinal von Faulhaber*. Regensburg, 1949.

Weizäcker, J., "Hincmar und Pseudo-Isidor," *Zeitschrift für die historische Theologie*, 28 (1858), pp. 327-430.

Werminghoff, A., "Die Fürstenspiegel der Karolingerzeit," *Historische Zeitschrift*, N.F. 53 (1902), pp. 193-214.

———, "Pseudo-Hinkmar," *Neues Archiv*, 30 (1905), pp. 471-472.

———, "Verzeichnis der Akten fränkischer Synoden von 742-843," *Neues Archiv*, 24 (1899), pp. 457-502, continuation for 843-918, *Neues Archiv*, 26 (1901), pp. 609-678.

Wieruszowski, H., *Die Zusammensetzung des gallischen und fränkischen Episkopats*, Jahrbücher der Vereinigung von Altertumsfreunden in Rheinland, vol. 127.

Wilmart, A., "Une catéchèse baptismale du IXe siècle," *Revue Bénédictine*, 57 (1947), pp. 196-200.

———, "Distiques d'Hincmar sur l'Eucharistie? Un sermon oublié de S. Augustin sur le même sujet," *Revue Bénédictine*, 40 (1928), pp. 87-98.

———, "Lettres de l'époque carolingienne," *Revue Bénédictine*, 34 (1922), pp. 234-245.

Wilson, H. A., ed., *The Gelasian Sacramentary*. Oxford, 1894.

Zwölfer, T., *Sankt Peter, Apostelfürst und Himmelspförtner: Seine Verehrung bei den Angelsachsen und Franken*. Stuttgart, 1929.

INDEX